Kaunda and Southern Africa

Image and Reality in Foreign Policy

STEPHEN CHAN

British Academic Press
London · New York

For Chanda
Ku-tuluka mtsuko woning'a

Published in 1992 by
The British Academic Press
110 Gloucester Avenue
London NW1 8JA

An imprint of I.B. Tauris & Co Ltd

In the United States of America
and Canada distributed by
St Martin's Press
175 Fifth Avenue
New York
NY 10010

1006491776

A CIP record for this book is available from the British Library

Library of Congress Catalog card number: 91-68014
A full CIP record is available from the Library of Congress

ISBN 1-85043-490-5

Printed & bound in Great Britain by
WBC Ltd, Bridgend, South Wales.

CONTENTS

ACKNOWLEDGEMENTS

This book has been under preparation since I lived in Zambia from 1980 to 1985 and owes an immense debt to information received from a great number of Zambians. They can only be acknowledged in a most general way here, but the acknowledgement is a grateful one. Several have read and commented on the manuscript and have spent time discussing my ideas with me.

A special one-day conference in 1990 of the Centre for Conflict Analysis was devoted to the problems I had in translating controversial research findings into a balanced manuscript. This involved both British and Zambian scholars and led me to revise totally my approach to the project.

A grant from the Economic and Social Research Council in 1989 enabled me to return to both Zambia and Zimbabwe in order to complete the bulk of my research. This book would not have been possible without the ESRC's help. A grant from the University of Kent in 1990 enabled me to make my eighth trip to Zimbabwe. The 1989 visit coincided with President Kaunda's first meeting with President de Klerk, and the 1990 visit coincided with major riots against Kaunda in Lusaka. Both visits were therefore opportune, so the ESRC and the University of Kent receive my thanks.

Lastly, I acknowledge the encouragement I have received at Kent from Professor A.J.R. Groom, who, while contriving to increase dramatically my teaching and administrative loads, nevertheless constantly cautioned me against finishing this project in a rush. Not rushing, although it has left a more considered manuscript, has however demanded great patience from my publisher, Dr Lester

Crook of the British Academic Press, I.B. Tauris. I thank him for
this.

I am aware that there remain faults in the finished work, but I can
attribute responsibility for these only to myself.

The book as a whole was completed in early 1991. However,
publication was deliberately delayed to accommodate a note on the
Zambian elections of 31 October 1991, which swept Kaunda from
power.

University of Kent
at Canterbury
1992

FOREWORD

I am extremely pleased to be able to write a foreword to this book. I should confess, at the outset, that I am least qualified to do so. The book itself is written by an intellectual of great ability. The author, Stephen Chan, commands immense respect in Zambia as a scholar of international relations.

Many Zambians readily recall him during his memorable stay in their country, both for his work at the University of Zambia, and for his prowess in karate when he was Zambia's celebrated National Karate Coach. The subject matter of his book concerns the foreign policy orchestrated by President Kenneth Kaunda, who until 2nd November 1991 was Zambia's leading political figure, and one of Africa's most prominent political personalities.

President Kaunda's overall involvement in Zambian politics spans a period of well over 40 years. Born on 28 April 1924 at Lubwa in Northern Zambia, he was educated at Lubwa Training School and Munali Secondary School, and taught at Lubwa Training School, where he was headmaster from 1944 to 1947. In 1950 he became the founder Secretary of the Lubwa Branch of the African National Congress (ANC), then the main nationalist movement agitating for political independence in Zambia, formerly known as Northern Rhodesia. Kenneth Kaunda went on to be the ANC's District and Provincial Organiser in 1951 and 1952 respectively.

His organisational abilities made an early impact within the ANC, and a year later he had been chosen as its Secretary General. However, Kaunda grew increasingly disillusioned of the ANC's pacifist strategy against colonial rule and resigned from it to form the Zambia African National Congress (ZANC) in 1958.

He had by this time figured prominently in the politics of independence in Zambia. Under his leadership, ZANC took a militant approach to the struggle against colonial rule. It was subsequently banned by the colonial government and Kaunda, together with some of his colleagues, was detained.

Whilst Kaunda was in detention, his loyal lieutenants formed the United National Independence Party (UNIP) in 1960. Upon his release from detention, Kaunda assumed formal leadership of UNIP as its president. This marked the beginning of Kaunda's ascendancy to political power. In 1962 he was appointed a member of the cabinet in the colonial government as Minister of Local Government and Social Welfare, a portfolio which he held until 1964 when he became Prime Minister of Northern Rhodesia.

The year 1963 had witnessed the dissolution of the Federation of Rhodesia and Nyasaland. Elections were held in that year but none of the political parties was able to master an absolute majority due to the complex constitutional and voting arrangements. None the less, a coalition between UNIP and ANC was struck, and Kaunda was invited by the then Governor of Northern Rhodesia in January 1964 to constitute a government as Prime Minister.

This signified that Northern Rhodesia was now firmly on its way to self-government. Upon Zambia's independence on 24 October 1964, Kenneth Kaunda's elevation to the position of President was a matter of virtual certainty. Even then, it was the manner of his ascendancy to the Presidency which was remarkably distinct.

The Independence Constitution by special provision endowed him as President of Zambia by name on 24 October 1964. In addition, President Kaunda was, and perhaps remains, the only leader in the Commonwealth who combined responsibilities of Head of State and Government upon his country's attainment of independence, for Zambia gained independent statehood with republican status under a Presidential and liberally democratic system of government.

Signs that President Kaunda coveted a one-party-based system of government were evident in his pronouncements as early as 1965. In his view, however, the one-party state would not come about by means of legislation, but by gradually wiping out, the opposition at the polls, as was the situation then in Tanzania.

President Kaunda's combined role as Head of State and Government since Zambia's independence is a crucial underlying factor to his early dominance of Zambian politics and of his image as the nation's father figure. It is an image which for a long time, and until now, enabled 'K.K.' – as President Kaunda has been fondly called – to hold the centre-stage of political power in Zambia.

In 1967, three years into Zambia's independent nationhood, President Kaunda outlined his vision of the Zambian polity in terms of 'Humanism'. This was to be the new nation's ideological and philosophical identity. As proclaimed officially, the philosophy of humanism contains the guiding values of Zambian society. It envisions the edicts of Zambian traditional society with a Christian-inspired outlook.

As originally profiled by President Kaunda, humanism placed man at the centre of human society and activity in Zambia. It portrayed man in simple terms as the common man: 'You, Me, and the Other Fellow'; and that man is central in all that 'we do, say, and think'. Underlying President Kaunda's teaching of humanism is the basic principle: 'Do unto others as you would like them to do unto you.'

Whether because of its simplicity or not, humanism has been prone to varying conceptions. While the centre-left of Zambian politics has pressed for a more scientific socialist perspective of humanism, the centre-right has seen it as a basis for pragmatism. Moreover, there is the common liberal, if not moralistic, conception of humanism as a warrant of generosity and forgiveness for wrongs committed by individuals against others and the state.

These conceptions evidence the proposition that humanism as a philosophy has either remained unconvincing, or has lacked a concrete identifiable core in philosophical terms. However, recent years – at least since the beginning of the eighties – have witnessed attempts to formulate humanism in a more sophisticated form.

Hence socialism is seen as the means through which humanism is to be attained. In this form, the main precepts of humanism have been identified as the five areas of human endeavour. The pertinent areas are categorised as: political and ideological; economic and financial; social and cultural; defence and security; and scientific and technological.

From the standpoint of humanism, these areas provide the framework of the ruling party's political thought, as well as the principal fields of political and government activity. In this sense, the five areas of human endeavour constitute the basis for the structural organisation of political and public administration in relation to the provision of public services.

Thus the Central Committee, which is the United National

Independence Party's policy making and advisory body, is structured in sub-committees corresponding to the five areas of human endeavour. Government ministries implemented policy under guidance from the respective sub-Committees. Likewise, the functions of local administration were also explicitly structured within these five areas.

If the structural organisation of the party and government was guided by humanism in accordance with the five areas of human endeavour, then the erection of a large, bureaucratic, cumbersome, and expensive administrative structure of government was a consequence of humanism.

In the economic sphere, the implementation of humanism was evident in state control or ownership of inefficient parastatals and co-operatives, state farms, and forms of workers' self-management projects, all of which are the equivalent of state capitalism. Within this context, gross inequities in wealth and power in Zambia have grown to such an extent that it is no longer possible to envisage that its socio-economic life is predicated on the needs of the common man.

Efforts to move from a state-controlled economy to a market-oriented economy have added hardship to the life of the common man. From the general point of view, therefore, humanism has seldom lived up to the expectations which it has itself engendered.

In his 27 years in power, President Kaunda was credited for presiding over unity and stability in Zambia. Viewed in this perspective, the case may well be made that he has bequeathed to Zambia the notion of a nation state. Moreover, to have remained in power for this length of time in a continent which is generally riven by political turmoil, turbulence, and internal strife is in itself an achievement of great measure. It testifies to the immense political skill which President Kaunda has repeatedly exhibited over the years.

As early as 1967, he managed to contain a tribal split in his party. It is true that then there was no threat to Kaunda's position as President of UNIP and Zambia. However, the general elections of 1968 showed that UNIP was not able to command support in some areas of the country, notably in Western and Southern provinces in which the opposition dominated. And in 1971, the split which was evident at the General Conference of UNIP in 1967 surfaced openly. The then Vice-President, the late Simon Kapwepwe, broke away from UNIP and formed his United Progressive Party (UPP) to challenge Kaunda for the national Presidency in the general elections which were to follow in 1972.

Some violent clashes which ensued in the by-elections held following the formation of UPP led to its proscription, and President Kaunda announced later in 1972 that his cabinet had taken the decision that Zambia would become a one-party state in order to end various un-Zambian activities.

The one-party state was introduced by legislative constitutional change in 1973. It was President Kaunda's political formula for containing threats to national stability, unity, and indeed his presidency. Former members of the opposition were invited to participate in the affairs of his ruling party and government, and some of them occupied high-ranking political office. In this way, much of the opposition was neutralised and contained. Nevertheless, Harry Mwaanga Nkumbula and Simon Kapwepwe (both now deceased) challenged President Kaunda for the leadership of the party in 1978. This challenge was nipped in the bud. President Kaunda's loyal followers within the party amended the rules concerning eligibility to contest the presidency of the party by requiring candidates to have been party members for at least five years. Kapwepwe was ruled out of the contest on this ground, and Nkumbula was simply not able to file his nomination papers at the General Conference of the party.

Other challenges to President Kaunda's leadership have been by means of attempted military coups in 1980, 1988, and most recently in 1990. In an act of political compassion and reconciliation predicated on the call for a fresh start, President Kaunda granted an amnesty to all the persons who had been involved in the coup attempts. In so doing, the image of a kind, forgiving President was superimposed over political strife in a continent where summary execution is the reward of a failed coup attempt.

During the years that he has been in power, President Kaunda played a visible role in international affairs in Africa, particularly with respect to Southern Africa. He was Chairman of the Front Line States in Southern Africa and, apart from Tanzania's former President Julius Nyerere, hc is the only other African Head of State to have served twice as Chairman of the Organisation of African Unity.

The sphere of foreign policy has been central to shaping President Kaunda's international image. When he became President in 1964, most of Zambia's neighbours, notably Southern Rhodesia (now Zimbabwe), Angola, Mozambique, and Namibia, were still under foreign domination. President Kaunda took the moralist stand that Zambia's independence was 'incomplete' as long as its neighbours remained colonised.

Thus Zambia provided a base for the liberation movements which waged armed struggles for independence in Angola, Mozambique, Namibia, Southern Rhodesia, and South Africa. In all these, and other post-independence conflicts in Southern Africa and elsewhere in Africa, President Kaunda has largely been involved in negotiations and political settlements of disputes both as a moralist and a mediator.

But against this background arose a potent challenge to his political longevity. In the face of concerted and popular-based opposition to his one-party system of leadership, President Kaunda had inevitably to concede in 1990 to the constitutional establishment of a plural political system. The first Presidential and Parliamentary elections under such a democratic political system since 1968 were held on 31 October 1991. Kaunda and his United National Independence Party suffered a heavy and stunning defeat at the hands of Fredrick Chiluba and the Movement for Multi-party Democracy which he heads.

The extent to which President Kaunda's leadership and government had long lost political legitimacy was evidenced in these elections by the lack of popular support for his Presidency and Party. The one-party system of government may have been a political cushion for a leadership that no longer commanded popular support. It is always said that the fallibility of great men in politics lies in their not knowing when to depart the political scene. President Kaunda proved to be no exception. In spite of consistently massive displays of public support for Chiluba, a former Trade Union leader, and his Movement for Multi-party Democracy, President Kaunda spurned calls to retire gracefully or to form a transitional government in conjunction with the opposition. He could have tactfully conceded to the latter demand – perhaps at some cost to his followers – but it would have enabled him to see through his five-year tenure in office until 1993 when next the elections were due under the previous constitution. In that way, he and his Party could have bought time, taken some of the opposition's steam, and prepared adequately for the elections. The outcome may still have been similar but the magnitude of his defeat would have been less severe. Moreover, he would have had sufficient time to take stock of the political odds against him, come to terms with it, and retire on his own terms.

In conceding defeat, Kaunda's manner of exit was most gracious and dignified. 'You win some, you lose some,' he said, and respectfully bid his Presidency farewell. For Zambia and Africa, this political scene looked like a fairy-tale. For 27 years President Kaunda had led his country peacefully, notwithstanding severe economic difficulties towards the last years of his Presidency. But to his credit, he also left it peacefully. An orderly mechanism for the peaceful transfer of political power, which Africa generally lacks, actually worked. It is a legendary example to all of Africa and will no doubt be Kaunda's most important legacy for democracy in Zambia and Africa as a whole.

The occasion of the outcome of the Zambian elections provides an appropriate opportunity for reassessing President Kaunda's role in international relations, particularly in the area of his foreign policy. Stephen Chan's book breaks new ground. As well as giving an insight into the mechanics of President Kaunda's foreign policy initiatives, Stephen Chan adds a further dimension to various versions of President Kaunda's role as international statesman. His book is timely and welcome and makes very interesting reading. Its analysis of the issues it raises and the approach it takes should be seen as an inspired academic inquiry. With these words, I warmly commend it to the reader and to students of Zambian politics in particular.

Chaloka Beyani.
Oxford, November 1991.

1

INTRODUCTION

This book is concerned with Kenneth Kaunda as an actor in southern African and international affairs, and with his formulation and execution of foreign policy. In this context, however, it is impossible to avoid discussion of his domestic policies – one is not unrelated to the other – but the focus of enquiry and judgement is firmly fixed on international affairs. Considerable attention is given to the differing international perspectives on Kaunda's performance as a statesman, on his motivations and underlying agendas, and on his successes and failures. The two broadest and most prevalent perspectives to have emerged describe Kaunda either as a noble statesman or as a collaborator with the forces of oppression. Other distinctions have also been made and this book is the first to identify them and discuss their merits. A basic step in ascertaining Kaunda's contribution to international affairs is to demystify the conflicting and often confused intellectual history that has grown up around him.

The book is not wholly an academic exercise however. For example, much of the source material is exactly the same as would be used in investigative journalism. In a very great number of third world studies there is often only one way to conduct any investigation, and that is to sift among rumours and personal experiences for a picture that might only be intuitively correct. I have gone as far as I can to minimise the worst effects of such investigation. Where I have reported only rumour, I say so. Otherwise, as far as possible, I have reported only information I have heard from more than one reputable source. By 'reputable' I mean persons with standing and direct, usually senior, involvement in the events they described to me. Even so, because

events are often controversial and my informants likely to be embarrassed or disciplined for discussing sensitive issues with me, I have
not cited any of their names. This means that readers must accept on
trust that none of their evidence has been fabricated by me and that I
have done my best to ensure that I have not anchored my arguments
on anything fabricated by others. Living in Zambia for five years, and
visiting regularly since, has given me the advantages of access to
politicians and officials, and some ear for what is credible and what
has been dissembled.[1]

The book, while clarifying certain academic problems therefore,
hopes to be an intelligent enquiry into Kaunda the statesman. As
such, it aims to interest those readers who, in spite of forcing a path
through the multitude of books on or by Kaunda, find themselves no
nearer a view of him that accounts for his whimsical, contradictory,
and hectoring delivery of himself and his beliefs. Nevertheless, the
book is also intended to be useful to those scholars involved with
southern African studies, foreign policy formulation, and mediation.

The book considers Kaunda's foreign policy both before and after
Zimbabwe's independence. Before independence, a free Zimbabwe
was the principal plank of Kaunda's foreign policy platform. After
independence, Zimbabwe competed for and successfully gained what
had been Zambia's crown of regional leadership against South Africa.
Robert Mugabe also quickly emerged as an intelligent and strong-
willed leader, and this meant that Kaunda's personality no longer held
centre-stage by itself. Simultaneously, Zambia's economic position
began seriously to worsen. These two unconnected events were
traumatic to Zambian self-confidence and policy. This book under-
takes, therefore, two major exercises in comparison. The first, as
noted above, concerns the different perspectives on the nature of
Kaunda as a statesman, and the second is to do with Kaunda's foreign
policy in two time periods – before Zimbabwe's independence in
1980, and after 1980. As such, it culminates a personal quest to
understand Kaunda in southern Africa that is now a decade old.[2]

---

[1] Nevertheless, for the problems of research see Appendix 1.
[2] From 1980, when I first arrived in Zambia, to the time of writing in 1990. The results
began to appear in the mid-1980s. See Stephen Chan: 'X for the Eagle', *Common-
wealth*, Vol. 26, No. 4, 1984; 'The Search for Peace – The Basis of Zambia's Regional
Policy', *Contemporary Review*, Vol. 248, No. 1444, 1986; *Issues in International Relations:
A View from Africa*, London: Macmillan, 1987, Chapter 21; 'Zambia's Foreign Policy
– Elitism and Power', *The Round Table*, 302, 1987; 'Kaunda as International Casualty',
New Zealand International Review, Vol. XII, No. 5, 1987; 'Zambia, Morality, and

The Singularity of Kaunda

The immediate objection to a study of this sort concerns its limitation. Is it only Kaunda who acts in international affairs for Zambia? Is there not a cabinet and parliamentary role in the formulation and discharge of foreign policy? In a one-party state, are there not powerful party secretaries or committees concerned with such matters? Or, within State House itself, does not the President of Zambia have expert aides who furnish him with specialist advice and recommendations? Outside the official apparatus, are there not journalists, professors, research institutes, or even dining clubs that debate foreign affairs and attempt to provide policy inputs? Are there no organised lobbies? The answer to all but the first of these questions is 'no'.

Allison has provided three models of how foreign policy might be formulated.[3] The first is known as the Rational Actor Model, in which states are regarded as unitary actors represented by their governments. They behave rationally and their actions are calculated responses to strategic problems. The second is known as the Organisational Process Model, in which the basic unit of analysis is the organisation and the range of effective choice is limited to organisational routines. The 'standard operating procedures' of a government determine the shape of policy and action. The third is the Bureaucratic Politics Model, in which there are many governmental actors, many organisations, and they do not necessarily act in a unitary manner, or cooperate, or even attempt to act rationally. Government decisions are the result of bargaining games: in short, of political in-fighting. I would like to argue here that the second and third models have no real applicability to Zambia. There is, firstly, no foreign affairs 'organisation' that plays any real role in policy formulation and implementation, so whether what passes as an organisation has standard operating procedures or not they have no effect. Secondly,

Mediation: A Problematic. Approach to Conflict Resolution in Southern Africa', paper presented to the Joint Convention of the International Studies Association and the British International Studies Association, London, 1989; *Exporting Apartheid: Foreign Policies in Southern Africa, 1978–1988*, London: Macmillan, 1990, pp. 65–80; 'Presidentialism in Lusaka and Harare', *Wasafiri*, No. 12, 1990. The publication of several of these papers in a single accessible volume will be accomplished in *The Decline of Kaunda: Essays of Praise and Complaint*, Canterbury: Kent Papers in Politics and International Relations, forthcoming 1991.
[3] Graham T. Allison, *Essence of Decision*, Boston: Little, Brown & Co., 1971.

not only is there no one organisation effectively involved with foreign affairs, there is no range of organisations. There is, therefore, no bargaining or in-fighting, since the actors that would normally bargain or fight do not exist, or lead polite and formalised existences. Only the Rational Actor Model is worthy of full study here, and that is on two assumptions. One is that Kaunda is in fact the unitary actor, not the wider Zambian Government. The other is that he behaves rationally. His rationality has, however, been questioned – even by his admirers. A component of one of his images has almost been an irrational nobility. I wish to discuss the contradictions perceived in Kaunda in the chapters that follow. In the remainder of this chapter, however, I wish to amplify my comments on the singularity of Kaunda.

The basic amplification rests on his constitutional position. He has enjoyed a constitutional pre-eminence as both executive president and party president, under a constitution that elevates the United National Independence Party above the government. The government is within the party's jurisdiction and implements what the party decides. Since Kaunda is party president and, as executive president, appoints the government, he is able to establish his agendas in both – so that the overlap in membership between UNIP Central Committee and cabinet, which might reduce the strict hierarchical view of party dictating to government, means very little in practice since both are hierarchically subordinate to Kaunda himself. As executive president, he is also commander-in-chief of the armed forces and is in charge of military appointments and promotions. Parliament can make few inroads against this monopoly of power and authority. Kaunda need not confine his choice of cabinet ministers to parliamentarians, nor his choice of officials to civil servants. Notwithstanding anything parliament, cabinet, or party might decide, Kaunda may, if he chooses, rule by decree. It has been a concentration of executive and political powers that makes the Gaullist Presidency pale by comparison.

Such powers need not be exercised in an authoritarian fashion. What Kaunda has is an immense capacity for patronage. Since he can hire and fire in any official sector, all official careers are dependent on his blessing for their development at senior levels. Kaunda periodically dismisses people from their positions, but very seldom from their livelihoods. 'Reshuffles' are frequent. Partially to accommodate a growing number of careers in recyclement, there has been a vast lateral expansion of the bureaucracy. Nominally, this bureaucracy is concerned with public administration and development, but it is also the president's repository of people not in need. Whether in need or not, all bureaucrats are paid and, above certain levels, attract housing and transport – these two benefits being otherwise in critically short supply. The critiques of the Zambian bureaucracy concern its size, duplication of functions, expense, and uselessness. If the president, however, can control an official's position, rank, prestige, salary, housing, and transport, not to mention a range of other benefits, then without a harsh word being said he is well placed to control their dissent from his policies.

The Ministry of Foreign Affairs is one repository among many. Firstly, diplomacy is not a graduate career – although the number of graduates is increasing – so the calibre of entrants to the ministry may depend on junior academic attainments, or criteria other than academic ones. At the senior levels, ambassadorships are the routine expectations of politicians out of favour. This means that there are numerous career diplomats, many at ambassador level, without assignments overseas. Too many chiefs and too many partially qualified indians at the ministry's headquarters in Lusaka have left a curious torpor in its corridors.

Coincidental with the lack of guaranteed university education within the ministry is the lack of full facilities for the study of international relations at the University of Zambia, so that even a graduate entrant may have no background related to his or her profession. The university offers one undergraduate course as an optional subject and, from time to time, has sought to mount an MA in international relations – but this has usually been understaffed and library-holdings out-of-date.[4] Moreover, ministry personnel have sought to avoid the local MA for fear of jeopardising their chances of being sponsored for an MA overseas. All the junior and, often, fundamental research work of the ministry is done, therefore, by essentially unskilled people. By the time they take their MAs, whether locally or elsewhere, their responsibilities have also changed.

This situation reflects the more fundamental problem of academic culture. No Zambian scholar has ever published a book on international relations. Effectively, the subject is invisible by being not fully

---

[4] When I was recruited to be coordinator of the foundation MA in International Relations, I found firstly that I had to teach it all myself, and secondly that no book in the library on the subject was less than ten years old. For some of my reactions to this, see Stephen Chan, 'International Studies in Africa – The European Connection', *European Consortium for Political Research News*, Vol. 2, No. 2, 1991.

in existence. If this problem of academic culture is reflected in students and graduates, then its meaning is that in neither the ministry, nor the party's research section, is there any sustained and sophisticated enquiry or interpretation. Nor is there assurance of basic knowledge and data. L. J. Chingambo found that knowledge of South African foreign policy processes is either rare or rudimentary, despite the fact that South Africa has posed Zambia's major foreign policy problems.[5] This was reflected in his respondents from governmental, scholastic, and journalistic callings. Even if the president insists or is accustomed, therefore, to taking his own decisions, then he must do so – and has always done so – without the benefit of expert professional advice.

The professional level exists as the civil service cadre within the Ministry of Foreign Affairs. The political level is represented by the cabinet Ministers of Foreign Affairs and Defence. If the professionals are not expert, then the politicians are often reshuffled so frequently that they cannot master their portfolios. The single exception has been Professor Lameck Goma, a former university vice-chancellor and scientist, who was Minister of Foreign Affairs for six years. His successors have had no such durability.

In the Zambian system, the policy level supersedes the professional and political levels, and theoretically has been monopolised by the party. The party has, however, the same problems of under-research at one level, and over-mobility at another. This leaves the executive level occupied by the president with his advisers. One former State House assistant to the president, Mark Chona, made a name in foreign affairs during the independences of Angola and Mozambique, undertaking a startling round of shuttle diplomacy, but no other presidential staffer has become known for his expertise or knowledge in this area. If he is unassisted, receives no proper policy, political or professional advice, how does Kaunda make foreign policy decisions? How does he operate out of his singularity? That also is a subject of the chapters that follow.

Having made all these points, it should be understood that Kaunda has maintained a fairly consistent set of foreign policy goals over the years. What they have been, and how rationally or irrationally they

5 Chanda Lloyd John Chingambo, 'Destabilisation and SADCC: The Politics and Economics of Economic Integration', unpublished Ph.D. thesis, University of Kent, 1990.

have been pursued, is discussed in what follows. The close to this introduction, however, should caution against two well-worn maxims in the field of foreign policy analysis. Firstly, Zambian foreign policy has not been simply a diminutive of the foreign policies of larger states; it has not been a policy with the same sort of goals, but with fewer resources.[6] Nor has it been a simple case of Kaunda substituting morality in the place of power, and rhetoric in the place of force. Hero or villain, his policies have been more complex than that.

[6] This is a point made of small states generally by Maria Papadakis and Harvey Starr, 'Opportunity, Willingness, and Small States: The Relationship Between Environment and Foreign Policy', in Charles F. Hermann, Charles W. Kegley Jr., and James N. Rosenau (eds.), *New Directions in the Study of Foreign Policy*, Boston: Allen & Unwin, 1987, pp. 421–3.

2

IN SEARCH OF KAUNDA

Kaunda's policies were complex and his personality remained enigmatic. This was well-displayed in 1990, when Kaunda was confronted by many crises, but none graver than the urban rioting that broke out in Lusaka in June. What began as a food protest soon took on the aspects of an uprising, and this uprising precipitated a hurried and unsuccessful attempt at a coup. Afterwards, Kaunda's remarks were vengeful. 'Those who live by the sword will die by the sword', he said, later adding that he might propose stronger penalties for coup plotters.[1] But the uprising had attracted international attention. British editorials judged that it was 'too late for him to save his reputation', and that his maladministration, vanity, and economic incompetence could no longer be offset by the 'aura of statesmanship' which he had retained 'for an undeservedly long time'.[2]

Kaunda did try to save his reputation in July. On the international front, he secured the release of Daphne Parish from an Iraqi jail, where she had been held because of her friendship with the *Observer* journalist, Farzad Bazoft, who had been executed on spying charges. Even though Zambian officials insisted it was the culmination of a lengthy process, and not an overnight stunt designed to refurbish his image, Kaunda made the most of the occasion by having Mrs Parish flown from Iraq to Lusaka, before sending her home to Britain, the roundabout route facilitating a press conference in which he could (and did) shine. Nationally, Kaunda released the prisoners taken in all

[1] *Times of Zambia*, 1 July 1990; and *Daily Mail* (Lusaka), 4 July 1990.
[2] *The Independent* (London), 29 June 1990.

three publicised coup attempts against him, that of 1980 involving
Edward Shamwana, that of 1988 involving General Christon Tembo,
and the most recent effort of 1990 in which Lieutenant Mwamba
Luchembe had, in official accounts, single-handedly taken over
Lusaka radio to broadcast the advent of a coup.[3] Blanket forgiveness
had overcome his earlier bitterness.

The release of Daphne Parish was not without its idiosyncratic
moments. Kaunda complained that the western media had been
responsible for the death of Farzad Bazoft in Iraq. Media pressure on
'my brother', Saddam Hussein, had been so intense that Saddam, so
as not to appear a pawn of the western press, had no choice but to
have Bazoft executed. 'I have no doubt in my mind that, if it had not
been for that vicious attack on him and on Iraq by the British
authorities and press, that man [Bazoft] might have lived, might have
been here with Daphne together.'[4] Kaunda seemed to suggest that
press attention on both Saddam and him had been wilfully spiteful
and misleading, and the intention of the press conference seemed to
be an attempt to vindicate them both by parading a freed Daphne
Parish. Whether this was the case or not, the choice of Saddam for a
'brother' could not have been more miscalculated as, the very next
month, Saddam invaded Kuwait and precipitated not only immense
international pressure against him, but a concerted international
recasting of his image. Yet Kaunda had not been caught in a trap of
opportunism, naming Saddam as his 'brother' simply for the occasion
of Mrs Parish's release. Zambia had supported Iraq in its conflict with
Iran, and Kaunda did indeed feel a close relationship with the Iraqi
President, renaming the prettiest street in suburban Lusaka Saddam
Hussein Boulevard. The problem is that, while it is perfectly possible
to view Saddam as a champion of the third world, prepared to stand
up against western domination of the world's interests, any such view
can only be limited by Saddam's ruthlessness. It is perfectly possible
that Kaunda misjudged the man, but such misjudgement would simply
add to the confused list of his attributes that arose from the events of
June and July 1990. In those two months he was a mediator,
successfully negotiating Daphne Parish's release; a generous victor,
forgiving his enemies who had sought to depose him; an object of
dissatisfaction and blame from his own people and elements of his

---

[3] *Times of Zambia*, 26 July 1990
[4] *The Guardian* (London and Manchester), 18 July 1990.

own army; an obstinate politician, monopolising power, and refusing to abandon it in the face of vigorous protest and the declining abilities of his government to provide services; a declared admirer of Saddam Hussein; and, through it all, two months of crisis, he was a man of decisiveness. Whatever one's preferred judgement of Kaunda, he did not panic and took a series of calculated steps which allowed him to emerge scathed but intact and still credibly the leader of Zambia.

The range of perceptions possible in that time, however, illustrates how difficult it is to pinpoint his personality. But, if Kaunda was decisive in an hour of crisis, then he was less so in the months leading up to it, toying with measures for constitutional change which could only have further centred power on himself and his UNIP. In March 1990, 14 proposed changes to the constitution were gazetted, including one which provided that only the party president could be president of Zambia.[5] A week later, he told the UNIP Fifth National Convention that the changes in eastern Europe were only temporarily mesmerising and that, in Zambia, the one-party state was there to stay.[6] In the beginning of April, however, parliament in a show of defiance failed to provide the two-thirds majority necessary to pass the second reading of the 14 proposals for constitutional change.[7] Prominent backbenchers, as had former UNIP luminaries at the Fifth National Convention, charged the government with a succession of failures, and the party with a hijacking of national power.[8] Clearly a mood of dissatisfaction was being expressed and, as a result, Kaunda promised to consider the backbench fears while on holiday.[9] In mid-May, Kaunda announced a referendum on a multi-party state, but spoke gravely against those who might seek such political pluralism, cautioning that it would be a recipe for tribalism.[10] Kaunda would himself lead the 'no' campaign, denouncing the scourge of multi-partyism and, in this way, he firmly identified himself with UNIP's record and staked the style, at least, of his own future on the referendum's outcome. It all seemed suddenly desperate and certainly stuff born out of isolation. If Kaunda had been in touch with national

[5] *Daily Mail* (Lusaka), 8 March 1990.
[6] *Times of Zambia*, 16 March 1990.
[7] *Daily Mail* (Lusaka), 5 April 1990.
[8] For the full text of one such speech, see Sikota Wina, 'An Open Letter to the Fifth Zambia National Convention', *Southern Africa Political & Economic Monthly*, Vol. 3, No. 7, 1990.
[9] *Times of Zambia*, 11 April 1990.
[10] *Times of Zambia*, 14 May 1990 and 25 May 1990.

feeling when playing with his 14 constitutional amendments, he would never have had them introduced in the first place. Once he took soundings of the political climate, he announced measures to safeguard his position by firstly placing it under threat. None of this was adroit and, as it turned out, it was not particularly convincing. In June, the riots came and Kaunda's tenure was threatened with violence.

In the wake of the riots and his successful crisis management, Kaunda postponed the referendum from October 1990 to August 1991. Even so, an opposition movement began to flower that included several former UNIP figures. Released detainees, who had been charged with coup-plotting, did not rule out their participation in the opposition, and UNIP itself began debating radical changes to the party's powers and the longevity of tenure of the party president.[11] Finally, under mounting public pressure, of the sort associated with the pro-democracy movements in eastern Europe, but largely untracked by television cameras in Africa, Kaunda abandoned the idea of a referendum and instead announced multi-party elections for October 1991 (see Appendix 3). What these changes will finally result in is unclear at the time of writing but, one way or another, they mean the end of a fully-monopolistic UNIP and the type of presidency occupied by Kaunda. The short-term history of this entire episode, from the introduction of 14 proposals to strengthen the UNIP grip on power in March, to debate on a radical loosening of this grip in August, to the September decision to allow a multi-party election, saw Kaunda having to move with a tide he had not anticipated. If, in crisis situations, he is decisive, then he can show less clarity of thought in longer-term political projections.

This seven-month cameo, while related firstly to domestic affairs, nevertheless has some resonance in international relations – not only because British editorials suggested that the domestic foundation for Kaunda's statesmanlike image had gone, but because other statesmen, politicians, and diplomats have never been sure with which Kaunda they were dealing. The range of responses to him has been immense. Lord Hatch, who met Kaunda at a very early stage and became a sort of British patron, was later a Labour Party spokesman on foreign affairs. His biography of Kaunda was extremely flattering and, on its first page, was the judgement that 'he comes within the category of

[11] *Times of Zambia*, 8–11 August 1990.

"philosopher-king" '.[12] By contrast, Lord Carrington, in his memoirs, recounted a dinner between Prime Minister Edward Heath and President Kaunda in which Heath had scolded Kaunda.

> Heath then relapsed into silence. The effect on Kaunda was electrifying. His eyes rolled, he clasped his arms, he swayed from side to side, intoning,
>   'My God, my God, my God! Never did I think I would hear a British Prime Minister speak to me like that! My God, my God, my God!'
>   His entourage took their cue. They folded their arms and swayed in unison, murmuring, 'My God, my God! How terrible, terrible!' This lasted several minutes.[13]

How The Singularity of Kaunda Arose

Carrington makes no further comment but, with the drollness of silence, he leaves his readers in no doubt that he found such behaviour ridiculous. Others have been bemused. The image of Kaunda visiting the late-Emperor Hirohito of Japan, and serenading him with the Zambian song, 'Tiendepamodzi' (let's all pull together), while strumming a guitar, is memorable mostly because of the flicker of amazement on the emperor's face – he, dressed in tails to host a reception, and Kaunda in his safari suit. But it is not merely an impetuous unconventionality that describes Kaunda. Lords Hatch and Carrington paint the same man. One portrait, the 'philosopher-king', has him full of intellectual idealism and dignity. The other has him standing on this dignity until a clown-like persona overwhelms him. It would be tempting to say that the true Kaunda lies somewhere between the images of king and fool, between king and minstrel, but this would be false. Kaunda's range encompasses both extremes. Nor does he lapse over time from one extreme to another: in a single presentation of himself he can be many persons. The man of compassion who weeps in public at the poverty of his people dabs at his eyes with an imported handkerchief. This does not make him a wicked man, but nor is he a saint; yet the literature on him tends to be uni-dimensional, concentrating on one of several extremes. Some of these extremes are

[12] John Hatch, *Two African Statesmen*, London: Secker & Warburg, 1976.
[13] Lord Carrington, *Reflect on Things Past*, London: Collins, 1988, pp. 254–5.

discussed in Chapter 5. For now, the immediate comment should be that the literature concentrates on Kaunda, and on almost no other Zambian. How did this singularity emerge?

Despite the British Government's opinion of Kaunda as an agitator during the campaign for Zambian independence, a view shared and publicised by the newspapers of the day, the image that eventually gained most currency within the British liberal intelligentsia and Labour Party was that of an engaging and charming young teacher who had emerged from the poverty and illiteracy of Northern Rhodesia to lead his people, with the utmost dignity and Christian compassion, to nationhood and freedom. This image was crafted in large part by his autobiographical account of the struggle for independence.[14] It is hard now, upon rereading his book, to accept it as the literary gem it was once thought to be. It is a very prosaic narrative, but its success came from what it narrated – Kaunda not so much confronting as confronted by a colonial authority which could not bend him. The simple style recounts a simple, uncomplicated, and largely low-key resistance; but its very simplicity and guilelessness seemed to a 1960s readership to be evidence against the complexities of evil, particularly colonial evil, and in favour of the humanity of the author and the justice of his cause. Although it was not this book that made him a philosopher-king, it added justice to the alloy of his crown.

The greater problem of this book is something Kaunda could not have predicted. Apart from two novels by Dominic Mulaisho,[15] for some time the State House economics adviser to Kaunda, there are no other Zambian representatives on the Heinemann African Writers Series, nor in any other western series. This situation is barely redressed by a study of local publishing. Very little creative literature has appeared and even its flow has tended to dry up in the 1980s as economic conditions have made paper, ink, photographic plates, and the other necessities of printing a great luxury. Very few books are now published in Zambia without the assistance of foreign grants, and these will be attached to academic projects that relate to foreign concerns about human rights, women's rights, and other questions of development. But even the little creative literature that managed to

[14] Kenneth Kaunda, *Zambia Shall be Free*, London: Heinemann, 1962.
[15] Dominic Mulaisho, *The Tongue of the Dumb*, London: Heinemann, 1971, and *The Smoke That Thunders*, London: Heinemann, 1975.

appear before the drought of the last decade was unexceptional – a
few adventure yarns – so that the great adventure of struggling for
independence towers on the Zambian literary landscape by default.
Nothing overshadows it because almost nothing else is there.

Quite apart from the question of what sort of Zambia is it that
contains no obvious great writers – nor, in 1990, a single shop devoted
to the selling of books – there is the question of the untested Kaunda
and, here, literature is a metaphor. The west has approached African
literature through the Heinemann series. Although now imitated, it
was invaluable and exemplary. If, within it, Soyinka and Achebe, for
example, represent Nigerian literature, Kaunda keeps high company.
But he is not remotely the writer they and others in the series are. He
is there because there are no other obvious Zambian candidates. To
some important degree, there are no candidates because there are no
willing or able publishers. If no-one publishes, the urgency to write
and share one's thought is diminished. The vehicle for sharing has
been diminished. Straitened economic times have now hit Heinemann, Longman, and other western publishers. Macmillan recently
suspended expansion of its African literature list. Caution allows an
international publisher only to consider those who have first been
nationally acclaimed. No writer is going to be acclaimed in Zambia in
the foreseeable future for the simple reason that no writer will be
published. Kaunda will stand alone, incomparable because he is
uncompared.

The metaphor of incomparability relates to Kaunda's political life.
Under a one-party state there is, of course, no opposition party. Lightheartedly, there is the evidence of national voting forms where a 'yes'
vote for Kaunda as president is entered alongside the symbol of an
eagle; a 'no' vote is entered alongside the symbol of a frog. In the
image stakes, Kermit is no match for Kenneth. But the fact of
cultivating a presidential image without opposing aspirants is disquiet-
ing: firstly because, in the event of rebellion against worsening
conditions in Zambia, Kaunda becomes the most visible target, and
the extent of any successful vengefulness may well reflect the extent
of his visibility; secondly, because of the way Kaunda arrived at his
unchallenged position. The way he out-manoeuvred both Harry
Nkumbula and Simon Kapwepwe, traducing the presidential prospects of Kapwepwe in particular, is an indication of a ruthless
politician rather than of incomparability solely by accomplishment. He

never allowed that accomplishment to speak for itself under challenge, destroying instead the challengers.[16]
In Kaunda's latest book published in the west, he presents himself as a tortured man having to balance idealism with ruthlessness.[17] I comment further on this book below. For now, it should be noted that Kaunda, by his own most recent hand, is a distance removed from the Kaunda who, again in his own hand, described in his Heinemann book the struggle against British rule and the injustices of that time.

Anecdote and Rumour

Against whom should one be ruthless but against one's enemies? Yet, for Kaunda, the high manifestation of idealism has always been forgiveness. There has been a tension in Kaunda's career between ruthlessness and forgiveness, expressed not only in his latest book, but in the long history of Zambian rumours about him. Rumours prove nothing, but a history of consistent rumours suggests something of the political atmosphere in which a one-party state must try to govern. If dissent is difficult and requires courage and sacrifice, scepticism, at least, will grow up in its place. People will distrust the good faith of those who rule. In Kaunda's case, people will distrust the hope that his forgiveness will always outpace his ruthlessness. Of late, forgiveness has been conditional, or extracted from him by the pace of events.

The last of the detainees from the 1980 coup attempt were released in July 1990, after the riots of June, and after they had spent nearly ten years in detention. It must be said that their trial had been conducted meticulously, and that Kaunda had commuted their death sentences, thus retaining Zambia's reputation for due process and Kaunda's for clemency. Full forgiveness took time, however. At the end of April 1990, Kaunda repeated his readiness to release Edward Shamwana. 'I only want him to be truthful and give facts to show he has genuinely changed.'[18] Kaunda required Shamwana to be contrite as a condition of his release. Forgiveness could come only after an admission of guilt and repentance. This has never been taken to

---

[16] Only after both men were dead did biographies appear. See Goodwin Mwangilwa, *Harry Mwaanga Nkumbula – A Biography of the 'Old Lion' of Zambia*, Lusaka: Multimedia, 1982; and idem, *The Kapwepwe Diaries*, Lusaka: Multimedia, 1986.
[17] Kenneth Kaunda, *Kaunda on Violence*, (ed. Colin Morris), London: Collins, 1980.
[18] *Times of Zambia*, 28 April 1990.

represent a delusion of godliness – or even priestliness. What the Lusaka rumour-mills concentrated on were accounts of prison conditions for the detainees, the physical and psychological pressures under which they lived, so that the rumours concluded, perhaps wrongly and maliciously, that Kaunda was determined to break them, to reduce them to contrition – so that he could then forgive them. In this case, scepticism had given way to a deep cynicism. The growth of such cynicism reflected the decay in morale as the 1980s progressed and, above all, the decay in lightheartedness. For the 1980s had indeed begun lightheartedly, with citizens expecting improvements in their lot after shedding the burden of sanctions and mobilisation against Rhodesia. The lighthearted, muddling, amateur spirit inherited from the British was most evident from the coup attempt.

Although the movement towards a coup in 1980 included a democratic dimension, it had other concerns. E. Chipimo, who had made a startling pro-democracy speech in Ndola in April 1980, was not among those afterwards charged with the coup. The coup had been wrongly conceived on two levels – in terms of both its rationale and execution. It sought a market economy and closer economic links with South Africa as the means of future growth and development. It was precisely in 1980, however, that Zimbabwe gained independence and Zambia's investment against Smith's regime could be redirected towards development. There had not been time to judge whether or not such redirection was successful. The Southern African Development Coordination Conference (SADCC) had been formally inaugurated that year precisely to provide a viable alternative to economic dependency on South Africa. Both national and regional regeneration seemed possible and, at the time of its conception, the coup seemed irrational. Its execution had been poorly planned, too loudly and often discussed at the Lusaka Flying Club, dependent upon a ragtag mercenary band being able to capture Kaunda and, that being the plan's critical and only strategy, the aim had been to have him sign a document relinquishing his official positions and agreeing to go into exile. Other accounts had the plotters undecided about Kaunda's fate and some said the plan had been to kill him. By and large, however, the plot seemed amazingly genteel and one could only speculate with what immense politeness the plotters might have asked Kaunda to sign along their dotted line. It might, perhaps, have been easier to forgive them, or to have forgiven them all earlier, than Kaunda finally managed.

Other attempts to gain power, according to the rumours, have been more comical. Here, the rumour circuit acts almost as an oral samizadt of satire, but there are many in high places who insist the story is true. It concerns a coup by magic and starred a highly-placed party official who, having consulted an 'inyanga' or witch-doctor, was persuaded that, by sleeping in the bed exclusively reserved for the president at a distant hunting-lodge, he would displace and succeed Kaunda. Somehow, Kaunda uncovered the plan and rushed to the lodge, arriving just before bed-time to confront the pyjamaed usurper. It was not so much that Kaunda himself believed in magic, but he saw its possibilities and meaning and, the tale goes, was extremely angry that his bed should have been sought as a prelude to his office. The offender was made an ambassador and packed off overseas.

The oral samizadt may be at times extraordinary, at times a species of magical realism not fully plumbed by any African writer, but it is often bitter and full of premonition. The 1990 food riots had their precursor in 1986. Some would say Kaunda learnt nothing from that episode, but the rumours say that he learnt something quite specific. Overwhelmed by remorse that his people could not afford to eat, Kaunda toyed with resignation and exile. A plane was requisitioned to fly himself and his family out. At this stage, General Christon Tembo upbraided Kaunda, reportedly with the words that, since he had created the mess in the nation, he should stick around to clean it up. Kaunda accordingly did, but had been twice shaken: firstly by the food riots themselves; secondly by the rare display of undeferential advice. He remembered in his heart the upbraiding a subordinate had delivered him and awaited the opportunity to assert the superiority of his position. Thus far, the account is all rumour and cannot be substantiated. That Tembo in some way became popular with the Lusaka crowds, however, is demonstrated by the reception he received after his arrest for plotting a coup in 1988. Driven to court in an open-topped landrover, Tembo and his colleagues were cheered, and the apparent approbation for him increased with the (unsubstantiated) story presented to the court of Kaunda holding a personal external bank account which disposed of dollar sums in the tens of millions.[19] Although unsubstantiated, the story was reported in the press and this fuelled antipathy to Kaunda since, somehow, he was rich while his citizens were poor. The story appeared in February 1990 and Kaunda,

[19] *Times of Zambia*, 15–17 February 1990.

seemingly unaware of the damage to his image caused by rumour and reportage, presented his 14 constitutional proposals in March.

The consistency of these and other rumours, anecdotes, and accounts – all circulating widely on the political and party circuit, repeated by friend and foe of Kaunda alike – is firstly that each individual story varies hardly at all from teller to teller. If it is a fabrication in the first place, no-one adds anything to it. Secondly, they all concern Kaunda's hanging on to power and beating down those who might challenge his tenure, or who overstep the boundaries surrounding his presidency. Kaunda has ruled Zambia since its independence in 1964. He has seemed perpetual. One of the justifications of his long reign, made by party followers and foreign admirers alike, is that he rules with true humanism. This is a philosophy devised by Kaunda, and it is this that has given him the title of philosopher-king.

In Search of Humanism

One of the attributes that endeared Kaunda to a liberal British constituency was his early decency. People were impressed by this, by his charm, and by his leadership qualities. In his first trip to Britain in 1957 he made many converts who have remained loyal to him, viewing him as embattled but principled. One of these was John Hatch, then head of the Labour Party's Commonwealth Section. Hatch became one of Kaunda's many biographers – not one of these biographies has been unadmiring – and he was able to view Kaunda not only as an independence leader but as a moral statesman: a statesman because of Kaunda's desire both to resist the unilateral independence of Rhodesia and to seek to subdue it, and moral because he did not consider cost above the principle underlying resistance. As early as 1967, not much more than a year after Rhodesian UDI, he had enunciated the founding precepts of humanism, an extraordinary and ecumenical mixture of Christianity, socialism, and African reference points. The central message of humanism was equality, and this provided a linkage between the pre-independence Kaunda and the later president. He resisted the British and Ian Smith for the sake of the same principle. Hatch maintained that 'the unique importance of Kaunda to Africa stems from his profound personal belief in the innate and equal worth of the human being'.[20] The construction of a social philosophy around this belief, as described in Chaloka Beyani's Foreword to this book, gave Kaunda the reputation not only of a thoughtful president but of a sage.

It was not just John Hatch and other British as well as Dutch writers who viewed Kaunda as a sort of philosopher-king. The Chinese did as well – at least insofar as they thought they might use this reputation for their own ends. In 1974, two years before Hatch's biography was published, the Chinese propagated their Three World Theory of international relations. Although this theory was short-lived, it remains the only attempt by a major power to theorise the post-war world. Its intent was to identify China firmly with the third world and its struggles and, if possible, act as its leader. Simply to assert such an identification would have been tactless. At the same time, to credit any non-Chinese with co-authorship of the theory would have been to dilute China's leadership ambition. The Chinese waited until just after a state visit to Beijing by Kaunda in 1974, mindful that Kaunda owed them a debt after they had built the Tazara railway for him, but more mindful still of his international standing as a social philosopher, before announcing their theory. They said that discussions with a third world leader – and Kaunda had been the only such leader to visit Beijing that month – had crystallised Chairman Mao's thought to such an extent that the theory, long dormant, could be formulated and announced to the world.[21]

Hatch's approach to humanism had a different utility in mind. In a way, he never departed from his 1957 desire to reveal Kaunda to the British public – a decent and upright man, able, and not a mindless native agitator. His 1976 book extended this desire to reveal Kaunda to the world. In 1982, he accepted an appointment at the University of Zambia to be both professor and director of the Institute of Human Relations. The term, 'human relations', was a euphemism for humanism, one necessary at the university, as made clear below, and one

[20] Hatch, *Two African Statesmen*. The Zambian edition cited here is John Hatch, *Kaunda of Zambia*, Lusaka: Institute of Human Relations, 1983, p. xiv
[21] The Chinese theory received remarkably little attention in the western academic press. For three exceptions, see Herbert S. Yee, 'The Three World Theory and Post-Mao global strategy', *International Affairs*, Vol. 59, No. 2, 1983; Stephen Chan, 'China's Foreign Policy and Africa: The Rise and Fall of China's Three World Theory', *The Round Table*, 296, 1985; and Peter Worsley, 'One World or Three? A Critique of the World-system Theory of Immanuel Wallerstein', in R. Miliband and J. Saville (eds.), *Socialist Register 1980*, London: Merlin Press, 1980.

recommended by Hatch himself. But it was also a term used by Kaunda in the past and summarises a culturally-based internationalism on his part. In 1967, he said that 'we have held, and we still hold, that Africa's gift to world culture must be in the field of Human Relations'.[22] If there was some irony in a British Labour peer and adult educationist lecturing Zambians on what was meant to be their national philosophy, there was also some need to give humanism intellectual flesh. It was not so much ironic as embarrassingly necessary. No Zambian scholar at the university had authored a book on humanism. Zambians not at the university had indeed attempted to do so;[23] the most spirited effort probably came from the Soviet-educated party official, Henry Mebeelo. Some years ago, fresh from his doctoral studies abroad, a scholar named Mwaipaya was asked by the party to analyse the philosophy of humanism, but his report was never published; suppressed – according to rumour – because it concluded that humanism was unscientific and irrelevant to Zambia. Before Hatch, two foreign academics, briefly at the University of Zambia, attempted to consider humanism. A Nigerian, Patrick Ollawa, wrote a book issued by a subsidy-publisher;[24] and a Dutchman, later a Netherlands senator, Bastiaan de Gaay Fortman, edited a collection of essays on it.[25] Even so, despite the limited number of academic treatises, and despite the lack of interest from Zambian scholars, students at the university were for years required to study this particular philosophy as part of their foundation years, and this undoubtedly contributed to the resentment described below. Hatch was something of a late or even last effort therefore. His mandate was to elaborate humanism, to relate it to appropriate academic disciplines, to make it, if not scientific, passably scholastic, to make it possible for there to be discourse on the subject.

Hatch became a curiosity about Lusaka. His appointment had raised disquiet among the university's academic staff, who, despite Hatch's track record at the Universities of Sierra Leone and Houston,

[22] Cited in Philip Brownrigg, *Kenneth Kaunda*, Lusaka: Kenneth Kaunda Foundation, 1989, p. 124.
[23] See Henry S. Mebeelo, *Main Currents of Zambian Humanist Thought*, Lusaka: Oxford University Press, 1973, and Timothy Kandeke, *Fundamentals of Zambian Humanism*, Lusaka: NECZAM, 1976.
[24] Patrick Ollawa, *Participatory Democracy in Zambia: The Political Economy of National Development*, Ilfracombe: Arthur Stockwell, 1979.
[25] Bastiaan de Gaay Fortman (ed.), *After Mulungushi: The Economics of Zambian Humanism*, Nairobi: East African Publishing House, 1969.

considered him not to be an outstanding scholar. Nevertheless, they did not object to his appointment since it was clear Hatch had the president's own endorsement. The Institute of Human Relations was located on a satellite campus and Hatch lived next to his office. The rift between him and the rest of the university was never closed because the two remained physically separate. The students, however, were far less reticent about voicing their disquiet. In a very real sense, the opening of the institute gave them a focus for protest. This protest had always been anti-party and, since the formation of the one-party state in 1973, the students had regarded themselves as an unofficial opposition. Their short-lived journal, *Trunza* (Truth in Zambia), had sought to provide exposés of the government; and they recalled the 1976 student riots against Zambian foreign policy – when the government was seen to be still supportive of UNITA in Angola, despite its South African connection – as an episode of heroism. In 1982, even though it was named the Institute of Human Relations, the students quickly realised that here was an outpost on their territory which was anathema to them. It was there to elaborate the philosophy to which they were opposed. A series of pamphlets was published, condemning first humanism, then all who subscribed to it. The students set about insulting the Zambian political leadership, denouncing humanism as a sham and a cover for those who both governed and were corrupt. Their major argument against humanism itself was that it was unscientific – but that was one of the reasons for Hatch's appointment in the first place. Their denunciation of the Zambian leadership, however, resulted in the closure of the university. The Institute of Human Relations did not begin its life with any clear sight of the good-will implicit in its name.

Nor did it continue its life with any academic distinction. It had been named the Institute of Human Relations because it was felt an Institute of Humanism would result in even greater student protest. The compromise name was soon attached to half-hearted or even halved publications. Hatch issued a Zambian edition of his joint study of Nyerere and Kaunda, but simply cut off the Nyerere part. His inaugural professorial address, although well-attended by luminaries, was a disappointment. It considered thought evoked by Konrad Lorenz's study of instinctual aggression in animal behaviour, and its relevance to human relations, in an entirely speculative manner that was devoid of reference to the huge academic literature surrounding what had become a very old and repetitive debate. The staff at the university felt that the address confirmed their views of Hatch's academic level, but I felt this was unfair. What it did was to confirm Hatch's academic age. He was from an earlier generation of thought, was certainly not a moral or social philosopher, and had not caught up. He was himself a most engaging and hospitable man, proud of his honours and his contribution to political life in Britain, proud that he had combined a political life with a university one, but he had been a wrong choice; and his own choice of a first staff member under him was also wrong – another non-Zambian who in turn set about alienating the academic staff by insisting he had come to do research and would not assist any hard-pressed faculty with a series of lectures. The institute simply became, rather quickly, unimportant. The question that arises from this cameo is whether or not humanism is itself unimportant. And why did the students, perhaps the future leadership of Zambia, find humanism not only objectionable but, even taking full account of pamphleteering rhetoric, repugnant?

The Foundation of Humanism

Although Kaunda had been a school-teacher, he was not well-educated. This was certainly not his fault. At independence, there were 99 Zambian university graduates, the majority of whom had relied upon private scholarships and support to study abroad. Some had studied in India, where the government, anxious to help third world countries emulate its own successful drive towards independence, provided official support. From the British Government there had been very little. To be a teacher or a clerk, therefore, was to be a member of an educated, or at least partially-educated, élite.[26] Progress beyond this level was almost comprehensively limited. Although Kaunda himself had the opportunity to study in India, he felt unable to remove himself from the independence campaign for the three or four years a degree would have demanded. When he came to Britain in 1957, he spoke English badly, having first to translate his thought from Bemba, and, even then, relied upon Biblical allusions to substantiate his thought. The impression, even from admiring biographies, is of an idealistic but naïve young man, educating himself in Britain by contact with the English and, most of all, with the Labour

---

[26] See P.C. Lloyd (ed.), *The New Elites of Tropical Africa*, London: Oxford University Press, 1970; and idem, *Africa in Social Change*, Harmondsworth: Penguin, 1975.

Party English; of an immense dignity despite the naïvety; and, inescapably, of charm, decency, and promise.[27] His English supporters did their work well enough so that, in the early years of independence, a persistent belief that Kaunda had gone up to Oxford held sway among the English public, and Kaunda's dignity of bearing helped to reinforce this false image.

The formulation of humanism, however, elaborated his decency but revealed the uneducated nature of his thought, his conviction that dignified leadership could inspire all the population, and a certain romanticisation of African history or his reinvention of it. This was all a superimposition upon the Zambian public, after the first imposition of national boundaries. Those national boundaries, the nationalism and nation-state that followed demanded symbols of cultural unity beneath the political cladding. Quite apart from artefacts in food and clothing – nshima or maize meal became regarded as the traditional national food, and the wrap-skirt chitenge became regarded as the traditional dress for women, even though both had been introduced for African consumption by European settlers – there was a need in Kaunda's mind for a social philosophy which acted both as a guide to the state and could be said to derive from African culture and tradition, particularly where they intersected with the messages of Christian love and charity and what Kaunda had picked up from British Labour Party socialism. If one were to ask what, in concrete terms, did Kaunda want, the answer would be that he wanted a Zambian version of the welfare state. If one were to ask who, even in summarised and second-hand terms, had influenced him, it would be his image of Harold Laski. If all this seemed ambitious and extraordinary, it was exactly this ambition that fired the western imagination of Kaunda in the early years of independence. There seemed a nobility within the ambition and people viewed him as a noble. This is the point: Kaunda was noble, not the Zambian people, for the message and application of humanism was paternalistic, top-down, with the exemplar, Kaunda, at the very top. For the west, Kaunda was also a noble Christian and he certainly secured the enthusiastic endorsement and help of several churchmen. His many books on humanism, none as well-written as his biography, owed greatly to the editing work of

[27] See Brownrigg, Kenneth Kaunda, Chapter 5; and Hatch, Kaunda of Zambia, pp. 40–45

Colin Morris.[28] In modern jargon, once Kaunda had established his image, it was properly 'handled'; he got 'good p.r.'. The western imagination of Kaunda, however, tends to ignore certain key aspects of humanism. In April 1967 Kaunda presented a small treatise on what he meant by humanism to the UNIP National Council. The foundation of his argument was a view of Zambian history which read like a cooperative movement in a pastoral paradise. Here, there was no war, tribalism, stratification, slavery, outcasting, and ruthless competition for food.[29] John Iliffe has presented a catalogue of how such things were very much present in the old nations that were welded into Zambia. He talks of rigorous stratification between ruler and ruled in the Lunda Kazembe kingdom in the Luapula Valley; of stratification also in the Bulozi kingdom, where the rulers grew long fingernails to prove they had no need to work; of the outcasting of lepers, epileptics, and the insane among the Lozi; of slavery and a view of slaves as sub-human in Bulozi; of slave-exporting by Kaunda's own Bemba people, often to the slave-importers of the Lozi; and of the strictures whereby food was distributed by the Bemba.[30] The catalogue is extensive beyond these examples, and includes accounts of orphans fending for them-selves, but Iliffe's work is very much a corrective to a common missionary view which generalised poverty, namely there wasn't very much, so all had very little. 'There are no poor among them, because all are so.'[31] The implication was of a communalism caused by negative factors. The assumption of many was therefore that, under positive circumstances, this same communalism would be found. This is the entire thrust of Kaunda's version of history, in the generalised missionary style. He ignores entirely the power relationships that

[28] The relationship is briefly described by Brownrigg, *Kenneth Kaunda*, p. 145, in which Kaunda dictates to his secretary, Gloria Sleep, and the work is edited by Colin Morris. It would be fair to say, however, that Morris is a very extensive editor; if not a co-author – since the basic *ideas* are Kaunda's – then the acknowledged 'ghost' who crafts the often rough ideas into a grammatical and logical flow. A selection of the results includes: Kenneth Kaunda (and Colin Morris), *Black Government? A Discussion*, London: United Society for Christian Literature, 1960; Kaunda, *A Humanist in Africa – Letters to Colin Morris*, London: Longman, 1966; and Kaunda *Kaunda on Violence*, (ed. Colin Morris).

[29] Kaunda's pamphlet to the UNIP National Council is excerpted extensively in Brownrigg, *Kenneth Kaunda*, pp. 124–5.

[30] John Iliffe, *The African Poor – A History*, Cambridge: Cambridge University Press, 1987, pp. 56–60.

[31] Vatican summary of missionary reports around 1590, cited ibid., p. 52.

arbitrated between the rich and the poor. If there exists in Zambia a contemporary power relationship between rich and poor, then Kaunda's 1967 treatise might be viewed as an intervening smokescreen between two periods of history which have both, in the minds of Kaunda's followers, been generalised and refused proper examination for the sake of maintaining a view of Kaunda's worth and the worth and authenticity of his thought.

The pamphlet presented to the UNIP Council said that, firstly, the traditional community was premised on mutual aid and that rulership of communal resources meant their fair distribution. Secondly, the traditional community was accepting and caring and made no outcasts of the old and infirm. Thirdly, the traditional community was inclusive so that community was denoted by the generalised use of 'mother' and 'father', titles which could be applied to all the senior members of one's family and which denoted in turn a parental responsibility that prevented any child from becoming an orphan. With this social and cultural heritage in mind, therefore, humanism occupied a place in a national tradition and could keep the modernising Zambia imbued with values that were both necessary and already structurally present in society. This presence, however, was not actual. If, then, humanism is a new construction, what strength has it?

Humanism as a Social Philosophy

The 1967 pamphlet on humanism was the first of three parts to Kaunda's vision of government. The second came in 1968 and was called the Mulungushi Economic Revolution. This set about the acquisition of majority shareholdings in large enterprises, including those of foreign companies, and sought to encourage a Zambian business and industrial structure by reserving government contracts in various sectors for them. The third came in 1969 and was called the Manifesto on Southern Africa. This followed a summit of 14 African leaders in Lusaka and, despite coming slightly more than three years after Ian Smith's UDI in Rhodesia, represented a first major foreign policy statement and triumph for Kaunda – a triumph because he seemed to be leading African opinion on the subject of decolonisation in southern Africa, and because the manifesto seemed to echo Kaunda's own thought. It was humanism applied to liberation. It rejected racialism, both as a means of oppression and as a rallying point for resistance. The problem was not white rule, but minority rule. It spoke of negotiations towards peaceful change, even if such negotiations made those in the resistance movements enter 'compromise on the timing of change'.[32] Briefly, it reflected that, since peaceful change seemed blocked, there was no alternative but to support those struggling against their oppressors. Then, as a prelude to later diplomatic action on boycotts and sanctions, it talked of the ostracization of South Africa from the United Nations and the remainder of the world community. The main points concerned non-racialism and negotiations, fighting shy of violence as much as possible.

There were other important contributions to humanism, such as the 1969 Matero Economic Reforms,[33] but those described above form a three-part vision of government – philosophy, economics, and foreign affairs – and they were given the mechanism for unrivalled implementation in 1973 with the establishment of the one-party state. In a word, the one-party state was concerned with unity: hence the twin slogans broadcast nightly on radio and television, 'One Zambia, One Nation', and 'UNIP means Unity'. The one Zambia was to be achieved by one party. The state, a consortium of some 70 nations, was to become dependent upon the party for its viability. Indeed, the immediate justification of one-party rule was the pressing requirement to overcome tribal divisions – although it must be said that Zambia was not in danger of fragmentation. It was in danger of having its politics tribally structured, with parties carrying particular tribal flags, but, at that stage, there was no serious suggestion that any of these tribes would seek to leave Zambia. The reality of the situation was that the state was safe. The idea of one nation, however, was not assured and it was this that Kaunda sought to guarantee. The mechanism of the one-party system owed greatly to his own thought, despite a canvas of public opinion.[34] And, although the system was publicly approved, the exercise in devising and imposing it had been accomplished in a top-down manner. In short, the artefacts of one nation, previously constructed and announced by Kaunda in a top-down manner – including humanism – required unopposed political muscle for them

---

[32] The Manifesto on Southern Africa is reproduced here in Appendix 2.
[33] See de Gaay Fortman, *After Mulungushi*, on the 1969 Matero Economic Reforms.
[34] For the process see Brownrigg, *Kenneth Kaunda*, pp. 132–3. Hatch, *Kaunda of Zambia*, p. 97, argues that Kaunda was 'forced to introduce the one-party state', and that it was an 'unpalatable decision', but this is a singular and forced reading since Kaunda had always hoped for a one-party state, but one occasioned by across-the-board electoral triumph rather than constitutional change.

to be assured of some form of adoption by a polity that had not known them before.

In a very real sense, Kaunda made a mark in the first ten years of his leadership: he announced a new national philosophy; he nationalised to a significant degree and centralised industry; he established a one-party state; and, as discussed in later chapters, he played an increasingly visible role in international affairs, resisting Ian Smith's UDI, resisting Edward Heath's arms sales to South Africa, and trying to lead African opinion. All of this was underlined with the justification of his thinking, with humanism, with the 'man-centred society' approach to all affairs. At home, he sought to educate the man at the centre of this society and, among other things, a beautiful university was constructed (although it didn't really look beautiful until the plants grew up to cover the concrete), to a large extent funded by public subscription. Everything seemed well-managed, at least to outside eyes, and the first major indication of fallibility and of one man playing the whole nation false came in 1975 with the Angolan crisis and Kaunda's desire to support UNITA. This also will be discussed later, but it was at this point that the students of the new university rose up and humanism received its first challenge both at home and by academics abroad. Till then, as William Tordoff has written, the Kaunda years up to Angolan independence could have been characterised by three great disengagements: firstly, disengagement from the Westminster model by means of the one-party state; secondly, disengagement from South Africa, particularly through the attempts to disengage from the South African rail system; and, thirdly, disengagement from foreign ideologies by the adoption of humanism.[35] All these things can be seen as the crafting of a true independence for Zambia, and as the demonstration of Kaunda's true nationalist inclinations and status. The first ten years, on balance, can only be counted a success, despite the cost of confrontation with Rhodesia and the attempt to disengage from South Africa. The appearance of principle in everything he did confirmed to his early British supporters that, in their Kenneth, they had found a truly great man. This was an era of largely undiluted praise.

Investigation of the achievements of this period, however, reveals that each had a fragile foundation and structure. Each will be

[35] William Tordoff, 'Zambia: The Politics of Disengagement', *African Affairs*', Vol. 76, No. 302, 1977.

discussed as the book progresses, but humanism was possibly the
most fragile of them all. It could never have existed or found even
polite currency without constant repetition of the word and its 'man-
centred' slogan by the party. In none of Kaunda's books, pamphlets,
or speeches does the definition of humanism rise above the platitudinous. Yet, if it could somehow become something practised, then
definitions would be unnecessary – if somehow everybody could love
their neighbour. It is as an ethic of great consequence, if it were ever
practised, that humanism has entered a peculiar literature. The
literature is peculiar because it is entirely uncritical; because it is
based on a simplistic pastiche of history; because it contains no
definitions; because it is simply hopeful; and because it says humanism
is great because the president who espouses it is great. I do not think
any work on humanism escapes this critique. As a social philosophy it
is certainly, as the students charged, unscientific.

Not that the students who protested the opening of Hatch's institute
were scientific themselves. Their brand of 'scientific' Marxist thought
was not peculiarly vulgar and deterministic – grist for the mill at
universities around the world – but peculiarly ironic (though probably
not consciously hypocritical), since almost all the protesting students
would shortly join the very élite they accused of sheltering under the
blanket of piety that humanism afforded. A more sophisticated critique
of humanism would take its assumption of a 'man-centred society'
and, instead of accepting that it is good, ask why it is better than other
sorts of society or ways of looking at society, or ways of looking at man
as a rational creature within it.

> The classical liberal's 'possessive individual man', the welfare
> liberal's 'man with basic needs', the Marxist 'labouring man in
> his sociality', the romantic ecologist's 'man in harmony with
> nature', the Christian humanist's 'man of brotherhood', the
> Freudian 'man of basic drives', Habermas's 'communicatively
> competent man', the contemporary pragmatist's 'man of
> ungrounded hope in the possibility of human community' – there
> are in principle as many possible interpretations of sovereign man
> as there are possible historical limitations that might be erected.[36]

---

[36] Richard Ashley, 'Living on Border Lines: Man, Poststructuralism and War', in James
Der Derian and Michael Shapiro (eds.), *International/Intertextual Relations*, Lexington, Massachusetts: Lexington Books, 1989, p. 266. The entire effort by Ashley is a
dense rebuttal of man's easy claim to be at the centre of anything to do with
statecraft.

To say 'this is the sort of aspiration that contains the sort of thought that considers that this is the sort of society for what I think is the ideal Zambian sort of man' is terribly limiting. It is a funnel. To voice a balanced criticism: it may or may not be a fine aspiration, but it is crude thought. It is a missionary style of thought in which certain key decisions have been made *a priori*. Despite or because of this, Zambians never became good humanists.

The students, however, had additional grounds for complaint. Humanism was meant, in the top-down fashion, first to be exemplified by the leadership. Kaunda had instigated a Leadership Code, and it was the widespread disregard for its tenets that provided ammunition for protest. The practice of humanism seemed often to comprise only Kaunda forgiving, or not even seeing, the misdemeanours of his colleagues. Forgiveness may be a Christian virtue, but it has resulted in a rich leadership, or a view of public service as an investment of one's time in order to acquire the funds and influence to establish business enterprises. Great private wealth is not a primary Christian virtue, and nor is it a humanistic one. The emphasis by humanism on cooperative enterprises for the sake of group livelihood and, hopefully, group prosperity seems mocked by a leadership that cannot display a single cabinet minister or member of the UNIP Central Committee who has remained poor. By contrast, such has been the lack of belief in cooperatives that, from my time in Zambia, I cannot think of a single cooperative that has been a longstanding success or that can be publicised as exemplary and worthy of imitation. The cooperative movement has for years been a dispirited nodule on the Zambian economic body, of neither economic consequence nor sightliness.

The student accusation, one which has considerable public support, is that the leadership is corrupt. Leaders are rich beyond what their salaries can provide, or what careful legitimate investment can usually provide, and certainly beyond what any leadership code would support. Here, apart from occasional scandals that are made public, the evidence is usually circumstantial. The accumulated wealth is visible, the process of accumulation the subject of rumours and suspicion.

President Kaunda has, himself, been the subject of such suspicion. How, when he makes substantial contributions to charity from his private purse, did he acquire such a capacious purse? As recounted above, at the 1990 treason trial of General Tembo, evidence submitted included reference to Kaunda's very large external account, denominated in US dollars. The court was also told that among the reasons for the planned coup were 'economic mismanagement' and 'leaders having external accounts'.[37] Whether true or not, such suspicion erodes public confidence that the leadership is in any way committed to the practice of humanism. Why then, the question is asked, should the public practise it?

The Party and Humanism

Humanism has never been so much practised as praised. Its officialisation, adoption by the party as national philosophy, has reduced whatever it was to a series of slogans and clichés, forever held aloft and never examined for inconsistencies. The president, the party, and the philosophy are so closely identified one with the other that to find inconsistencies in one is to find them in the rest. From the outset, however, observers have doubted the bona fides of the one-party state. Although, in 1974, shortly after its introduction, Jan Pettman felt inclined to accept the justifications given – the need for national unity[38] – the reviewers of her book included not only those with doubts but those with accusations.[39] Already, in the mid-1970s, some viewed an emerging and corrupt élite with foreboding, and saw the one-party state as the élite's method for self-preservation and self-perpetuation.

It would be wrong, however, to suggest that Kaunda himself saw the one-party state in such self-interested terms. If he has never been able to define humanism, the construction of the new state, the so-called 'second republic', saw his attempt at least to apply what he felt, and to match an apparatus with what basic outline of thought had emerged. It was, at least partly, a sincere exercise. In his man-centred society, Kaunda saw five categories of human endeavour. These are the political (including legal matters and foreign affairs), the economic, the social and cultural, that concerned with defence and security, and the scientific and technological. Accordingly, the Central Committee of the single party was divided into five sub-committees, each concerned with one of these categories. This taxonomy of human endeavour has stuck in Kaunda's mind, so that the 1980 Local Administration Act apportions the concerns of local government

[37] *Times of Zambia*, 17–30 January 1990.
[38] Jan Pettman, *Zambia: Security and Conflict*, Lewes: Julian Friedman, 1974.
[39] Graham Mytton, review of Pettman, *African Affairs*, Vol. 74, No. 294, 1975, pp. 111–12.

according to the five categories. Whether such categories are all-inclusive or not – and they cannot be unless included in each one of them are the pathological and oppositional, room in short for the reverse decor of all neat and tidy government – the point here is that the apparatus of policy and government reflects something of the apparatus of humanism.

But it has not been very successful. No non-partisan account views it as having been so, and even assessments that bend backwards to be objective can only conclude in desultory terms:

> that the single party cannot represent all walks of life in society equally, even though it aims to do so. The Zambian experience suggests that the one-party system has been fairly successful in integrating regional groups. But as social differentiation in society became more acute and was intensified by economic crisis, the state party in no way reflected the diverse interests of peasants, workers, private businessmen and others. Its prime focus was the ruling élite of party and state functionaries, drawn from all regions. Hence its increasing lack of credibility and popularity.[40]

That whatever animating role humanism had in government has become of service only to an élite is evident from the 1980 Local Administration Act. According to this act, only UNIP members could vote UNIP officials into local government posts. This led Rodger Chongwe, the distinguished African jurist, to comment that one-man one-vote democracy had been 'buried' by this act.[41]

If Kaunda himself still clings to some remnant of humanism, it is only after his own long night of the soul. His book, *On Violence*, released in 1980, was something of a confession on the perils of leadership and the dirty art of government. Even Zambian reviewers, writing for the western academic press, noted the president's slide from idealism to despair.[42] Others, however, were excoriating, pulling no punches, and wrote that the book was a confession of too little

[40] Peter Meyns, 'The Road to One-Party Rule in Zambia and Zimbabwe: A Comparative View', in Peter Meyns and Dani Wadada Nabudere (eds.), *Democracy and the One-Party State in Africa*, Hamburg: Hamburger Beitrage zur Afrika-Kunde, 1989, p. 202.

[41] *Times of Zambia*, 25 May 1990.

[42] Mwizenge Tembo, review of Kaunda, *The Journal of Modern African Studies*, Vol. 19, No. 2, 1981.

substance, which had come too late, and after too much misrule.[43] If the book had been a plea for understanding, it did not work. Yet there is something contradictory even here. In 1980, this book seemed to plead for understanding; in the same year, the Local Administration Act passed into law to 'bury' democracy. The book described the difficulties of even the president's adherence to humanism; the act reiterated the categories of humanism's man-centred society. How many ways can the president have it? Is he, at the last, merely stubborn? What has happened in the decade since book and act? Through the focus of foreign policy, these questions are addressed in what follows.

[43] Particularly R.V. Sampson, review of Kaunda, *African Affairs*, Vol. 81, No. 325, 1982.

3

A BRIEF HISTORY OF SOUTH AFRICAN REGIONAL POLICY

Zambia became independent in 1964. Ian Smith made his Unilateral Declaration of Independence (UDI) for Rhodesia in 1965. From the outset, Zambian foreign policy was reactive. Events determined its shape. Supporters of President Kaunda have, however, staunchly insisted that his sense of principle determined its content. The Zambian response to events is discussed in the next chapter. The aim of the present chapter is to describe the animation behind events in southern Africa.[1] For it would be wrong to think that UDI established a region in which it was a case of Zambia against Rhodesia. It would be wrong also to consider a situation where Zambia faced a white south – Rhodesia and South Africa. Zambia in fact faced a largely white region. To its south, west, and east, white-ruled territories covered a greater area than the independent states, disposed of greater wealth, and possessed greater military forces. In fact, Botswana and Lesotho did not gain independence until 1966, after UDI had been declared, and Swaziland not until 1968. Zambia was determined by the pace of history to be the first frontline state and, although joined in due course by Botswana, Lesotho, and Swaziland, these three states retained close monetary and trade ties with South Africa and could only develop independent foreign policies gradually and cautiously. Zambia had, therefore, the first fledged foreign policy of the independent region and, despite support from Tanzania to its north and, to a more ambiguous extent, from Malawi, it was Zambia that bordered a multiplicity of white-minority regimes. To its south were the Rhodesia

---

[1] As such, it draws on some of my earlier work: Stephen Chan, *Exporting Apartheid*.

of Ian Smith and the Namibia of South Africa; to its west and east were the Portuguese territories of Angola and Mozambique. The fact of being almost surrounded gave the appearance of a Zambia embattled. The impression of principle certainly derived from the fact that Zambia opposed minority-rule. It would be fair to say, however, that this impression also benefited by contrast with the difficulties and violence on its northern borders. The chaos of Zaïre meant that Africa desperately required the projection of reasonable and moral leadership. This sub-agenda was doubtless present in the support given to Kaunda and Nyerere, and, over time, was apparent in the attention given the philosophies of humanism and *ujamaa* – both reasonable and moral – the fact that both men wrote books (both were therefore literate and Nyerere, translating Shakespeare, was clearly well-read), and the fact that both were essentially pacific. The combination of proofs of principle – philosophy, books, contrast with the wild black north, contrast with the white-minority east, west, and south – and pacific resistance were the ingredients used in Zambia's public foreign policy and by Zambia's international support. It seemed a flimsy defence, although that made it seem all the more heroic, against a region that appeared structurally opposed to what Kaunda was meant to stand for.

The first structural element was laid considerably before Zambia's independence. Zambia was created as a landlocked colony. The colonial transport structure predetermined a flow of goods southward, eventually to the ports of South Africa, with imports travelling north from these ports along the same lines of rail.[2] Other lines of rail to the west and east ran through Angola and Mozambique, in short through other minority-ruled territories, and the main line east ran through Rhodesia in any case before even reaching Mozambique. Opposition to minority rule meant, from the beginning, attention to the fact of vulnerability in the areas of communications, transport, the export of commodities (and hence the earning of foreign exchange), and the import of necessities. The minority regimes, opposed by Zambia, controlled Zambia's important lifelines. Even without the oppositional politics of the region, economic competition would have still placed Zambia in a dependent situation. Zambia might well have been the

2 See Simon Katzenellenbogen, 'Zambia and Rhodesia: Pioneers of the Past – A Note on the History of Railway Politics in Central Africa', *African Affairs*, Vol. 73, No. 290, 1974.

'nub of a network of strategic highways',[3] but the nub did not control any of them.

The second structural element was part of South African strategic planning and grew out of its desire to protect itself from the encroachment of black-ruled states. This desire was an extension into foreign policy of its domestic policy of separateness, of apart-ness or apartheid. The Purified National party had come to power in South Africa in 1948 and, throughout the 1950s, established all the principal pillars of apartheid: the Prohibition of Mixed Marriages Act of 1949; the Immorality Act of 1950; the Group Areas Act of 1950; the creation of reserves or 'Bantu Authorities' in 1951; and, in 1959 under Verwoerd, the Promotion of Bantu Self-Government Act, which identified the 'eight homelands' and enshrined the idea of separate development. By the mid-1950s, however, it became clear that Britain and France were set on the idea of granting independence to their black colonies – although it must be said that, already by the eve of World War II, Malcolm Macdonald of the British Colonial Office had been envisaging a much earlier independence for them than had previously been thought possible.[4] Recognition of this had, however, been clouded by a South African view of world opinion that was withdrawn and naïve. Smuts had been embarrassed and surprised that, despite his involvement in the founding of the United Nations, the new world body thought South African racism objectionable. So it was that, even as British colonies in Africa began achieving independence, the hope in Pretoria was still that, somehow, the process could be slowed down. Malan lobbied Britain hard with this in mind, but to no effect. Ghana became independent in 1957, Nigeria in 1960.

As late as 1961, Verwoerd was trying to attach conditions to diplomatic contacts between South Africa and the emerging continent, among them the effective veto of black African embassies in Pretoria. Ghana had, in fact, been prepared to explore the idea of reciprocal diplomatic links with South Africa but, in 1961, joined with the Afro-Asian caucus in the Commonwealth – Nigeria, Tanzania on the eve of independence, India, Pakistan, and Ceylon – and prompted South Africa's withdrawal from that body.[5] Verwoerd's difficulties in extend-

[3] Guy Arnold and Ruth Weiss, *Strategic Highways of Africa*, London: Julian Friedmann, 1977, p. 163.
[4] John Flint, 'Planned Decolonization and its Failure in British Africa', *African Affairs*, Vol. 82, No. 328, 1983.
[5] Derek Ingram, *The Commonwealth Challenge*, London: Allen & Unwin, 1962.

ing full diplomatic recognition and courtesies to the new states served only to radicalise their policies towards his regime. The former British colonies began to view the Commonwealth as an instrument by which they could further heap pressure upon it. As the 1960s progressed, more and more African states became independent, including Zambia in 1964.

If the 1950s, therefore, saw the institution of domestic apartheid, the 1960s saw the South African regional policy of a *cordon sanitaire* gain salience and urgency. In broad terms, the policy looked like this: Botswana, Lesotho, and Swaziland could, because of their economic links and vulnerabilities, be kept neutralised; South Africa would not concede control of Namibia; Angola and Mozambique would not be surrendered by Portugal; in the early 1960s, there remained only the question of how Rhodesia might complete the jigsaw. It would not be wholly accurate to suggest that South Africa prompted UDI in 1965. Ian Smith's Rhodesians certainly consulted Pretoria, but the action was one very much determined by the white settler government and its own racist obstinacy. Nevertheless, when it came, it was accepted gratefully by Pretoria. The *cordon sanitaire* looked firmly in place. By the end of the 1960s, it seemed to both Pretoria and Washington that nothing could shift it. One of Henry Kissinger's first tasks as National Security Advisor was to chair the National Security Council Interdepartmental Group for Africa, and its report of August 1969 concluded that liberation groups in Angola, Mozambique, Rhodesia, Namibia, and South Africa would be unable, in each case, to overthrow the minority regime.[6] Each country of the *cordon sanitaire*, and South Africa itself, was safe. This is to see the strategy in broad terms. Looked at closely, what the South Africans were attempting to structure was something quite astonishing.

Africa as a continent is not much given to buffer states. They are difficult to put and keep in place. Southern Africa was the only exception, and it is not difficult to give the white-minority regimes around South Africa the appellation of buffer state. They were, however, only the second tier of a buffer state structure.[7] The 1959 Promotion of Bantu Self-Government Act, identifying eight 'home-

---

[6] The NSC report is reprinted in B. Cohen and M.A. El-Khawas (eds.), *The Kissinger Study of Southern Africa*, Nottingham: Spokesman, 1975.

[7] See Sheridan Johns, 'Southern Africa: Buffer States without a Conventional Buffer System', in John Chay and Thomas E. Ross (eds.), *Buffer States in World Politics*, Boulder, Colorado: Westview, 1986.

lands' or bantustan 'states', put in place the first tier. Separate development, or development isolated from the centres of white interests, provided the ultimate policy to a decade of inventing the formal system of apartheid. With domestic apartheid, or a system of isolating black from white interests, in place by the end of the 1950s, the 1960s saw the parallel isolation of South Africa from the emerging continent. A band of minority or controllable states provided a thick land-mass of isolation and quarantine.

There was thus a domestic foundation and springboard for foreign policy unique in the post-war world. The development of both domestic and foreign policies owed not only to the South African Government and the National Party but also to their dominating Afrikaner ideology of racial superiority. At first glance, it might be thought that Kaunda sought a Zambian equivalent in the troika of government, party, and humanism, in order to give consistency to domestic and foreign affairs – and indeed he might have sought just this – but there was a fundamental difference. If humanism was top-down, it was at least public. In South Africa, the ideology of racial superiority had its own clandestine governance and, far from being disseminated by an élite, the apparatus of this ideology chose the élite in the first place. In the late-twentieth century, histories of secret societies, lodges, and blood-oaths seem picturesque and marginal. The Afrikaner Broederbond (brotherhood), however, did dominate all National Government policy from 1948 until about the late-1960s. Its influence began, perhaps, to decline under Vorster,[8] but Botha was himself a leading member, as is the brother of de Klerk. The Broederbond of today has emerged from factional disputes and splits but still exercises a fascinating influence over what is meant to be public life. In February 1987, one of its working documents, 'Basic constitutional conditions for the survival of the Afrikaner', was leaked. It envisaged a form of black majority rule, under a black head of state, albeit with major provisions to protect white interests.[9] This established for the first time to the public that the Broederbond had evolved from a white supremacist organisation to a more pragmatic white protectionist one. The document laid down the outline principles with which President de Klerk

[8] See Deon Geldenhuys, *The Diplomacy of Isolation – Southern African Foreign Policy Making*, Johannesburg: Macmillan for the South African Institute of International Affairs, 1984, pp. 171–5.
[9] David Beresford and Patrick Laurence, 'Broederbond Plan for Black Power', *Guardian* (London and Manchester), 5 February 1987.

has been negotiating with Nelson Mandela. Indeed, de Klerk's coming to power was much approved by the Broederbond and one of its former chairmen, Gerrit Viljoen, was appointed Minister of Constitutional Development – in charge of reform – following the publication of the National Party's 'Plan of Action', a document inspired by the Broederbond envisaging the five years after 1989.[10] Since then, the Bond has been active, trying to heal the rift between the National Party and the far right and, in April 1990, it circulated a further working paper which proposed, among other things, an Afrikaner conference as a prelude to constitutional negotiations, and highlighted an interesting list of 'unacceptabilities'. Apartheid, or forced separation, was unacceptable. However, forced integration was also unacceptable.[11] If this seems like trying to have it both ways, it is a mighty departure from its original thought which expressed the conviction that the white man should have it all ways. Its early blood-oaths were chilling, its power of endorsement or even selection for public office extensive; membership conferred exclusivity and pedigree. It had, in short, all the reach often imagined for the Masons – but without the broad range of masonic mysticism, just the concentrated aim of white, rightful white, domination forever.[12] No history of South African policy, domestic or foreign, can ignore the Bond. Nothing in Zambia could parallel it.

All this is to say that South African foreign policy formulation has its own peculiar structure and rationale, its own animation. Later, towards the end of the 1970s and throughout most of the 1980s, the Broederbond as an unconstitutional actor was augmented, some would say partially or even largely supplanted, by the rise of the military. This is discussed below. The military, however, intensified the instruments of coercion and dependency already in place. South Africa always had the strongest armed forces, always had the strongest economy, the strongest manufacturing base, controlled the traditional

[10] David Beresford and Patrick Laurence, 'De Klerk's Cabinet Reveals Secret Society's Comeback', *Guardian*, 12 September 1989.
[11] David Breier, 'Secret Broeder Document Calls for Afrikaner Summit', *Sunday Star* (Johannesburg), 27 May 1990.
[12] See Stephen Chan (with Lloyd John Chingambo), in *Exporting Apartheid*, pp. 10–13; J.H.P. Serfontein, *Brotherhood of Power: An Exposé of the Secret Afrikaner Broederbond*, London: Rex Collings, 1978; Ivor Wilkins and Hans Strydon, *The Super Afrikaners: Inside the Afrikaner Broederbond*, Johannesburg: Jonathan Ball, 1978; Brian Bunting, *The Rise of the South African Reich*, London: International Defence and Aid Fund, 1986, Chapter 3.

routes to the sea. Zambia faced both a buffer and conditional access for its exports and imports across this zone that was to prevent the black man's rule from spreading further south.

The intensification of coercion and dependency, even at an early stage, meant academic reconceptualisation of where South Africa stood in the world. In 1968, Larry Bowman argued that South Africa should be viewed as a subordinate state system, by which he meant that it was largely autonomous within the global international system and that it maintained its regional pre-eminence through unequal economic linkages, tying black- and white-ruled neighbours alike to it and its policies.[13] This view has its major rival in forms of world system theory and dependency theory, discussed in Chapter 5, in which a world capitalist system, or an international capitalist class, has distinct interests in South Africa. In this formulation, South Africa becomes one part of a wider structure. The Bowman view, by contrast, gives considerable autonomy to South African policy within the southern African region. Later scholars, working in this mould, have maintained that even when, by force of arms and negotiation, Mozambique, Angola, and Zimbabwe gained independence, South Africa was still able to determine how viable these countries might be. I include myself in this group,[14] and the analysis of the present chapter conforms to this view, with evidence presented below. What it meant, however, and what was faced by Kaunda, was that the foreign policy of *cordon sanitaire* had three major structural components.

1. It established a buffer state system constructed in two tiers, the internal tier of bantustans, and the external tier of white minority-ruled states and controllable black-ruled states like Botswana, Lesotho, and Swaziland.

[13] Larry W. Bowman, 'The Subordinate State System of Southern Africa', *International Studies Quarterly*, Vol. 12, No. 3, 1968; but cf. I. William Zartman, 'Africa as a Subordinate State System in International Relations', *International Organization*, Vol. XXI, 1967; also Kenneth W. Grundy, *Confrontation and Accommodation in Southern Africa: The Limits of Independence*, Berkeley: University of California Press, 1973; for a recent discussion, see Paul B. Rich, 'The Politics of Southern Africa: Security Complex or Regional Sub-system', paper presented to the British International Studies Association Annual Conference, University of Kent, 1989.

[14] For a summary of my views, see Stephen Chan, 'Southern Africa Security and the South Atlantic', paper presented to the Colloque Internationale Géopolitique et Géostratégie dans l'Hemisphere Sud, Université de la Réunion de l'Océan Indien, 1990; and a wider expression in *Exporting Apartheid*. See also Murdhi Awad Nassar Al-Khaledi, 'Coercive Diplomacy: The Nkomati Accord between Mozambique and South Africa', unpublished Ph.D. thesis, University of Kent, 1990.

2. It was established by a ruling structure that had considerable
   depth, through government, party, and Broederbond – government and party being publicly answerable to at least a white
   electorate, but the Broederbond being answerable to no constitutional or public device. The formulation of alternative policy
   could be no easy thing.
3. It established a southern African state system largely determined
   by South Africa, and more determined by South African policy
   than by any policies from without the region. In policy terms,
   South Africa enjoyed great autonomy. In practical terms, what
   this meant for South Africa's independent neighbours, like
   Zambia, was that recourse to outside powers and authorities was
   likely to prove fruitless.

These are the realities that Kaunda faced upon independence. UDI
in Rhodesia, therefore, should not be read as instigating a struggle
between Zambia and Rhodesia, but as completing the South African
policy for the region. All declarations of principle aside, Kaunda could
never have contemplated an unequal struggle with South Africa itself.
That is why the 1969 Manifesto on Southern Africa, referred to in
the last chapter, sought so strenuously to avoid emphasising armed
struggle. What Kaunda sought is discussed in the next chapter. In the
meantime, as the mid-1970s approached, challenges to South African
autonomy were beginning to loom within the region.

The Birth of Total Strategy

Where both Pretoria and Washington had been deficient in their
forecasts for the region was over the willingness of Portugal to remain
in Angola and Mozambique indefinitely. They had assumed that the
Portuguese Government, and hence its policy, would be long-lived.
The 1974 coup in Portugal, followed by the sudden independences of
Angola and Mozambique in 1975, surprised everybody. It must be
said that Pretoria's immediate reactions were not belligerent, but were
concerned instead with a loose idea of regional *détente*, not fully
specified but negotiable, and perhaps centred on a mixed government
in Rhodesia – the concept behind the later Smith/Muzorewa administration – thus preserving a watered-down *cordon sanitaire* with the
black-ruled states being voluntarily compliant, like Botswana, Lesotho,
and Swaziland, refusing to lend support to liberation movements

within South Africa and being rewarded by economic cooperation (under South African leadership) rather than coercion. South Africa would, in its domestic politics, be left to its own devices. Both President Khama of Botswana and President Kaunda of Zambia were interested at least in the prospect of negotiation, with, as the next chapter relates, Kaunda making more of the running.

If this was a hurried vision of the future, events soon forced an almost extemporaneous South African foreign policy. Regional *détente* depended upon compliant governments. In Angola, however, as the Alvor Agreement among the three contending liberation movements (MPLA, FNLA, and UNITA) collapsed, it soon became clear that the MPLA had greatest military capacity and could soon overwhelm its rivals. Here was a Marxist movement, heavily armed by the Soviet Union, supported by Cuban personnel, operating from the Angolan capital of Luanda, and marching south. The South African bogey, black communists, had taken militarised flesh in South Africa's own region.[15] This, in the South African imagination, would be the polar opposite of a compliant government.

In August 1975, South African troops moved into Angola. What their exact objectives were is unclear. They could not have hoped to replace the Portuguese as the colonial power. If they took the capital and either stayed there or installed a preferred government, they would have had to defend it from those who held the countryside and harassed their supply lines and communications. Getting to Luanda in the first place, through the Cuban and MPLA lines, would have meant supply difficulties even before an assault upon the city, and getting through those enemy lines could never have been assumed. The South African Defence Forces (SADF) would be facing for the first time a black army and its communist allies. In November 1975, after some initial successes, the forward lines of the SADF met the Cubans. Although, afterwards, both the MPLA and independent Africa hailed the confrontation as a great defeat of South African might, the truth would seem to be that there was indeed a South African retreat, but not a defeat as such. From my interviews with military and diplomatic personnel present in Angola at the time,[16] a South African column of 2,000 men wandered, somewhat ineptly, into

---

[15] For one detailed account, see J.A. Marcum, *The Angolan Revolution: Vol. 2, 1962–1976*, Cambridge, Massachusetts: MIT Press, 1978.
[16] Author's interview with US military and diplomatic personnel present in Angola in 1975.

a Cuban ambush. The ambush was so arranged that, normally, the South Africans would have been trapped or wiped out. It appears that the Cubans, themselves ineptly, failed to close the trap and the South Africans were able to withdraw in relatively good order.

Certainly the South Africans now considered the Cubans not to be as formidable as they had feared, although the SADF would have learnt its own lessons about what constitutes good reconnaisance. But, while regrouping, the South African military fell victim to political considerations. Fearful of another Vietnam, the US Congress in December 1975 voted to withhold arms from UNITA and the FNLA – fighting like (in the case of UNITA with) the South Africans against the MPLA – and the US message to Pretoria was made clear. If the SADF sought to take Luanda, it could expect neither military nor political support from Washington. A struggle against an African army could be confined to the region. An assault against Cubans implied a global context in which one superpower had to calculate its commitments against the other. Throughout, Pretoria had assumed support from Washington. This was now being withdrawn; the Soviets – after a short lull – were increasing their arms shipments to the MPLA; there were by December 1975 about 10,000 Cubans in Angola. It would be a hard road to Luanda. In January 1976, South Africa withdrew its forces.

Although it was not a defeat, it was a military humiliation. The SADF withdrew without achieving any of its objectives, and perhaps without ever thinking through exactly what they were in the first place. It was also a political humiliation, since Pretoria had been rebuffed by Washington. It was, finally, a humiliation of strategy, since the *cordon sanitaire* – although not dismantled – had been seriously breached. The search for a policy to prevent such humiliations, therefore, became of great importance. The policy had to have military, political, and strategic strengths; it had either to appeal to Washington or, at least, dissuade Washington from reacting against it; and it had either to shape the region or, at least, distort its shape sufficiently for Pretoria to be the dominant power – an unchallenged hegemony. Finally, it had to have a diplomatic dressing, so that the international community could not so easily say that the region had been shaped solely by South Africa's force of arms.

The changes in policy began with the 1977 Defence White Paper and the 1978 coming to office of Prime Minister P. W. Botha. This began the so-called era of the 'securocrats'. Botha had been Minister of Defence and brought to power with him an array of generals and defence personnel. This is to look at matters on the surface, however – and also seems to exempt civilian policy-makers from what followed. At first glance, it seems the civilian positions had been overrun. They had been weak in the first place. Eric Louw, as Minister of External Affairs, had only in the 1950s established an Africa Division within his ministry, and its predictive powers had always been limited. However, as noted above, no matter how strong a ministry was, policy could always be at least influenced from non-constitutional sources, particularly the Broederbond. As it turned out, in 1975 'the Department of Foreign Affairs found itself largely excluded from decision making on South Africa's Angola venture'.[17] It had been an operation conceived by the military under P. W. Botha's Defence Ministry, and even the Broederbond was, to an extent, surprised – establishing its own regional policy unit only after the withdrawal from Angola. Despite this, to view the era that followed as one of isolated militarised policy-making ignores a certain integration of the Afrikaner élite. Botha had been a leading figure within the Broederbond, and its reach was such that the senior military officers would also have been members, as would have been senior civilian officials. In short, after the shock of Angola, the Afrikaner establishment rallied around the military option for future policy. Although scholars like Jack Spence have consistently argued that there existed a distinct pluralism in foreign policy inputs, he himself quotes from Seiler that there was a 'hazardous reality: cabinet ministers, civilian officials and military officials are in general agreement about coercive policies'.[18] The planning and execution of policy became militarised, but both the constitutional and non-constitutional arms of government supported the policy that emerged. If any sector dissented, it was never – until the end of Botha's tenure, after almost a decade of military and coercive economic action that devastated southern Africa – a sustained dissent. When, finally, it was sustained, it was because the 'Botha doctrine' was seen as having failed. While it was succeeding, there was never outrage.

A great deal of work has appeared on the military apparatus that

---

[17] Geldenhuys, *The Diplomacy of Isolation*, p. 79.
[18] J.E. Spence, 'South Africa's Military Relations with its Neighbours', in Simon Baynham (ed.), *Military Power and Politics in Black Africa*, London: Croom Helm, 1986, p. 303.

was accumulated and deployed in the Botha years,[19] but, although excellent work has also been done on how the military constructed policy,[20] this knowledge has been less in the public eye than the trail of devastation that policy wrought. The system of policy formulation used by Botha was finally formalised in the 1984 constitutional changes. These changes included the introduction of a tricameral parliament, giving Asians and 'coloureds' – but not blacks – a limited voice alongside the white chamber, so that most attention (and indignation) was directed towards it. What was also created was the State Presidency, a position Botha occupied and which gave him greater powers than the premiership. The presidential apparatus, however, has not been widely publicised outside South Africa. Power was concentrated in four cabinet committees which, given the new centralisation of executive authority in the presidency, bypassed cabinet in order to report directly to the president. There was thus no system of constitutional check and balance against these committees. The most powerful of them was the State Security Council. This met fortnightly in closed session. Unlike the other committees, it had its own secretariat – so it bypassed the civil service as well. Its meetings preceded cabinet meetings, both were chaired by the president, but the president merely reported orally to the cabinet the recommendations (effectively the decisions) of the State Security Council. All matters of security and foreign policy were covered by the SSC, and it could effectively expand its brief as widely as it wished. Seated on the Council were selected senior ministers, but also the senior military officers. This sort of arrangement suited Botha, an 'organisational virtuoso', who placed great emphasis on expert planning and technocratic skills.[21] What it came to mean, and what it already meant well before the process was given constitutional cover, was that military experts and security technocrats – hence the South African epithet 'securocrats' – played a determining role in the country's foreign policy but, as noted above, there was wide support for the coercive policy they espoused.

[19] E.g. Gavin Cawthra, *Brutal Force – The Apartheid War Machine*, London: International Defence and Aid Fund, 1986.
[20] E.g. P.H. Frankel, *Pretoria's Praetorians: Civil-Military Relations in South Africa*, Cambridge: Cambridge University Press, 1984; Kenneth W. Grundy, *The Militarization of South African Politics*, Oxford: Oxford University Press, 1987.
[21] Kenneth W. Grundy, *The Rise of the South African Security Establishment: An Essay on the Changing Locus of State Power*, Johannesburg: South African Institute of International Affairs, 1983, p. 15.

There was unity within the governmental apparatus, at least in broad terms, and no sustained or effective dissent in detail. As time passed, there developed debate and manoeuvring over the limits of policy – not over policy itself but over the thresholds beyond which it could no longer be internationally justified, or beyond which it might start becoming regionally counter-productive. On the latter point, there was always a fine line between a destabilised frontline state, and one which could no longer function. The desire was not to overthrow states – in which case Pretoria might have to support the new states that emerged, and support could become more expensive and its results less measurable than destabilisation – but to constrain them, demoralise them, narrow their resources, prevent them from mounting any effective campaign against Pretoria, sometimes terrorise them, occupy parts of them. Internationally, the justifications were addressed primarily to the US, whose own military planners would recognise only too well a doctrine of carrying a fight to one's enemies. The South African justifications numbered four.[22] Firstly, Pretoria protected the sea-lanes around the Cape of Good Hope. Secondly, Pretoria produced minerals strategically vital to the west. On both counts, therefore, Pretoria was a guardian of western interests. Thirdly, these interests were threatened by the spectre of advancing communism, of which the Cuban military presence in Angola was now a proof. Having been highly agitated by the Cuban presence at first, Pretoria now sought to utilise it as cover for the South African regional policy,[23] so that, as well as being a guardian of western interests, Pretoria portrayed itself as a bulwark, a rampart in a fight that had already begun. Fourthly, South Africa was clearly the strongest power in the region. It made geo-strategic sense to deal with Pretoria. With whom else could the US deal? Who else had the capacity to deliver, to hold down the region in the name of the west?

Although much has been made of the Reagan doctrine of constructive engagement, and how this gave a cloak of permission to Pretoria to proceed with its regional policy, the history of US objection to South African foreign policy is a meagre one.[24] The 1969 Kissinger

[22] See Larry W. Bowman, 'The Strategic Importance of South Africa to the United States: An Appraisal and Policy Analysis', *African Affairs*, Vol. 81, No. 323, 1982.

[23] See Robert M. Price, 'Pretoria's Southern African Strategy', *African Affairs*, Vol. 83, No. 330, 1984.

[24] See Paul Rich, 'US Containment Policy, South Africa and the Apartheid Dilemma', *Review of International Studies*, Vol. 14, No. 3, 1988.

report, noted above, recommended against an active US involvement on the continent – since it seemed then that the Soviet Union was not planning any great involvement of its own. The Soviet and Cuban support for the MPLA in Angola reversed this assumption, but it was significantly easier – cleaner and less costly – for the US to allow Pretoria to counter this presence than to do so itself. The difference between December 1975, when the US signalled its lack of support for Pretoria, and the post-1978 Botha era was the intensification of the cold war. The Soviet Union invaded Afghanistan in 1979, so it seemed to be committed to a bellicosity first signalled by Angola. Moreover, unlike 1975, the South Africans were not aspiring to take Luanda, merely to choke it. It is doubtful whether any US administration would have halted what the South African Government and its military called 'Total Strategy' – or, beyond gestures, sought to halt it. The international justifications of South Africa were well-pitched and, in the US, well-received.

The Unleashing of Total Strategy

Total Strategy was meant to be South Africa's reply to a perceived total onslaught. Using all means available against the enemy – military, economic, social, and psychological – it was meant to strike against him at all times and in all places. It was thought to have been derived from the work of the French General, André Beaufre, who in turn conceived his thought in the colonial war against Algeria.[25] The notion of a total onslaught suggested that South Africa was surrounded on all sides and had to fight on all sides, just as the idea of a *cordon sanitaire* suggested that South Africa might be isolated on all sides from an encroaching black tide. Neither departed from the central Afrikaner metaphor of the laager, the encircled waggon-train of the voortrek. The continuity of this metaphor meant that one strategy did not have to succeed another overnight and, indeed, what was left of the *cordon sanitaire* seemed worth persevering with. South Africa retained Namibia. Ian Smith's government retained Rhodesia. Both, however, now faced greater threats. The MPLA Government meant that SWAPO could open a proper military front in Namibia, establishing bases in the new state of Angola. The independence of Mozam-

---

[25] André Beaufre, *An Introduction to Strategy*, London: Faber & Faber, 1963; and *Strategy of Action*, London: Faber & Faber, 1967.

bique meant that what became Robert Mugabe's ZANLA guerillas could leave Zambia, where their military forays into Rhodesia had been constrained to a low level by President Kaunda, and could open a front from Mozambican bases. What was left of the cordon required fortification. Even so, the idea of a form of independence for both Namibia and Rhodesia, under a form of black rule that was simultaneously acceptable to the international community and compliant to Pretoria's foreign policy and security requirements, gathered strength. This would reduce the expense of military build-up, and peaceful neighbours would at least be more predictable than those caught up in war. The experiment with the Smith/Muzorewa Government of Rhodesia/Zimbabwe in 1978–9 was a serious though tentative attempt to see if this variation on the cordon – compliant black governments rather than fortified white ones – could work. International insistence on a contested election in Rhodesia that involved all parties, including those of the guerilla armies, led Pretoria to accept the independence formula negotiated in 1979 at Lancaster House. Even then, the South African hope was for a Muzorewa victory and the continuation of compliance. The unexpected victory of Robert Mugabe's ZANU party, however, together with the inauguration in 1980 of the Southern African Development Coordination Conference (SADCC), a formal attempt by the majority-ruled states to achieve greater economic independence from South Africa, meant the final death of the *cordon sanitaire*.

Elements of Total Strategy had been applied before 1980 and, of all the frontline states, Angola had been the most persistent target. Davies and O'Meara have given an excellent account of the different phases and time-periods of Total Strategy,[26] and most commentators agree that the 1980–1 period saw its full-blooded application. There have been many accounts of what Total Strategy accomplished, particularly in military terms,[27] and it is important to suggest that none

[26] Robert Davies and Dan O'Meara, 'Total Strategy in Southern Africa – An Analysis of South African Regional Policy since 1978', *Journal of Southern African Studies*, Vol. 11, No. 2, 1985.

[27] See Joseph Hanlon, *Beggar your Neighbours – Apartheid Power in Southern Africa*, London: James Currey, 1986; idem, *Apartheid's Second Front – South Africa's War against its Neighbours*, Harmondsworth: Penguin, 1986; Victoria Brittain, *Hidden Lives, Hidden Deaths – South Africa's Crippling of a Continent*, London: Faber & Faber, 1988; Phyllis Johnson and David Martin (eds.), *Destructive Engagement – Southern Africa at War*, Harare: Zimbabwe Publishing House, 1986; Paul L. Moorcraft, *African Nemesis – War and Revolution in Southern Africa 1945–2010*, London: Brassey's 1990.

of them has been overstated. What has been understated is the strategic pattern behind South Africa's war against its neighbours.[28] Southern Africa is a varied region. In 1980, the two leaders with greatest international respect were Kenneth Kaunda of Zambia and Robert Mugabe of Zimbabwe – Kaunda because he had been perceived as seeing principle through to its successful conclusion, the overthrow of Ian Smith's UDI and the independence of Zimbabwe; and Mugabe because he had emerged, through a heavily monitored democratic process, from a guerilla past to a politics of racial reconciliation. Their two countries were also strong economically – in regional terms challenged only by Botswana. And, in geographical terms, Zambia and Zimbabwe were the centre of southern Africa. They had, therefore, special strengths but also a special vulnerability. Being the geographical centre, they were landlocked and depended on rail routes through other countries. Control of those routes meant that Pretoria could exercise economic leverage on them both. Because of the international respect both leaders enjoyed, however, this leverage could be applied gradually, almost subtly, with a view not so much to destabilisation as to the constraint of hostility in foreign policy and an openness to negotiation with Pretoria.

Apart from the Tazara rail between Zambia and Tanzania, which has never operated at full capacity, the rail routes of Zambia and Zimbabwe ran either through South Africa itself or through Angola and Mozambique. These two latter countries, with forms of Marxist government, had not gained major western friends, particularly Angola. They were, therefore, diplomatically exposed. Military options were applied to them by Pretoria, in the knowledge that international protest would be sparse. This was both to destabilise their governments and militarily to interdict the rail routes upon which their neighbours depended. In Mozambique, the military option was exercised through the recreation of a proxy force. The MNR or RENAMO had been first brought into service by Ian Smith's Rhodesia, as a means of sabotaging the activities of the post-1975 FRELIMO Government.[29] After Zimbabwe's independence, South Africa moved

---

[28] This strategic pattern is a central concern of my work in *Exporting Apartheid* and in earlier work. See, inter alia, Stephen Chan, 'Contemplating the 1990s – Towards a Pattern in South African Regional Policy', *Royal United Services Institute Journal for Defence Studies*, Vol. 132, No. 2, 1987; and 'The Militarisation of South African Regional Policy', *New Zealand International Review*, Vol. XIII, No. 3, 1988.

[29] Ken Flowers, *Serving Secretly – Rhodesia into Zimbabwe 1964–1981*, London: John Murray, 1987.

to take over and refurbish RENAMO and, with far greater logistical and communications support and advice over strategic planning, its new version of RENAMO was considerably more effective than its Rhodesian predecessor. In Angola, a proxy force also existed, and this was Jonas Savimbi's UNITA. It was not, however, an equivalent to RENAMO. It had been a bona fide liberation force, continued to enjoy popular support in its own territorial base, and had a political programme. It wanted to create something, but first it had to overthrow the MPLA. In allying itself with South Africa, it compromised severely its original credentials, but those credentials still carried a faint echo and Savimbi, a considerably complex man,[30] could not be easily typecast as a thorough villain. By contrast, it has always been difficult to find anything redeeming to say about RENAMO, and tales of its bandit atrocities are well-documented – although some suggest that it has now developed a genuine programme and should be viewed differently.[31] It had no discernible programme at the time of its recreation however.

For a variety of reasons, South Africa chose not to depend solely on a proxy force in Angola. Firstly, the geographical terrain was such that obtaining control over the Benguela railway would be much more difficult than control over its Mozambican counterpart, the Beira line. In Angola, the line to Benguela was long and, although cutting it at one point only and maintaining that cut would not have been difficult, the strategic objective was both to control the railway and to view it as a form of border. Below it, the bulk of southern Angola was to be a UNITA and South African preserve. If the MPLA wanted it, it would have to mount a military operation as if it were launching an invasion of its own territory. Secondly, precisely because UNITA had a political programme, its point of origin had not been manufactured by South Africa. It could not be as easily manipulated as RENAMO, it enjoyed US support and supplies and was, to a limited extent, independent of South African logistical control. Thirdly, the Cubans were in Angola and the South African Government wanted to be seen by the world, particularly the US, as directly confronting the communist threat, and the SADF felt it had, in any case, its own point to prove in engaging

---

[30] Fred Bridgeland *Jonas Savimbi – A Key to Africa*, Edinburgh: Mainstream, 1985.
[31] See e.g. Lloyd M. Sachikonye, 'UNITA and RENAMO: "Bandit" Social Movements?', *Southern African Political & Economic Monthly*, Vol. 3, No. 7, 1990. At the time of going to press, several articles on the same theme have begun appearing in the western Africanist scholarly press.

Cuban forces. The South Africans therefore invaded Angola with its own armoured columns, with aerial support from bases in South Africa and Namibia, maintaining a semi-permanent bridgehead often several hundred kilometres inside Angolan territory.

Control of substantial portions of both Angolan and Mozambican territory, denial of it or denial of its productive use, not only placed immense pressures upon the MPLA and FRELIMO Governments – defence costs and budgetary deficits, loss of agricultural productivity, infrastructural damage, civilian as well as military casualties, refugees, destruction of health and education facilities, loss of investment, and decline in national morale – it also meant that the strategic map of southern Africa depicted a pincer movement around Zambia and Zimbabwe. Without ever needing to mass upon their frontiers, South Africa made its threat clear and, meanwhile, effectively controlled the land transport systems of both countries as they sought access to the sea.

Already economically tied to South Africa by way of currency and customs links – quite apart from considerations of company ownerships, technological dependence, market catchments, and remittances – Botswana, Lesotho, and Swaziland did not escape military attack. Although never on the scale suffered by Angola and Mozambique, periodic raids on their cities caused great damage. It was never clear exactly why South Africa should attack countries that were so clearly dependent and generally compliant. Although the excuse given was attack upon ANC targets, it was difficult to see these countries as major military bases of the ANC, and it was difficult to view the often widespread destruction that resulted from SADF attack as surgical or even roughly selective. The real aim seemed to be intimidation and an attempt to reinforce 'good' behaviour that was lacking, appallingly, in subtlety. An attack against Maseru, the capital of Lesotho, in December 1982 left such devastation that even strategic commentators in South Africa who had published foreign policy options lists, which had included forms of economic coercion and military operation,[32] protested its unnecessary and unconstrained nature.[33] A suburb was flattened.

[32] Deon Geldenhuys, *Destabilisation Controversy in Southern Africa*, Johannesburg: South African Forum Position Paper, 1982; 'Some Strategic Implications of Regional Economic Relationships for the Republic of South Africa', *ISSUP Strategic Review*, January 1981; 'The Destabilization Controversy: An Analysis of High Risk Foreign Policy Options for South Africa', *Politikon*, Vol. 9, No. 2, 1982.

[33] Geldenhuys's call for restraint was even noted by one of his severest critics; see Hanlon, *Apartheid's Second Front*, p. 104.

Faced with attacks on Gaborone in the mid-1980s, Botswana established its own defence forces to patrol its frontiers – not to keep the SADF out, but to ensure that any ANC personnel residing in Botswana stayed in. Evidence of guerilla infiltrators coming from Botswana could only have brought further attacks. To this extent, South African policy was successful as neighbouring countries sought to exhibit some form of behaviour acceptable to Pretoria. What, however, were the specific objectives in state behaviour that Pretoria had in mind and which Total Strategy was meant to deliver?

The Underlying Aims of Total Strategy

Zambia and Zimbabwe, as the strongest frontline states, had to feature in Pretoria's plans for the region. Destabilisation in Angola and Mozambique meant a pincer west and east of Zambia and Zimbabwe. Sporadic military intimidation to the south of these two countries, against Botswana, Lesotho, and Swaziland, were also signals and warnings *pour encourager les autres* – to remind Zambia and Zimbabwe of the limits upon their regional initiatives before Pretoria's interests were invoked. Pretoria had its own long-term plan for the region, and this included its plans for Zambia and the then newly-independent Zimbabwe.

If Total Strategy derived from a French approach to war against Algeria, the diplomatic and political aims of it all were similar to those of the pre-Gorbachev Soviet Union towards the Warsaw Pact. This might have meant the resurrection of a buffer policy, indicating that, despite transformations in strategy, Pretoria had still its original concept of the region in mind. By this time, however, as the remainder of this chapter suggests, the objectives were both more complex and more sophisticated – if only because the region had become more complex and sophisticated, not to mention independent – though derived from the idea of buffers. Within the Warsaw Pact there was not only the one Pact, the one treaty. In addition to the central multilateral treaty, each individual Warsaw Pact member had signed its own bilateral treaty with the Soviet Union. The bilateral treaty reinforced the multilateral treaty and vice versa. There was, in a very real sense, no escape from the Pact as it was first conceived, and, under the provisions of this sort of double-treaty arrangement, an eastern European state operated under various measures of permission from Moscow.

Pretoria's plans for southern Africa, although partly analogous to the schema outlined above, were not as formalised. It never envisaged, for instance, the formation of a bloc or an alliance. It did envisage, however, a series of formal instruments. Each member of the region was to sign some form of treaty or accord with South Africa. The commonalities in them would be two-fold: firstly, they would all be signed with South Africa so that, throughout the region, there would be a uniform acknowledgement of South Africa's centrality; secondly, they would all renounce violent acts against South Africa so that, throughout the region, there would be an established limit to protest and resistance against the apartheid-state. In a region not therefore at war, even in an anomic and surly peace, Pretoria would then complete its economic domination and reconstruction of southern Africa. The first steps to achieving such underlying aims would be, by both military and economic coercion, through Total Strategy in fact, to force the so-called revolutionary states – Angola and Mozambique – and the region's weaker states – Botswana, Lesotho, and Swaziland – to sign treaties or accords. This would leave Zambia and Zimbabwe both surrounded by states who had signed, and diplomatically isolated because they alone had not. Eventually, through the manipulation of pressures, the last two would also sign.

By the end of 1983, military pressures against Angola and Mozambique had led both to consider overtures from Pretoria concerning accords. The Nkomati Accord between South Africa and Mozambique, signed in March 1984, is the more famous – written about both with the hope that Mozambique might extract something real from it,[34] and in sanguine terms as a triumph for Pretoria's Total Strategy and coercive diplomacy.[35] The problem in reading the Nkomati Accord is that, at first sight, both sides pledge the same undertakings. The accord is not best read as an unequal treaty, i.e. one between unequal powers, although Mozambique was significantly less powerful and had been partly rendered that way by South Africa. The accord has become infamous because, although both sides pledged the same undertakings, only one side honoured its signature. Both undertook not to support or harbour groups bent on violence against the other. Mozambique promptly expelled all but a mission-sized contingent of

[34] See some of the work in Ibrahim S.R. Msabaha and Timothy M. Shaw (eds.), *Confrontation and Liberation in Southern Africa – Regional Directions after the Nkomati Accord*, Boulder, Colorado: Westview, 1987.
[35] E.g. Al-Khaledi, 'Coercive Diplomacy'.

ANC personnel. Pretoria certainly desired this as it lessened the number of borders across which the ANC could operate. But South Africa did not promptly end its support for RENAMO and, at time of writing, RENAMO still poses a significant threat to the Mozambican Government. There is a huge literature suggesting that, despite the intentions of the South African Government, parts of the SADF, acting autonomously, were responsible for this continuing support. In addition, Portuguese businessmen who had lost their holdings to the FRELIMO Government were meant to have stepped up their support for RENAMO. In any case, RENAMO had sufficient stockpiles of equipment to last at least a year after Nkomati was signed.

These are apologetics. In 1984, the same year as the Nkomati Accord, constitutional changes in South Africa gave immense powers to a state president who was determined to govern through his State Security Council first, and his cabinet only secondarily. It seems inconceivable that the centralised convergence in the SSC of both civilian and military power could have been unaware or could not have stopped an 'autonomous' wing of the SADF from carrying out a massive programme of logistical and advisory support, not to mention field direction, for RENAMO. The entire complaint against the SSC is that it centralised power with 'securocrats' responsible to no-one but the president, and it would seem disingenuous to insist that this apparatus could not keep track of itself as it planned its control of all South Africa and southern Africa. As for the Portuguese businessmen story, it is true that such support for RENAMO exists, but it is difficult to see how it was coordinated and wealthy enough to take the place of the South African state in supplying a guerilla army with sufficient fire-power to destabilise an entire country. Although, by 1989, South African support of RENAMO had finally declined, it was still evident. From my information, it would appear that the most significant recent equipment of RENAMO had been in the form of a radio-communications system that allowed coordination of all its operations throughout Mozambique, and the ending therefore of fragmented operations on isolated fronts.[36] The truth of the matter is that, as far as Mozambique was concerned, South Africa had forced an accord upon the FRELIMO Government, had not honoured its side of the bargain, and was happy to watch and measure the

---

[36] Author's interview with western officer assigned to Mozambique, October 1989.

discomfiture of that government as it dared not repudiate the accord in case it worsened even further the destabilisation that continued.

The role of Kenneth Kaunda in the lead-up to the Nkomati Accord has not been much investigated; it is, however, considered in the next chapter. His role in the contemporaneous Lusaka Accord between Angola and South Africa is more immediately clear since, at the very least, he provided Lusaka as a kind of 'neutral ground' for the treaty. The Lusaka Accord, although fitting Pretoria's aim for a series of treaties, was different from Nkomati. Although requiring measures to be undertaken on both sides, to demonstrate each side's lack of violent intent against the other, the South African obligations could be much more clearly monitored – since it involved the withdrawal of South African forces from Angolan soil. There were three major undertakings within this accord.

1. South Africa would withdraw its forces from Angola.
2. Angola would control the activities of SWAPO.
3. This would be conditional on South Africa's making progress towards Namibian independence under Security Council Resolution 435.

The Lusaka Accord thus had more immediate regional implications, involving Namibia as well as the two signatories. It was signed in the territory of a third party, thus suggesting a mediatory or facilitative role. And it stipulated actions that were conditional, i.e. South Africa had to be seen to be doing something; and actions that were quite visible – a South African armoured column left in Angola would be far more visible than a clandestine equipment of RENAMO. It was, lastly, a treaty between two states who could both dispose of considerable military resources and, although South Africa had been destabilising Angola, it had been required to use considerably greater firepower and investment than in Mozambique. It was, in every respect, a better accord than Nkomati. Even so, South Africa was happy with it, at least as a sign of progress towards its diplomatic aims for the region. To extract something from the Cuban-assisted MPLA Government might surely be a stepping stone to future accords with Angola.

After the conclusion of the Lusaka and Nkomati Accords, signed in February and March 1984 respectively, Swaziland announced that it had secretly signed its own treaty with South Africa two years earlier – so the beginnings of the regional design became apparent. With the three accords accomplished, Pretoria began a slow withdrawal from Angola, taking a year to do so and, in this way, testing the patience and tolerance level of the MPLA Government – just as it set about testing to what extent the Mozambican Government would abide by the Nkomati Accord while South Africa dragged its feet, or did nothing at all about its side of the bargain. Even so, slow withdrawal from Angola was better than no withdrawal at all and it seemed that at least some coerciveness was being removed from the South African regional policy. The less coercive atmosphere led to the coining of the term, 'pax Pretoriana', apt since it was clearly a peace that depended on South Africa and left Pretoria in a position of economic dominance, not to mention military readiness. But it seemed, to some at least, perhaps Kaunda among them, that a negotiable future lay in store for southern Africa.

In 1985, seeking to take advantage of the pax Pretoriana, the MPLA and its Cuban allies launched a major offensive against the UNITA positions in southern Angola. If this had been successful, then the MPLA Government would have rid itself of both the South Africans and its internal opposition. This, however, would have been an act of independence within a region which Pretoria considered that it dominated. With the SADF out of Angola, UNITA played the useful role of keeping the MPLA occupied and of preventing any national economic development in Angola. Unlike the other southern African states, Angola was not economically dependent on Pretoria. Of the SADCC grouping, only it and Tanzania had no trade links with South Africa. It had, moreover, the potential to become a relatively strong economy – unlike Mozambique [37] – and, as such, might in time have provided some economic alternatives to what Pretoria offered. UNITA's role in destabilising the country helped to prevent this from happening. In addition, since UNITA had become so firmly identified with South Africa – not a client like RENAMO but a heavily-subsidised ally – it would not help Pretoria's case, if ever it sought future partners of this sort, to have UNITA put to the sword. As the MPLA and Cuban offensive, based mainly on armoured columns, gathered momentum, it seemed indeed that this time UNITA could be destroyed, and the South African State Security Council had to make a swift decision.

---

[37] Author's interview with western ambassador, Harare, September 1989, in which he assessed the economic futures of the frontline states.

The end of the pax Pretoriana was signalled as squadron after squadron of South African planes bombed the MPLA offensive to a halt. The South Africans had first withdrawn from Angola in 1976. The Defence White Paper which laid the conceptual foundation for Total Strategy was published in 1977. P. W. Botha, who had been minister of defence, became prime minister in 1978, relying heavily on military advice from those who had served him in his earlier portfolio. Although military measures against surrounding states began to be used, the 1978–9 period was essentially the last stand of the *cordon sanitaire* strategy, played out in the Smith/Muzorewa Government of Rhodesia/Zimbabwe. The failure of this effort, together with the formal inauguration of SADCC in 1980, led to the first phase of Total Strategy. This culminated in 1984 with the Lusaka and Nkomati Accords. A pax Pretoriana was launched throughout the region as, meanwhile in South Africa itself, constitutional changes enshrined the Botha method of government with its presidentialism and militarism. Throughout the pax Pretoriana, the military option was always at the president's ear. After the Angolan offensive of 1985, Total Strategy entered a further phase.

By the end of 1986, Lesotho had signed an accord with South Africa – but only after a coup precipitated by Pretoria had installed a military government; Botswana, seeking to avoid an accord and what it represented, nevertheless issued a declaration that covered ground similar to that of the accords. There were rumours that, secretly, Zimbabwe had signed an accord, but there is no evidence of this. The year 1986 was also the one that the Commonwealth members of the frontline states sought to hit back at Pretoria, by mounting the first stages of the international sanctions campaign. A Group of Commonwealth Eminent Persons arrived in South Africa to seek negotiations on the ending of apartheid. If the Eminent Persons found no scope for negotiation, they were set to recommend sanctions. Pretoria launched short, almost demonstration, attacks against Botswana, Zimbabwe, and Zambia, even while the Eminent Persons met with President Botha. The attacks against Zimbabwe and Zambia were a signal to Kaunda and Mugabe that even their countries could no longer assume immunity from the military application of Total Strategy. Towards the end of 1986, shortly after the Non-Aligned Movement summit in Harare, Samora Machel of Mozambique died in a plane crash, and some saw in this the hand yet again of Pretoria,[38] signing off a traumatic year for the region with a threatening flourish.

The year had not all been Pretoria's. As noted above, a sanctions campaign intensified within the Commonwealth. A Non-Aligned summit had been held in Harare and, if nothing else, it offered the spectacle of international solidarity close to home. Zimbabwe decided to send its own troops into Mozambique to guard the Beira railway against RENAMO attack, thereby picking up the military gauntlet long thrown down by Total Strategy. But there were limits to all of this. The British refused to apply sanctions and, in any case, there were grave doubts as to whether the frontline states could themselves afford to participate in the campaign they had initiated. The Non-Aligned summit had discussed the notion of a third world force being sent to southern Africa to defend it against Total Strategy, but even the Non-Aligned membership saw its own rhetoric for what it was and the force, far from materialising, never left the pages of general and often extemporaneous speeches. In entering Mozambique, the Zimbabweans were careful not to commit themselves to battling RENAMO at large – although they did later achieve some major, though isolated, successes against it – but only to the limited stabilisation programme surrounding the rail route. The South Africans were anxious not to intervene directly against the Zimbabweans, firstly for fear of making them heroic martyrs in the eyes of the world and, secondly, because of the commitments entailed in opening up their own second front. The SADF was back in Angola, and achieving successes there. An SADF operation in Mozambique would have detracted from that effort. Instead, the South Africans noted the limited objectives of the Zimbabwean intervention, considered that RENAMO, even if occasionally defeated, would continue to destabilise the country-at-large, and assessed the Zimbabwean strength if ever a showdown was required. The Zimbabweans had no air-cover. The South Africans thought that the Zimbabwean economy was such that any lengthy commitment to Mozambique would bleed Mugabe's exchequer dry.[39]

The South Africans thought that these areas of resistance could not

[38] For my comments on Pretoria's involvement, see *Exporting Apartheid*, pp. 52–4.
[39] Michael Evans, 'The Security Threat from South Africa', in Colin Stoneman (ed.). *Zimbabwe's Prospects: Issues of Race, Class and State in Southern Africa*, London: Macmillan, 1988; and idem, *The Frontline States, South Africa and Southern African Security – Military Prospects and Perspectives*, Harare: University of Zimbabwe, 1986.

defeat their total Strategy. What did, finally, drag it to a halt was a combination of overarching pride, the last Soviet and Cuban campaign, and American diplomacy. The SADF and UNITA had waged a very successful campaign in 1987, denying space to the MPLA and consolidating its control over much of southern rural Angola, leaving only a few towns in assured government control. As 1987 closed and 1988 began, the Soviet-equipped MPLA and its Cuban allies prepared for their annual offensive – only this time it was clear that, in the new foreign policy of Gorbachev, this effort was to be the last throw of the dice. After this, investment in the Angolan conflict would be scaled down and, if victory was not gained, the probable future would have been two Angolas under the northern MPLA and the southern UNITA. The idea of a last throw of the dice meant two things. It meant that UNITA had to resist the offensive and prepare a proper de facto government – if only for initial propaganda reasons. And it meant that the MPLA offensive was bigger, better prepared, better equipped, and – with Soviet and Cuban advisers thick on the ground – better led than before. For it would be a mistake to conceive that war in Angola had a guerilla nature. It certainly had a fair number of guerilla operations but, for some time, major conventional engagements involving armour and air support had occurred regularly. A decisive conventional campaign was now planned on both sides.

The SADF and UNITA were confident they could hold ground against the offensive. What UNITA wanted in addition, however, was to take and hold the strategically important town of Cuito Cuanavale. This would serve it as a capital after the MPLA offensive had failed and be a sign of its triumph. It would be to the streets of Cuito Cuanavale that Savimbi would bring his foreign guests and have them ride in limousines to his executive mansion. Having a capital would be a sign of victory. But what this did in the context of battle-planning was to focus the campaigns of both sides around one town. The MPLA, Soviets, and Cubans decided to reinforce Cuito Cuanavale in depth. Something out of a Warsaw Pact manual emerged in the jungle. The town was ringed with layers of mine-fields. It was given an air defence of layered ground-to-air missile units. What this meant was that, on land or in the air, the attackers would have to penetrate a defence established in lines that reinforced one another. Breaking through one line or layer would mean having to break through the next, and so on.

The fixation on Cuito Cuanavale meant a curious inversion. The

MPLA offensive became a defence. Where UNITA might have succeeded by diffusing an MPLA attack, making it spread out over a number of targets and countering on various flanks, it now found itself preparing a concentrated attack. For UNITA, Cuito Cuanavale was not necessary in military terms and, as it turned out, it was a military mistake to insist upon it. The first South African calculations were that the town could be taken. The problems on land could be overcome simply by using the UNITA troops as the 'grunts' – they would be the ones going through the mine-fields. The SADF would follow. When they calculated an attack by air, however, the projections changed. The South Africans thought they could launch a successful aerial attack on the town and provide aerial support for the ground operation. However, given the air defences installed by the Soviets and Cubans, it would cost an unacceptable number of aircraft or, in the jargon of it all, airframes. This was worrying in itself but what became even more worrying was the realisation that, for this last throw of the dice, the Soviets had despatched a squadron of latest generation MIG fighters – almost certainly piloted by Soviet officers. For the first time since 1975, the SADF would not have air superiority. The new MIGs could outfly and outgun the South African Mirages, Jaguars, and Cheetahs. The South African air attack never materialised. If Cuito Cuanavale was to be taken, it had to be by land.[40]

There are a number of journalistic accounts of the battle and, although one otherwise well-informed series of reports exaggerated the scale of fighting – it was not the largest conventional clash ever seen in Africa,[41] otherwise one must take a reduced view of the north African battles of World War II – it was nevertheless not insignificant. But the town was never taken; indeed, it is probably the case that the town was never attacked – in the sense of a committed onslaught. A number of skirmishes, including armoured clashes, took place on the fringes of the town and in the countryside around. Both sides attempted to out-manoeuvre the other, so that the 'battle' was not static but one of seeking positions: one side seeking positions from which to attack the town, the other denying such positions. In this war of positioning, a large SADF contingent fell victim to a pincer and found itself surrounded. This time, unlike 1975, the Cubans had

---

[40] Account given to the author by a western ambassador, Harare, September 1989.
[41] See e.g. some of Victoria Brittain's features in *Guardian* (London and Manchester) in April to June 1988.

closed the trap and were poised to destroy the SADF units – which contained a number of white soldiers. The Cubans did not, however, move in for the kill. Their hesitation was a deliberate signal, no doubt ordered from Havana and Moscow, and conveyed not only to the South Africans but to the US that the time was appropriate to negotiate a future for this part of the region. Unable to take Cuito Cuanavale, unable for some years to come to bridge the technological gap that had suddenly appeared in air superiority, unable otherwise to rescue its surrounded troops, and unwilling to face the consequences in public opinion if sizeable numbers of white soldiers were killed, Pretoria responded to US Assistant Secretary of State Chester Crocker's diplomatic initiative for a series of negotiating sessions. Ten formal sessions followed in the second half of 1988.[42] The South Africans withdrew from Angola. Namibia became independent. Gorbachev's last throw of the dice had succeeded and, for this, one must credit at least partially a strategic mistake by UNITA.

Since the agreements of 1988, and the coming to power in South Africa of President de Klerk in 1989, South African foreign policy has changed its application. It no longer relies on Total Strategy. But it has not changed in its essential strength. It is still, notwithstanding its withdrawal from Angola, the strongest military power in the region, and the strongest economic power. The approach of de Klerk is discussed in Chapter 6, but his long-term aims are not so radically different from those of his predecessors – although the means may be different – to suggest that a new epoch has unequivocably begun.

Conclusion

What Total Strategy sought can be summarised as follows:

1. It sought not so much a ring of buffer states as a constellation of dependent states that acknowledged, in formal diplomatic terms, the fact that Pretoria was the regional hegemon. These states would be not only dependent, but integrated into the South African economic system. The entire region would therefore become an economic community, but not one of equal members.

---

[42] For a good description of the negotiating stages involved, see G. R. Berridge, 'Diplomacy and the Angola/Namibia Accords', *International Affairs*, Vol. 65, No. 3, 1989.

2. It would have been established by a South African constitutional machinery that was, nevertheless, unanswerable even to the white electorate. The State Security Council was answerable to the president alone. Within the SSC, there was at least residual Broederbond influence, reinforcing the condition of unanswerability. The civilian constitutional machinery that was answerable was complicit with this presidential, militaristic, and secretive troika.

3. As with the *cordon sanitaire* strategy, it sought to establish, and for a time did establish, a region more determined by South African policy than by any policies from without the region. This South African autonomy was militarily underscored and, through a series of accords, was given some diplomatic credence. Politically, diplomatically, and economically, the region was to be achieved in its totality by Total Strategy.

The idea of a constellation of states, a term used by the South Africans themselves, underlay strategy and, indeed, it would be fair to ask whether this central premise of South African foreign policy can be abandoned. An analogy to the idea of a constellation might be the 'co-prosperity sphere' sought by the Japanese before World War II. Under Total Strategy, the first phase of the constellation would have been complete when all southern African states, including, finally, Zimbabwe and Zambia, had signed accords with Pretoria. A second phase may have been an accord between Pretoria and SADCC as a whole. SADCC would then have become Pretoria's instrument for integrating the region according to its own design. This would not have been economically detrimental to the southern African states. In fact, South Africa could have been the engine for their growth. The consequences, however, in terms of politics, principles, and pride would have been considerable. Any negotiation with South Africa, while Total Strategy was at its height, could only have been over the level of coerciveness superimposed on top of this basic aim of integration under domination.

The questions that must be asked of Kaunda's attempts to negotiate a future for southern Africa that did not, unlike the aftermath of Cuito Cuanavale, depend on the impact of arms, relate to his readiness to accept this sort of South African domination. Or, did Kaunda conceive of the South African hegemony as being not wholly one-dimensional?

Did he feel that exchanges and bargains were possible, so that a dominated and limited pluralism within the region was possible and even worthwhile? If this is what he felt, what sort of other dimensions did he seek to create?

4

THE ZAMBIAN FOREIGN POLICY RESPONSE

The Zambian foreign policy response was not unsophisticated, though it seemed often simple and sometimes wilful. Later, it seemed treacherous and, after Zimbabwe's independence, to diminish in consequence. All these impressions, I shall argue, were wrong. However, these interpretations of foreign policy provide a series of time periods. The decade 1965–75 was meant to have been marked by a moral stand, pure and simple, sometimes irrational but still principled, against the 'white south'. This decade began with Ian Smith's UDI in Rhodesia, and ended with the granting of independence by Portugal to Angola and Mozambique. It was precisely the independence of Angola that heralded an analysis of Zambian foreign policy as treacherous, as collaborating with South Africa's. The touchstone to this school of thought was Kaunda's reluctance to abandon his support of UNITA, doing so only when it became irrefutably clear that UNITA was itself collaborating with South Africa. The underlying rationale to this approach was the evidence of a Zambian élite class having been formed, and having monopolised power through the one-party state. The analysis then proceeded on the basis that international relations are essentially the product of class collaborations across state lines. Therefore, the Zambian ruling class was an agent for an international capitalist class and, therefore again, a cousin at least of the South African capitalists. After Zimbabwe's independence in 1980 which, according to the class analysis, Zambia did as much to hinder as to help, Zambia's regional role diminished and, through Kaunda's insistence on his mediatory exercises, his meetings with South African politicians and presidents, it actually became an impediment to a unified foreign policy of all the frontline states. There are thus three time periods involved, 1965–75, 1975–80, and 1980 to the present. The interpretations of foreign policy sketched in this paragraph will be taken up more fully in the next chapter. The current chapter will begin with a discussion of history. It should be noted from the last chapter, however, that what Kaunda faced, what he sought to address in his foreign policy, was complex and powerful.

UDI in Rhodesia

It was not appreciated as complex and powerful at the beginning. For Kaunda, foreign policy was a learning process, and it is fair to say that, at the outset, he was bewildered and unsure at the pace of events and, secondly, that he placed Rhodesian UDI at the centre of his policy. This did not last, and it is certainly incorrect – and a disservice to Kaunda rather than an admiration of him – to say that, from 1965 to 1980, his was only a policy of moral principle suffering, with the unrequited patience of Job, the vicissitudes of regional wickedness. He had more up his sleeve than noble suffering. He was not helplessly afflicted.

When Rhodesian UDI was declared, the Commonwealth Secretariat was but a few months old, having been created by membership demand to provide an alternative to the British centre of the Commonwealth and, specifically, because the newly-created Afro-Asian caucus within the Commonwealth did not trust Britain to deal strongly with the rebellion of white settlers in Rhodesia rumoured from the early 1960s.[1] When UDI came, one of the first acts of the new secretariat was to organise an emergency heads of government meeting in Lagos. This took place in early 1966 and was the first Commonwealth summit held outside London and the first not arranged by the British Government. Its situation in Lagos was a symbol of African concern over UDI. Yet, it must be said that, at this meeting, Kaunda made no impact. He assumed no leadership role. He seemed then to have no real policy over Rhodesia.[2] To be fair, the other African leaders had

---

[1] On the creation of the Commonwealth Secretariat, see J. D .B. Miller, *Survey of Commonwealth Affairs – Problems of Expansion and Attrition 1953–1969*, London: Oxford University Press, 1974, pp. 397–401; and Derek Ingram, *The Imperfect Commonwealth*, London: Rex Collings, 1977.

[2] Account of senior Commonwealth Secretariat official, related to the present author, London, October 1990.

no clear policy either, except that Britain was at fault in not crushing the rebellion and that it should now do so. Harold Wilson was able to argue that his policy of sanctions would do exactly that, the same argument that he carried to all other international fora. But the meeting did extract two major concessions from him. The first was that there should be no recognised independence of Rhodesia without majority rule. Secondly, although it was recognised that Rhodesia was a British responsibility, it was also a Commonwealth concern. Thereafter, successive British Governments took this as a defence against criticism – nobody's responsibility but ours, so it's up to us to formulate and discharge policy – and successive Commonwealth summits took it as a mandate to challenge and scrutinise British policy as an expression of concern.

Harold Wilson would not have anticipated what a history of Commonwealth challenge he was unleashing but he, like his successor, Edward Heath, thought poorly of Commonwealth strength and regarded it as a chore to attend the biannual summits.[3] Year by year, however, Kaunda's sense of foreign policy improved and the articulation of this policy came with the 1969 Manifesto on Southern Africa. It had taken more than three years after Rhodesian UDI, but the message of the manifesto was clear: negotiations were more important than violence; South Africa should be ostracised from the international community (so South Africa was seen as more important than Rhodesia); and Kaunda had emerged as a leader of African opinion. This leadership role was evinced in 1970, when Kaunda became Chairman of both the OAU and the Non-Aligned Movement, and then in 1971. Edward Heath had become British Prime Minister having, in his election campaign, entertained the idea of selling arms to South Africa.[4] It was Kaunda who led an OAU delegation to London to seek to persuade Heath against such sales, and Kaunda again who played a major role at the 1971 Commonwealth summit in

---

[3] See Elaine Windrich, *Britain and the Politics of Rhodesian Independence*, London: Croom Helm, 1978.

[4] Even years after, former aides to Heath insisted that he had never moved to sell arms to South Africa. Their definition of 'arms', was, however, narrow. The present author was publicly challenged during his address to the New Zealand Institute of International Affairs, Wellington, 11 September 1986, by the British High Commissioner to New Zealand, who had been with Heath at the 1971 Singapore summit. He insisted, 15 years on, that what had been proposed for sale were not arms, but unarmed helicopters. The fact that these helicopters could easily be armed and, indeed, were designed to be armed, was a point excised from his intervention.

Singapore, where Heath was subjected to prolonged and, often, ill-humoured debate on the subject. Although Heath never backed down in so many words at the Singapore summit, the idea of arms sales to South Africa was afterwards never carried through. The argument at Singapore had left a bitter taste in an organisation that still considered itself a club. Kaunda proposed, therefore, that the summit should not end on a negative note, but should agree on a vision for the future. What emerged, and in fact allowed the summit to conclude with amazing cordiality, was the Declaration of Commonwealth Principles – a document of rather generalised liberalism, but which was adopted by all the heads of government present, and has been taken ever since to represent the aims and objectives of the Commonwealth, with some scholars even arguing that it provided the Commonwealth with the equivalent of a charter. [5] John Hatch was wrong, however, in writing that Kaunda had already drafted this declaration before Singapore began, that it was argued over at length in and out of session, and that it was finally approved 'with minor amendments' and stands 'as an historic witness to Kaunda's international vision'.[6] What really happened was that Kaunda proposed in general terms the desirability of a Commonwealth statement of principle, but the draft that emerged and was agreed was very largely the work of Emeka Anyaoku, the Commonwealth Secretariat's conference secretary, now Commonwealth Secretary-General.[7] Kaunda had come a long way in foreign policy, but not as far as had been claimed for him. That his policy was still incomplete and unrefined can be seen from the crisis in rail links that dominated the mid-1970s.

This crisis began in 1973 and raises several questions. The first and second of these are 'why had it taken so long to arise?', and 'what had been the character of Zambian regional policy before the crisis?' The third question is 'why did Kaunda react the way he did?', and the fourth is related to the South African attempt to solve Kaunda's problems: 'why did South Africa want to help Kaunda?' The fifth and overarching question is important to the debate on Kaunda, so often

[5] This is a point first made by Sir William Dale, *The Modern Commonwealth*, London: Butterworths, 1983, and developed by myself in Stephen Chan, *The Commonwealth in World Politics – A Study of International Action 1965 to 1985*, London: Lester Crook, 1988.

[6] Hatch, *Kaunda of Zambia*, p. 104.

[7] Account of senior Commonwealth Secretariat official, related to the present author, London, October, 1990.

seen to be suffering because of principle at this point, and is simply 'what was noble and principled about his policy, and what was extemporaneous and, basically, whimsical?' Upon Rhodesian UDI, Zambia certainly had to make some harsh adjustments. It is worth pointing out, however, that in the late 1960s, international copper prices had begun to decline and, since this was overwhelmingly Zambia's major export, providing some 97 per cent of all export revenues, the economic constraints of that time could not have been laid solely at Rhodesia's door. A number of new and expensive pieces of infrastructure had certainly to be put into place. For instance, the Maamba mine in Zambia's Southern Province was geared up to replace Rhodesia's Wankie as the main source of coal and coke. But it would be incorrect to say that UDI immediately dislocated or threatened to dislocate the Zambian economy. Zambia continued to use the railways that passed southward through Rhodesia, on to South Africa, and the international community understood that, in Zambia's landlocked position, exemptions from the sanctions policy could be claimed. Not only did Zambia claim them, neither Rhodesia nor South Africa made any sustained threat to choke off the transport lifelines. In fact, it would be fair to say that, on the matter of transport, a frosty cordiality was maintained. There wasn't much scope for other communications: only seven telephone lines existed between Lusaka and Salisbury; but each side signalled clearly enough to the other that their coexistence and cooperation, though frosty, at times tense, could continue. In short, from UDI in 1965 until 1973, eight years, it must be said that, despite having to make some concentrated infrastructural adjustments in a short space of time, Zambia had suffered a little less than Kaunda's plaintiff pleading to the west suggested. In that time, Kaunda had developed some foreign policy expertise. In the wake of the 1969 Lusaka Manifesto, he took his fight into the fora provided first by the OAU and Non-Aligned Movement, and then by the Commonwealth. He stressed negotiations and he came to view South Africa as the major player in the region. In 1971, he campaigned against British arms sales to South Africa, emerging as a major (but certainly not a determining) Commonwealth figure. He maintained a public relations campaign throughout this period as an aggrieved participant in southern Africa, calling for justice on the grounds of Zambia's suffering – but he had not yet offered any major stakes in his quarrel with Ian Smith. The character of Zambian regional policy had been, therefore, strangely ambivalent: diplomatically active but also very pragmatic and well-mannered. This suddenly changed.

In 1973, after a border incident, Smith abruptly closed the Zambian/Rhodesian border. This was meant to generate publicity for the Rhodesian account of the incident, and to act as a large, though clumsy, signal to Lusaka that Smith's patience with border 'provocations' was wearing thin. Ten hours later, Smith proposed to exempt copper from this closure and, three weeks later, he proposed to lift the closure entirely. Smith had come under some pressure from Pretoria to reopen the border, but he had probably not sought an indefinite closure in any case – just long enough to make a point to Kaunda. To the surprise of Salisbury and Pretoria, however, and the rest of the international community, Kaunda refused to accept the reopened border, saying that Smith was 'too hostile a neighbour', and could not be trusted – though, in the matter of cross-border traffic, Kaunda had trusted Smith for eight years.

No-one knows exactly why Kaunda responded in this way. It was a decision for which no preparations had been made, and this certainly did lead to increased economic hardship as the scramble to find an alternative outlet to the sea began. The Tazara railway, being built between Zambia and the Tanzanian port of Dar es Salaam, despite a Chinese and Zambian work-rate that has entered local legend, could not be ready until 1975. Kaunda, therefore, sent his country's copper northwards then west through Angola on the Benguela railway. The problem here was that, having suddenly decided to cease dealing with one minority regime, he had now to deal with another. Angola was still under Portuguese rule and, in many ways, it might be said that Portuguese racism was greater, at least more insidious, than that of others – offering the prospect of certain rights, but only to Africans who had reached a certain stage of 'assimilation', economically integrated, educated, and culturally whitened. The Benguela route, however, could not cope with 27,000 tons of Zambian copper a month in addition to its normal traffic and, by the end of 1974, Kaunda had to suffer the revelations of English newspapers that, despite the many protestations of principle he had made over the transport issue, Zambia had been secretly using Rhodesian railways to move copper to Mozambican ports. Mozambique was not yet independent so, from having to use rail through two minority regimes in 1973 – Rhodesia and South Africa – Zambia was using rail through three – Angola, Rhodesia, and Mozambique. It seemed nothing had been gained and, in terms of dislocation, missed delivery dates, and lowered national income, much had been lost.

By the end of 1974, however, it had become apparent that changes would be possible in Angola and Mozambique. The Portuguese coup had brought to power officers who were prepared to divest their nation of African colonies. This meant that a new power structure would become apparent in the region, something appreciated by both Kaunda and South African Prime Minister Vorster. The Victoria Falls conference of 1975 brought both men face to face – in (ironically) a railway carriage parked in exactly the middle of the bridge that linked Rhodesia and Zambia across the Victoria Falls gorge. There, Vorster offered to vouchsafe the reopening of the border and ensure that Smith never closed it again; but, again, Kaunda refused to accept this. Perhaps he had in mind the prospective viability of the new Tazara link to Dar es Salaam, operational from October 1975, but when questioned by Vorster about his refusal to use a reopened frontier with Rhodesia, Kaunda replied, perhaps jocularly, 'Julius won't let me do it.'[8] If it was jocular, it hid a serious reservation on the part of Julius Nyerere, and this is discussed below. On the matter of rail links, however, although Kaunda refused Vorster's offer, it soon became clear that Tazara, like Benguela before it, could not cope with the volume of Zambian traffic. After its completion, the line was never properly maintained and, consequently, has not run at anywhere near its full capacity. In addition, Dar es Salaam proved a very slow and inefficient port. By this time, Benguela was no longer possible either as an alternative or supplement, as the Angolan civil war brought it to a standstill. In October 1978, almost exactly three years after the opening of Tazara, rail links with Rhodesia were restored – the agreement to do so being signed by rail authorities rather than government leaders – and Zambia began exporting copper and fertiliser, through Rhodesia, for shipping from Port Elizabeth in South Africa. The rail saga which had run for five years, 1973–8, had begun dramatically, and ended without ceremony. Kaunda had never thought through his policy on transport routes. To this extent, if principle had been involved, it had been given extemporaneous expression.

The 1975 Victoria Falls conference was the first meeting between Kaunda and any South African premier; it also marked the culmina-

8 Geldenhuys, *The Diplomacy of Isolation*, pp. 271–2, fn. 194.

tion of a long-held ambition of Vorster's, and was a further step in the slightly longer South African campaign of wanting some contact with Zambia. In 1964, shortly after independence, Kaunda offered South Africa an exchange of diplomats. This was not extraordinary since, as early as 1959, even Kwame Nkrumah of Ghana was interested in the establishment of full diplomatic relations. As noted in the last chapter, South Africa rebuffed all such efforts. In 1965, however, the then South African Prime Minister, Verwoerd, began suggesting to Zambia the possibility of regular non-diplomatic contact. Nothing came of this; Verwoerd died in 1966. Kaunda, to mild South African astonishment, sent his widow a gracious note of condolence – and the South Africans read this as a statement of peaceful intent in Zambian foreign policy, which it may certainly have been even though Kaunda wrote that his condolences had been conceived solely as a Christian act. Nevertheless, Vorster as the new prime minister pursued the idea of links with Zambia and, specifically, the idea of a summit meeting between himself and Kaunda. Kaunda did indeed meet with Vorster's representatives more than once and the Zambian version of the South African agenda included the information that South Africa wanted to discuss 'what compromise Zambia would prefer on the Rhodesian issue'.[9]

A summit was almost arranged in 1971, but was never held because of a late reluctance to go ahead on Kaunda's part. The year 1971 was, however, as noted above, one in which Kaunda was flexing his diplomatic muscle internationally. Heath's desire to sell arms to South Africa ended whatever residual faith Kaunda had in the British, and the episode confirmed Kaunda's discovery of 1970 – with the chairmanships of the OAU and Non-Aligned Movement – that he could rely upon himself to make an international impact, and to propose African initiatives for an African problem. Some writers have stressed that, until the Heath episode, Kaunda had felt deepening depression over British foreign policy towards Rhodesia and, during Harold Wilson's office, had felt betrayed by the Labour Party that had once been so affectionate towards him.[10] This was particularly so after Wilson's discussions with Smith on board the British warships, *Tiger* and *Fearless*. Kaunda felt that the terms almost agreed on both

[9] Quoted in Sam C. Nolutshungu, *South Africa in Africa – A Study of Ideology and Foreign Policy*, Manchester: Manchester University Press, 1975, p. 235. See pp. 226–43 for excellent background to this issue.
[10] E.g. Hatch, *Kaunda of Zambia*, p. 100.

occasions would have sold out the prospect for true majority rule in Rhodesia. Yet, as Nolutshungu has pointed out, if Kaunda had really expected the British to do anything dramatically different from what it in fact did, including negotiating with Smith on the warships, and seeking to persuade Pretoria that it should encourage Smith to cooperate, 'then the Zambian Government seriously misunderstood the nature of its political situation in southern Africa'. It could not rely on the British Government 'to play a part wholly alien to British southern Africa policy'.[11] Zambia was thus on its own and this was a central part of the lessons of foreign policy that Kaunda was learning up to 1971. Certainly, from studies of the Wilson government, it appears that Kaunda and Zambia were not on Wilson's list of priority items, even where Rhodesia was concerned. Paul Foot's excellent chapter on Wilson's Rhodesia policy mentions Kaunda not at all.[12] It would be wrong to emphasise too strongly, however, Kaunda's reliance on Wilson. As mentioned above, Kaunda required time to find his foreign policy feet, and this would have been the case whatever Wilson did. By 1970 and 1971, he was certainly an assured actor and, thinking through the pros and cons of meeting with Vorster, may have decided at the last moment that such a summit could solve nothing. It was better to concentrate as he had on building a coordinated international pressure against both Rhodesia and South Africa, whereas a meeting with Vorster could detract from this campaign by giving the appearance that fruitful negotiations, without fully-developed international strength behind the Zambian position, were possible. Kaunda needed international support to countervail the obvious South African strengths in the region.

For South Africa would have welcomed the formula put forward at the *Tiger* talks of December 1966. It would have 'stabilized the economic situation, without any immediate revolutionary upheaval, and removed the threat of international economic sanctions from the area'.[13] Talks in 1971 would not have seen any fundamental South African advance from what the Zambians had rejected in the British proposals of 1966. It would not have been so much 'what compromise

---

[11] Nolutshungu, *South Africa in Africa*, pp. 242–3.
[12] Paul Foot, *The Politics of Harold Wilson*, Harmondsworth: Penguin, 1968, Chapter 8, although on p. 249 the chapter is prefaced by a denunciatory quote from Simon Kapwepwe, then Zambian Foreign Minister, charging Wilson with becoming a racialist.
[13] Ibid., p. 278.

Zambia would prefer on the Rhodesian issue', as what compromise best suited the South Africans. After 1971, Kaunda was involved in his railways project of 1973–8 and, in its early stages, would have been unwilling to be seen seeking South African help. Publicly at least, it was meant to be a stand of Zambian principle, self-sacrifice, and independence. Even at the 1975 Victoria Falls conference, Kaunda rejected South African offers of help on the rail-routes question. But why was that conference held in the first place?

The conference was not all sweetness and light and, despite the emergence in due course of some jocularity, it also included acrimonious exchanges. Kaunda warned Vorster that he was sitting on a powder-keg, and Vorster, in expounding the cultural-not-racial theory of divisions in South African society, said to his face that the Zambian President didn't know what he was talking about.[14] But it had been Vorster again who had sent the signal of seeking a summit. After the 1974 coup in Lisbon, and with the prospect of regional change of some sort, whether the South Africans liked it or not, Vorster made a remarkable speech. It echoed Harold Macmillan's 'wind of change' speech almost one and a half decades earlier and was, indeed, also described as being about the 'wind of change'. He said that southern African leaders faced 'a choice between peace' on the one hand, and the 'escalation of strife' on the other. The cost of conflict would be 'too high for southern Africa to pay'. Kaunda's reaction was that this represented the 'voice of reason for which Africa and the rest of the world had been waiting'.[15]

To an extent, the rhetoric on both sides was ritualistic, concerned both with sending signals and international public relations. Vorster's echo of Harold Macmillan was probably deliberately evocative of that first wave of African independence and hope for the future. It was important for him to characterise his own hopes for the future in that positive light, and to suggest that the independence of Angola and Mozambique might herald a regional wave of peace and cooperation. Underlying this evocation were two possible aims of the South African regional agenda. The first was that he could have been sincere, in which case a *détente* between South Africa and Zambia would be the first step in achieving both a regional peace and a regional shape acceptable to both Pretoria and Lusaka. The term

14 According to Brownrigg, *Kenneth Kaunda*, p. 130.
15 Quoted in *Africa*, No. 51, October 1975, p. 16.

'regional shape' here implies a domination of southern Africa by Pretoria and Lusaka. They would be the two poles of power, so that regional hegemony would be exercised according to how that power was balanced. The problem here was one for Zambia – since it didn't really have the resources to sustain a balance of power. Hegemony would have drifted, probably rather quickly, towards South Africa. In short, South Africa would retain a significantly altered *cordon sanitaire*, except that it would no longer consist of minority-ruled colonies, but dominated good neighbours. To use an institutional metaphor, it would be a headmaster and Zambia a head-prefect. The latter would have some autonomy and even powers of initiative, but would always be answerable to the former. South Africa would have, essentially, its ring of compliant states. For Zambia, however, a stabilised region was an important goal, and if it were stabilised with Pretoria and Lusaka as the two most important powers, even if any real balance of power could only be nominal, that would not be a loss, but could even be seen as an advance on the situation that had prevailed up to 1974. Moreover, some movement towards majority-rule in Rhodesia would be included in the agenda; at least something might be negotiable there; in the short term, this would end Zambia's problems of social order in hosting sometimes unruly exiles, and end also its border tensions with Rhodesia; and, in the long term, it could solve a major problem of the region. If all this could be negotiated, who knows? Perhaps Pretoria might wish eventually to negotiate changes in its own domestic structures. For Zambia, the risks in talking with South Africa seemed worth taking, even if only in the light of an immense optimism.

The second possible South African aim might be seen more cynically as simply to talk for the sake of appearing to talk, creating a good impression while playing for time.

When Kaunda remarked to Vorster that he could not accept a reopened border with Rhodesia because 'Julius won't let me do it', this remark was less lighthearted than it might have appeared. Julius Nyerere had deep reservations about the South African aims, was concerned in case Kaunda might be duped by Vorster, and particularly concerned that, in his commitment to negotiation, Kaunda might concede too much, give too much away, get too little in return. Nyerere had, in fact, established lines – and not just railway lines – across which Kaunda was not to step. In November 1975, Nyerere gave an extraordinary speech at Oxford University in which he laid out, with the precision Kaunda never mastered, his view of the South African objectives.[16] I summarise it here.

1. At first, independence in Mozambique seemed to achieve what the Lusaka Manifesto could not. South Africa offered talks which included the future of Rhodesia, and not just whether majority rule should come but how. South Africa seemed willing to 'deliver' Ian Smith on the matter.

2. Vorster viewed *détente* and constitutional settlement in Rhodesia as providing advantages for South Africa: an end to its costly role in breaking sanctions; an end to its military assistance to Rhodesia which had attracted international attention.

3. Vorster sought some concrete returns for his goodwill over Rhodesia, principally from Mozambique to do with South African interests in the Mozambican transport and harbour system, electricity supply from Cabora Bassa, the flow of migrant workers to South African mines, and border security.

4. Behind these specific short-term objectives lay another set of aims: the buying of time to promote its brand of 'independence' for Namibia and the bantustans; the promotion of South Africa's view of the region, a so-called 'United Nations of Southern Africa', with Pretoria as its political and economic centre. This would reduce the UN lobby against South Africa and, with the reduction of international pressure, South Africa could maintain its domestic structures – using its good-neighbourliness as a smokescreen.

5. A negotiated settlement in Rhodesia would mean no military victory for African guerillas there and, therefore, no inspiration from that quarter for a guerilla campaign in South Africa itself.

If Nyerere was right, then South African gains from negotiations would centre around its own internal security, and time to shape its own external environment. Gains for the majority-ruled region might include Rhodesia. Kaunda may have lacked Nyerere's precision, but there is no reason to suspect that he was unaware of these things. The question really revolved around just how far Vorster really would deliver Smith. Here, there are contrasting views. Certainly Ian Smith

---

16 Julius Nyerere, *Some Aspects of Liberation – A Speech by President Nyerere at Oxford University on 19 November 1975*, Dar es Salaam: Government Printer.

himself considered Vorster to be serious. In a BBC interview, he said that Vorster's message was 'clear and unequivocal', and meant that Rhodesia had no choice but to accept majority rule – although this was to be along the lines of the Kissinger plan of the time, which had, in Smith's account, the blessing of Julius Nyerere. Smith said that Vorster 'was of the opinion that he could work with the black leaders to the north of us'. In return those black leaders 'were going to accept South Africa and their philosophy'. So the outline of the trade-off in Smith's mind was clear. The black leaders got Rhodesia and South Africa got left alone. Smith remarked to Vorster that South Africa wouldn't be left alone for long.[17]

If Smith was right in his recollection that Nyerere accepted the Kissinger plan of 1976, then it seems that Nyerere himself, despite his Oxford speech, saw possibilities in *détente*. In his commentary on events, however, Zdenek Cervenka poses a less positive view. 'The only price Vorster was prepared to pay was to deliver Rhodesia to the conference table, but not to force it to accept *a priori* the condition of black majority rule. On this point he completely shared Ian Smith's view that this would never happen because of the disunity of the Rhodesian Africans.'[18]

This represents part of the playing-for-time-and-reaping-goodwill scenario.

Whichever view was correct, neither mattered in the end. Alarmed by events in Angola, South Africa was losing interest not so much in the concept of *détente* but in the prospect that it might cover the entire region. As mentioned in the last chapter, the transition from *cordon sanitaire* to Total Strategy was not made overnight. So also, *détente* was not abandoned in its entirety overnight. Thus Vorster still had hopes of a *modus vivendi* with Kaunda, he was open to the Kissinger plan to the extent of placing at least some pressure on Ian Smith, but he had also sent his troops into Angola. War with one part of the region and *détente* with the other could not work. The foreign policy confusion in Vorster's last years in office would not be repeated in the Botha reign of power and regional terror.

The events of this period, however, close a chapter in the history of

[17] Ian Smith in an interview with Michael Charlton, in Charlton, *The Last Colony in Africa: Diplomacy and the Independence of Rhodesia*, Oxford: Basil Blackwell, 1990, pp. 3–5.
[18] Zdenek Cervenka, *The Unfinished Quest for Unity: Africa and the OAU*, London: Julian Friedmann, 1977, p. 128.

Kaunda's reputation. His Victoria Falls conference with Vorster was seen by many as a collaboration with the enemy. This must certainly be an unfounded judgement since, as discussed above, there was the possibility of gains as well as risks. Judgement on how sincere Vorster was is problematic, but Nyerere seemed to take at least a cautious, sceptical, but not fully dismissive view – a view which fluctuated over the months of 1975 and 1976. Kaunda was certainly sincere, and not demonstrably naïve. The railway issue aside, Vorster never found him simply a repository of faith, hope, and principle. So, any judgement of Kaunda on the basis of Victoria Falls must tend towards the positive. Kaunda's support of UNITA in the Angolan civil war, however, poses a weightier question. When the UNITA matter is added to the meeting with Vorster, and other events are thrown into the mix, such as the departure of Robert Mugabe and ZANU's army from Zambia to operate more freely from Mozambique than Kaunda had allowed from his borders, then there seems to be an amount of circumstantial evidence which could fit a pattern. This pattern is unflattering to Kaunda. I consider this below, but it is worth making the point early that the gathering of circumstantial evidence works both ways. The frequent Rhodesian bombings and commando raids against Lusaka in 1979 do not suggest the fruits of collaboration. When it comes down to it, the pattern is all. How to think about patterns of thought is the subject of the next chapter.

From Angola to Zimbabwe

Two important points emerge from the independence of Angola. The first is that all three liberation groups, the victorious MPLA, the FNLA, and UNITA, were exactly that – groups that had fought for liberation. All had established their bona fides and all had eventually been recognised by the OAU. The Alvor Agreement of January 1975, established by the departing Portuguese and these three groups, providing for a share of power and eventual elections, drew continental acceptance. The second point is that all three groups had suffered divisions, or internal quarrels, or had experienced a recent history of intervention at the hands of others. This last condition certainly applied to the MPLA. In December 1973, the Soviet Union had suspended aid to Neto, the MPLA leader, and thrown its weight behind the Chipenda faction in an abortive coup, thinking that Chipenda might make a more malleable ally. At that time, China had

20 military instructors in Zaïre, training FNLA personnel. The overall stakes changed dramatically in April 1974 with the coup in Portugal. By August 1974, China had 105 instructors in Zaïre and, by October, Moscow had healed its rift with Neto. The elevation of tension within Angola encompassed the Sino-Soviet rivalry, but also spread out to involve the entire region and alarm those beyond it. Into the power vacuum left by the Portuguese entered the foreign policies of Zaïre, Zambia, South Africa, China, Cuba, the Soviet Union, and the USA.

None of these foreign policies, as applied to this period, was particularly well-rehearsed. All of them, except those of Cuba and the Soviet Union, suffered reverses. Cuban and Soviet foreign policy in Angola was successful, but at the price of a lengthy committal of military personnel and material. Once in, it was hard for them to leave. By June 1975, the Alvor Agreement had disintegrated amidst civil war. By July, the first Cuban contingents had arrived. In the same month, the FNLA, reinforced by 1,400 Zaïrean regulars, had tried to seize Luanda from the MPLA and failed. In the same month again, the US had sent $60 million of military aid to UNITA. In August, South African troops had crossed into Angola and, in September, alongside UNITA, had made strategic gains. The Soviet reply in October had been to airlift massive Cuban reinforcements to the MPLA. The Cubans and South Africans had clashed by November and, in December, the US Congress had voted to withhold arms to both UNITA and the FNLA. Faced with a lack of US support, South Africa had withdrawn its troops in January 1976.

It seems extraordinary that, in the mêlée of conflicting, often improvised, foreign policies – involving commitments, mistakes, and reversals by major powers – a school of thought should have developed that accused Zambia of a fully sensible collaboration with western capital. The speed and confusion of events were such that the capitalist powers involved could not secure collaboration between each other, South Africa finding itself unable to count upon US support. The claim that, beneath the surface of confusion, there existed a deeply-rooted structure of class-based interests and, therefore, class-based collaboration, is fully discussed in the next chapter. Briefly, however, the immediate accusation of 1976 was as follows. South Africa supported UNITA. Kaunda had met with Vorster to discuss the future shape of the region. Zambia supported UNITA for as long as continental African policy, expressed within the OAU, allowed. Therefore, complicity existed among South Africa, UNITA, and

Zambia. The University of Zambia riots of 1976, expressing this view and lambasting Kaunda's role in it, led to the closure of the university and the arrest of several student leaders, who were detained for a year without trial, on presidential order.[19] The harsh treatment of the students and the expulsion at the same time of some expatriate lecturers led to further charges of intolerance and the trammelling of free speech, and both charges could be sustained. Beyond this, however, the student uprising lent a romantic aura to the critique of class domination in Zambia, and the students, at least, saw themselves as involved in a class struggle. This view of themselves could not be sustained. That they provided an oppositional voice is true, but they were hardly class warriors: not a single arrested student leader has failed to enter professional life, and none of them has played a visible role in more recent opposition to Kaunda. Viewing them as young, ideological romantics, however, should not detract from the fact that, shorn of an international class analysis, a Zambian desire for collaboration with South Africa existed. It was not a desire to collaborate with western capital as such, and it was probably not very sensible given the direction of events as 1975 hurtled to its close, but the pace of events had confused more than just Zambian foreign policy; so it would be fair to say it was a collaboration that had set out to explore possibilities for the region, but that Zambia remained stubbornly faithful to these possibilities even when all chance for their materialisation had gone.

Even writers sympathetic to Kaunda say that he talked too long to the South Africans and too late, past the point when negotiations could change the direction of events.[20] At the end of 1975, he was still encouraging Joshua Nkomo to talk with Ian Smith. But that encouragement, and the Victoria Falls conference as a whole, should be seen in a particular context. Throughout much of 1974 and 1975, Kaunda's policy had been, by consultation and negotiation, to secure a peaceful region. His State House aide, Mark Chona, conducted a tireless shuttle diplomacy – largely unsung and barely recorded – between Lisbon, Pretoria, Washington, and the various liberation groups.

[19] The actual arrest authorisation was signed by Sunday Kazunga, then a senior aide to the president. Copies were shown to me by the student leaders concerned. After a year's imprisonment without trial, the students were barred from re-entering university for a further three years – then were finally allowed to resume their studies.

[20] William Tordoff, 'Zambia: The Politics of Disengagement', p. 68.

Kaunda's position at this time should not be seen, therefore, as merely responding to a South African initiative concerned with *détente*, but as activist in its own right – seeking to amalgamate the policies of the different interested parties into a proposal for a peaceful region. At some stage, he would have had to meet with Vorster since, of all the countries in the region, Zambia and South Africa were the most involved in diplomatic initiatives for its future. The justification was that no stone should be left unturned, particularly that stone against which the region's hopes might founder.

Even so, Kaunda's residual hopes for UNITA, that it might have a place in the government of Angola, compromised him, moving him beyond negotiation with South Africa and towards the quite legitimate charge that he was talking to a military enemy. The South African military support of UNITA was sufficient to tip Nigeria, a normally conservative state in OAU councils, towards the MPLA, and it was Nigeria that helped sponsor a resolution calling for a change in OAU policy in January 1976, from support of all three liberation groups to support only of the MPLA. Zambia had been a sponsor to another draft resolution, condemning South African intervention, but also that of all other non-African powers, and not preferring any Angolan party above another.[21] Although the OAU meeting came to a deadlock on the issue, the MPLA victory soon put paid to any further arguments. In February 1976, the OAU admitted the MPLA Government of Angola as its 47th member. Zambia finally recognised the MPLA Government in April 1976, after the student riots had taken place. In a way, Zambia's tardiness in accepting the MPLA as the sole Angolan representative was a desultory tailpiece to the OAU's own history. It was the OAU Liberation Committee that had sought a common position among the three Angolan parties up to January 1975, so that they might have appeared unified in the independence talks with Portugal. However, as far as the MPLA itself was concerned, the OAU was also responsible for its own internal unity. In August 1974, the Chipenda faction had still not been defeated, and it seemed likely that the MPLA might split into three. Acting for the OAU, it was a troika of the Congolese President Ngoubi, Nyerere, and Kaunda that restored unity to the MPLA. To view Kaunda as against the MPLA is, therefore, incorrect. To view him as being alarmed by the escalation

[21] The two draft resolutions are outlined in Cervenka, *The Unfinished Quest for Unity*, pp. 145–6.

of violence, in a region he had hoped would be both independent and peaceful, is closer to the truth. The key to this sort of region was a live-and-let-live policy with South Africa – but South Africa would be considerably less ready to let live with a communist government, supported by communist troops, on its doorstep. To preserve the sort of region he had hoped for, Kaunda sought to prolong the viability of UNITA as a player for at least a share of power in Angola. It was a policy he found hard to abandon and, at the end of it all, it was a policy that was wrong; it was not necessarily wrong at the beginning.

The difficulties of typecasting could be applied not only to Zambia, but to China. Both the FNLA and UNITA enjoyed Chinese support.[22] China took considerably longer to recognise the MPLA Government than Zambia, yet China could not be easily brushed with the paint of collaborationism. The same China that supported UNITA also supported Robert Mugabe and helped Zimbabwe to independence. The Soviet Union that had thrown considerable weight behind the MPLA also favoured Joshua Nkomo, operating out of Zambia, and hoped he would win the Zimbabwean crown. At this point, nothing of the conflicting foreign policies in southern Africa was particularly logical. The Rhodesian conflict, however, and the question of who supported which Zimbabwean liberation group, now enters the picture.

Zambia has often been accused of clearly favouring Nkomo in the divisions that afflicted the Zimbabwean guerilla movement, and this is true. The corollary of this is that it also deliberately constrained the forces of Robert Mugabe while they were in Zambia, and this also is true. But this was not because of conspiratorial reasons to do with class interests. Nkomo was indeed the more conservative of the two leaders, but he was supported as well by the Soviet Union which, as observed above, had helped bring the MPLA to power. Nkomo was perhaps the leader thought more likely to achieve a Zimbabwean independence that would not lead to South African destabilisation of the new country, and the region that supported it. Perhaps Kaunda thought also that any future possibility of *détente* might be better prosecuted with Nkomo as the leader of Zimbabwe. These are all suggestions that argue for Kaunda's conservatism in the sense that he still sought a region achieved by negotiation rather than force of arms, and that he supported pragmatic leadership rather than anything 'revolutionary'.

[22] For a good account of the Chinese involvement, which seemed often enigmatic, even inscrutable, see E. Ted Gladue Jr., *China's Perception of Global Politics*, Washington DC: University Press of America, 1982.

Such, a debate, by itself, ignores the history of the liberation groups in the mid-1970s, which was one of division. In addition to the competing claims of Nkomo and Mugabe, were those between Mugabe and Sithole. The latter two were engaged in a power struggle for control of ZANU, and it should be pointed out that the frontline states generally, not just Kaunda, supported Sithole. In December 1974, both ZANU and Nkomo's ZAPU were persuaded by the southern African states to join in an umbrella African National Council, led by Muzorewa, but this was done grudgingly. In March 1975, however, Herbert Chitepo, probably the most senior figure within ZANU, regardless of the claims of both Mugabe and Sithole, and acknowledged internationally as such,[23] was assassinated. Kaunda had several members of the ZANU executive arrested and imprisoned. Although it has been claimed that Kaunda was here persecuting ZANU, the murder of Chitepo has remained an unsolved mystery, and there is nothing as yet that fully exonerates at least some part of ZANU from the assassination. Sithole sought to exploit Kaunda's crackdown on ZANU for his own ends, but merely alienated his former support within the frontline states by so doing. April 1975, therefore, saw Mugabe and Edgar Tekere leaving Zambia for Mozambique, taking a great number of ZANU personnel with them. There, they linked up with guerillas who had been operating from Mozambique since 1972, although without very great strategic success. Mugabe became acknowledged as their leader and the crafting of a proper command structure and strategy, along with the independence of Mozambique and its willingness to allow the guerillas to establish a proper base structure, facilitated a major escalation of the struggle against Smith's government. This escalation, which can properly be dated from 1976, followed the history of division and quarrel outlined above. To maintain that Kaunda refused to support Mugabe would be accurate only after first acknowledging the feuding of the liberation groups on Zambian soil, and then acknowledging that Mugabe took some time to establish his leadership of ZANU, and only really did so in 1977 – by which time he was operating out of Mozambique. It should also be pointed out that Nkomo, Mugabe, and

---

[23] Chitepo was certainly the most active on the international circuit at that time, indefatigably drumming up support for ZANU in the most remote of places. He reached, for instance, New Zealand in 1973, on a lecture tour arranged by the New Zealand University Students' Association when I was president of that organisation.

Sithole had all been released from Rhodesian prison as part of the drive towards *détente*, and as a by-product of the decision by Kaunda and Vorster to hold talks.

The argument that, by preferring Nkomo to Mugabe, Kaunda was also not serious about guerilla war is likewise open to question. It is true that Nkomo never threw all, or even the majority, of his military resources into the battle for Zimbabwe. This was at least partially Nkomo's caution and hesitation as much as Kaunda's. Some of this caution had a military base. The achievements of Mugabe's ZANLA forces owed something to trial and error, and many guerilla contingents were sacrificed in the process by which the ZANLA high command grew in sophistication.[24] The battle of Chimoio in 1977, for instance, precipitated by a (largely successful) Rhodesian attack against a ZANLA transit, recuperation, and refugee complex inside Mozambique, has entered Zimbabwean military legend because of the heroism with which the surprised defenders sought to hold their ground. But they were surprised, and were able to be surprised because of the lack of rudimentary security and surveillance procedures undertaken by the ZANLA command.[25] By 1978, Nkomo's ZIPRA guerillas had begun larger-scale operations within Rhodesia, even though it is fair to say that the spheres of separate ZIPRA and ZANLA operations had been more-or-less carved out as early as 1976. In southeastern Matabeleland and the western Midlands, there were clashes between ZIPRA and ZANLA forces as late as 1979 – to the delight of the Rhodesian army, who then sought to play one off against the other – so the war was then a competitive one.[26] But the war was also directed against the Rhodesian forces, and the firefights between ZIPRA patrols and Rhodesian ones, and the somewhat less than equal

[24] Author's interviews with Rhodesian, ZANLA, and ZIPRA officers throughout Rhodesia during the British Governorship, January to March 1980, including interviews with the Rhodesian Joint-Operational Command at Umtali on the Mozambican border. These interviews were followed by others with former ZANLA officers and combatants who became the author's students in Lusaka towards the end of 1980.
[25] Author's interviews with ZANLA officers who survived Chimoio, 1980. For comments on this by a former high-ranking officer, see John Mawema, 'The Liberation of Zimbabwe: ZANLA Guerilla Strategy and Regional Support', unpublished MA dissertation, University of Kent, 1990.
[26] Author's interviews with ZIPRA, ZANLA, and Rhodesian Joint-Operational Command officers, Bulawayo and Gwanda, January and February 1980. Some of the interviewees were cross-examined on their information by Commonwealth Observer Group officers from Canada, Nigeria, and Bangladesh, in my presence; and the author also sought the opinion of British Commonwealth Monitoring Force officers on this subject. There was no dissent from any quarter over this information.

confrontations between ZIPRA personnel and Rhodesian helicopters, have their own place in the overall history of the armed struggle.[27] In October 1976, Mugabe and Nkomo merged their forces into the Patriotic Front. Although this alliance was never realised on the battlefield and, although it was reluctantly done on Mugabe's part,[28] it was a recognition at least that both parties and both men had something of a common aim.

What this overall history means in terms of Kaunda is simply that he was never against liberation by war. He was for liberation without war, if it could possibly, even remotely, be achieved. In 1977, Smith delivered a warning to Kaunda on the dangers of hosting a ZIPRA that was now beginning to establish itself within the Rhodesian borders and, from 1978 to 1979, while Kaunda continued his search for a negotiated settlement, Smith's airforce bombed Lusaka, his commandos attacked chosen targets within the city, and, on one such raid, destroyed Nkomo's house on the intelligence that he was still in it. (He wasn't and Nkomo's own account is probably apocryphal, saying he escaped through the toilet window – adding a variation to the metaphor of a camel and the eye of a needle.) During these raids, the Zambian military and, even at one stage in 1979, the mass mobilisation of the adult urban male population were ordered not to return Rhodesian fire without direct orders from State House in Lusaka. This was an order which the Zambian military sought, on occasion, to defy,[29] but the Zambian resistance did generally remain doggedly pacific. This pacifism was not so much an expression of Kaunda's humanistic principles, as an expression of his fear that South Africa might be tempted to join the conflict – which would then be escalated beyond any hope of Zambian or other frontline state control.[30] This is not the fear of a collaborator with South Africa but, rather, that of a leader who is aware that, whereas in peace some cooperation and at

---

[27] The author attended the first 'reconciliation party' in Bulawayo, just after polling had closed in the independence elections of March 1980, in which both Rhodesian and ZIPRA officers were present. Some recognised one another, to their consternation and then delight, from having stared at one another in brief close encounters between low-flying helicopters and ZIPRA ground forces. 'God must have prevented me from pulling my trigger that day so that we might meet again tonight.' It was very emotional.

[28] See Chapter 7, pp. 155–6.

[29] Author's interviews with students conscripted in 1979, Lusaka, 1981. For an additional comment see my *Exporting Apartheid*, p. 120, fn. 98.

[30] Author's interviews with Zambian ministers, Lusaka, 1980 and 1981.

least nominal balance of power with South Africa might be possible,
in war it would be a depressingly different situation.

Throughout the 1976–9 period, Kaunda kept up his involvement
in the search for a negotiated peace. The main efforts in this search
concerned the 1976 talks in Geneva, where, serviced by the Commonwealth Secretariat, Mugabe and Nkomo sat as the Patriotic Front, and
Ian Smith's government sat opposite; the 1977 proposals of the Anglo-
American initiative; and the round of diplomatic activity in 1979 that
culminated first in the Lusaka Commonwealth summit, and then in
the Lancaster House talks. The various negotiations are well related
elsewhere,[31] and my own comments about the Commonwealth role,
and Kaunda's within it, appear in a later section of this chapter. This
is, however, usually seen as the orthodox history of Zambian foreign
policy in this period, concerned primarily with negotiation. Above, I
have sought to suggest that Kaunda's foreign policy up to 1976 had
more than one dimension; that, after 1976, negotiating was not a
complete substitute for fighting; and that Zambian foreign policy was
not something at the behest of others. I would like to return to
Kaunda in the Commonwealth below, but his activity there straddles
the independence of Zimbabwe, and it is better to see it as a whole.
In the meantime, I would like to move on to what his policy was, and
what it has been taken to be, in the wake of Zimbabwean independence
in 1980. That year was, it will be recalled, also the prelude to the full-
blooded application of South Africa's Total Strategy.

From Zimbabwe to Namibia

The era of Total Strategy had two major parts of three years each,
from 1981–4, and from 1985–8. The first part ended with the signing
of both the Lusaka and Nkomati Accords, and the advent of the so-
called pax Pretoriana. The second part ended with the South African
defeat at Cuito Cuanavale, and was followed by ten rounds of formal
negotiations from May to December 1988. The results of these talks

---

[31] E.g. in Windrich, *Britain and the Politics of Rhodesian Independence*; Charlton, *The Last
Colony in Africa*; Jeffrey Davidow, *A Peace in Southern Africa – The Lancaster House
Conference on Rhodesia, 1979*, Boulder, Colorado: Westview, 1984; Anthony Verrier,
The Road to Zimbabwe 1890–1980, London: Jonathan Cape, 1986; with the best
opposed point of view to these overall orthodox treatments being the first two
chapters to Ibbo Mandaza (ed.), *Zimbabwe – The Political Economy of Transition
1980–1986*, Harare: CODESRIA, 1987.

were South African withdrawal from Angola, and independence for Namibia in 1990. In the meantime, in 1989, P. W. Botha was replaced as State President of South Africa by F. W. de Klerk. One of the first things de Klerk did was to visit Zambia for a summit with Kenneth Kaunda. This meeting propelled Kaunda back into the limelight as a leading figure in southern Africa and is fully covered in Chapter 6. From 1986, with the hosting of the Non-Aligned Movement summit in Harare, the Zimbabwean decision to send troops into Mozambique, and the death of Samora Machel, Robert Mugabe had emerged as the pacesetter among the leaders of the frontline. Kaunda did very little of real consequence from 1986–9. To an extent, that was a period of war against Total Strategy, starting with the limited but plainly daring Zimbabwean decision to secure the Mozambican railway to Beira, and ending with the large-scale conventional battlefield of southern Angola. This is not to say that Kaunda did nothing. He pursued the theme of peaceful change, albeit in the context of sanctions against South Africa – describing it as the last instrument of pressure before blood flowed – and was active in the Commonwealth on this issue. But, on the same subject, at the 1986 Non-Aligned summit in Harare, he had sounded pessimistic, cautious, and all the running at that gathering was made by Mugabe. The coming to power of de Klerk, a man against the 'securocratic' style of government achieved by Botha, meant a new entry point for Kaunda's diplomacy. The last years of Botha, however, had seen the second phase of Total Strategy. It was force of arms that brought it to a close. Kaunda was not a major figure here. He was far more so, but controversially, in the first phase of Total Strategy and in the lead-up to the pax Pretoriana.

This should not detract from some true consistency throughout the 1980s. Both the ANC and SWAPO were permitted to maintain their head offices in Lusaka, even though periodic rumours flew about various curtailments of ANC activities and personnel. Nevertheless, in the wake of the release of Nelson Mandela, it was from Lusaka that other ANC leaders returned; and, at independence celebrations in Windhoek, it was Kaunda – of all the many leaders present – who received the greatest cheers when he mounted the podium.[32] Nor might this have been solely for his diplomatic support and hosting of SWAPO-in-exile. In Chapter 7, I relate various accounts of other support. Having said that, it would be true to point out that, over the

---

[32] Author's telephone conversation with Namibian Foreign Affairs personnel, 1990.

period 1980–4, those who charge Kaunda with collaborationism, of a complicity with South Africa, have greater evidence than the period leading up to 1980 ever provided. Here, an immediate distinction should be drawn. There is no evidence that Kaunda supported the South African destabilisation of the region. When it came to the reformulation of the region, giving it a shape suitable to South Africa, then Kaunda appeared either cooperative or naïve.

Zambia's relations with the new Zimbabwe and, particularly, the somewhat strained relationship between Kaunda and Mugabe – despite public shows of cooperation – is discussed also in Chapter 7. Here, the emphasis remains with the Zambian response to South African foreign policy, although the discussion of Chapter 7 might be prefigured by noting that Mugabe did not approve of Kaunda's diplomacy with South Africa. This may have been part of a surliness born of his dislike of Kaunda in the pre-independence days – Mugabe had felt compelled to leave Zambia for Mozambique – and, certainly, some surliness was evident in the early days of Zimbabwean–Zambian relationships. Kaunda was only able – only invited – to make his first state visit to Zimbabwe in July 1981, more than a year after independence, and only after Machel and Nyerere had made their own state visits and been accorded the accolades of sponsors of liberation. Machel and Nyerere had broad Harare boulevards named in their honour. Kaunda's name was appended to a dusty road by the railway station. In the history of Zambian rail links through Rhodesia, this was probably an appropriate if bitter reminder of a foreign policy gone wrong.[33]

Mugabe was not the only frontline leader in disagreement or bemused by aspects at least of Kaunda's foreign policy, particularly his penchant for negotiations with South African politicians, and his readiness to meet with the South African Prime Minister himself. In April 1982, Kaunda conferred with P. W. Botha in Botswana. The summit was held there at Kaunda's request and, though obliging Kaunda with a place to park – the summit was convened in motor coaches, not rail carriages, though discussions took place across a

[33] Although Zimbabwean officials insist no slight or insult was intended. The road named after Kaunda fits into a grid of roads named after heads of government who assisted liberation. But none of the many Zimbabwean officials I bearded on this issue ever made this explanation without first broadly smiling. Diplomats in Harare assured me it was designed to be insulting, and Zambian officials in Lusaka attempted to dismiss it as unimportant Zimbabwean childishness.

table so arranged that both Kaunda and Botha sat astride the Botswanan/South African border – the Botswanan President then politely and studiously distanced himself from the entire episode.

No official reason has ever been given for the summit, nor official account released, although Kaunda later told Brownrigg that the idea had been placed in his head by a New Zealand journalist, that after the journalist's story appeared Botha sent an envoy to Lusaka, that Botha had requested Kaunda to open the meeting with prayer, that the meeting was cordial, and that he had gone to the summit because of the Biblical injunction to love his neighbour.[34] Kaunda has repeatedly made a practice of invoking Biblical sanction for his policies, although whether this is for public effect or genuinely felt is a matter for debate. His press statements of the time suggest firstly an apocalyptic view, followed by an accommodating one. 'If the lid does blow off we will all get burnt . . . we still condemn apartheid, and there can be no compromise on that issue, but we still view South Africa as an independent state ruled by people who are Africans in every sense of the word.'[35] In the run-up to the summit, therefore, Kaunda was careful to send a signal of reassurance to Botha's constituency. There would be a place for whites in South Africa – but the situation was threatening. Afterwards, he explained that 'speaking directly to Botha will enable us to analyse the situation in a cool and honest manner. That is why I felt it was worthwhile to talk to him.' On his talks with Vorster and Smith in the past, he said that Zambia 'did the dirty work on behalf of the Organisation of African Unity while the glory went to Africa'.[36] The two are not, however, on the public information available, really comparable. The talks with Vorster in 1975 had a clear agenda, but Kaunda could only say in 1982 that talks with Botha would help analysis – as if he had no other way of gathering and assessing information.

There does seem to have been an agenda unrevealed at the time. One of the eight-strong Zambian delegation to the 1982 summit, the cabinet minister Punabantu, told Al-Khaledi in 1988 that the talks did soften South African foreign policy: 'We had the Angolans and South Africans worked [sic] out some kind of programme for the withdrawal of S.A. troops from Angola . . . that [Lusaka Agreement] went on

34 Brownrigg, *Kenneth Kaunda*, pp. 130–1.
35 *Herald* (Harare), 19 March 1982.
36 *Herald* (Harare), 29 April 1982.

beautifully . . . we even had the S.A. Foreign Minister and the Defence Minister came [sic] to Lusaka.'[37] This refers to the Lusaka Accord of 1984, discussed in the last chapter. At first sight, therefore, it appears that Kaunda and Botha were considering the question of treaties between South Africa and members of the frontline states. Some caution is necessary here, since other pressures were at work. The South African push into Angola of December 1983 (Operation Askari, designed to enlarge the South African occupied territory) encountered extremely stiff opposition from both MPLA and SWAPO contingents, and South African losses were far greater than projected. Moreover, attempting to link the Lusaka Accord to the Nkomati Accord is problematic. As early as December 1982, the Mozambicans themselves had been broaching the idea of a border security agreement.[38] There was also a great deal of US pressure in this period for some sort of agreement between Mozambique and South Africa. Punabantu went on to tell Al-Khaledi that Kaunda had not been 'part or parcel of the process' which led to Nkomati.[39] Nevertheless, a suggestion that at least a very broad outline for the future region was discussed, one which afforded South Africa a sense of security (letting them feel African 'in every sense of the word'), and one which sought to guarantee the frontline states a sense of safety from South Africa, seems not unreasonable.

After the Lusaka and Nkomati Accords, Kaunda claimed in several Zambian newspaper statements that the agreements had been the fruit of his dialogue with Botha. This may have been as much to do with public relations as reality, but there is the evidence of Punabantu over the line of descent from the Botswana meeting to the Lusaka Accord. Whatever the genealogy of the accords, Kaunda sought to follow them up. While doing so, he also made public his view that Nkomati was a setback, a sign of weakness which should not be glorified.[40] He reiterated this opinion at the Arusha summit of the frontline states that discussed Nkomati.[41] But, at Arusha, he also proposed a summit between the frontline states and South Africa. This was rejected.[42] It

---

[37] Al-Khaledi, 'Coercive Diplomacy', p. 301.
[38] Dr Mota Lopes, aide to President Machel from 1982–6, in an interview given to Al-Khaledi, 'Coercive Diplomacy', p. 174.
[39] Ibid., p. 181.
[40] *The Financial Times* (London), 7 April 1984.
[41] Punabantu to Al-Khaledi, in Al-Khaledi, 'Coercive Diplomacy', p. 235.
[42] *Guardian* (London and Manchester), 28 May 1984.

was left to Mozambique, in a series of statements, to defend Nkomati as the harbinger of a new, safer region with a better-behaved, more peaceful South Africa. Meanwhile, Kaunda went ahead with another extraordinary meeting between himself and representatives from Pretoria. What appears to have happened is as follows: (1) against the wishes of other frontline leaders, Kaunda met with Botha in 1982; (2) the Zambian follow-up of that summit culminated in the Lusaka Accord of 1984 – a stronger Accord than that of Nkomati, as discussed in the last chapter; (3) Nkomati rapidly followed the Lusaka Accord, catching Zambia by surprise, but Kaunda used them both as a conflated example of the fruits of Zambian diplomacy; (4) Kaunda had doubts about Nkomati and expressed them but felt, nevertheless, that a bandwagon might now be rolling and sought to exploit it; (5) he sought to do so despite frontline scepticism.

In May 1984, Kaunda hosted in Lusaka representatives both of SWAPO and the internal Namibian parties, together with the South African Administrator-General for South West Africa. This was an amazing enough cast in itself, and Kaunda sought to achieve some unity among all the Namibian parties. The Administrator-General, who had played some role in keeping them disunited in the first place, alternated with Kaunda as chairman of the conference. At one stage, seeking to impose all his moral authority – or simply in a process of attrition – Kaunda occupied the chair for a continuous session of 20 hours.[43] The conference failed to reconcile the disputing parties and was never repeated.

Other initiatives were more positive in their outcome. In 1985, a group of white South African businessmen met ANC officials in Lusaka and, although Pretoria publicly frowned upon their visit, it seems that official messages were sent through them. This meeting prefigured the 1987 Senegal conference of ANC leaders and white South Africans. These two gatherings carried forward a process that began in 1984, when Professor Hendrick van der Merwe of the University of Capetown and Piet Muller of *Die Beeld* newspaper came to Lusaka, ostensibly on a private visit, but carrying messages from

---

[43] The author lived in Lusaka at this time and was kept informed of events in the conference by FLS diplomats who, not admitted as observers, sought to piece together the conference proceedings from the periphery. The author also viewed the cable traffic at this time between FLS embassies in Lusaka and their capitals.

Pretoria; they also carried messages back.[44] One of the outcomes of the 1982 Botswana meeting at least had been the agreement to keep each informed of the other's thought, and a system of informal diplomacy was expedited through couriers. Work towards the Lusaka Accord could, therefore, proceed, even though military difficulties might have caused South Africa to agree – from its point of view – to a weaker accord than what it achieved in Nkomati. But the Lusaka Accord was by no means a setback for South Africa. Followed swiftly by Nkomati and the Swazi announcement of its own accord with South Africa, it seemed that the strategy of tying the region into Pretoria by a series of treaties had been well-begun. Peace in the region was by virtue of South Africa's permission – thus the pax Pretoriana.

For Kaunda, however, the elusive image of *détente* was again proferring itself. What had been destroyed by the Angolan war of 1975–6 now seemed possible in the South African withdrawal from Angola of 1984–5. But, as noted above, the pax Pretoriana was short-lived. Any possibility of *détente* fell apart as the South Africans once again entered Angola in force. Zimbabwean troops in Mozambique found evidence of South African support for RENAMO guerillas, despite the Nkomati Accord.[45] On every front, South Africa escalated the war and, in 1986, Lusaka itself was given a short, sharp warning as bombs were dropped on a refugee centre the South Africans insisted was an ANC base.[46] The road from Botswana 1982 had come to its end.

Was Kaunda therefore a hindrance to the policies of the other frontline states? The answer to that is 'no', since they had no other policies of their own which could be said to be undermined by Kaunda's. Was Kaunda treacherous? Again, the answer is 'no', since he pursued a policy that, with its emphases on negotiation and personal trust, was at least consistent and well-meant. Was he naïve? He was at least

---

[44] On this visit they had dinner at my house and were quite candid about the reasons behind their coming. It was the first time, Muller said, he had dined in multi-racial company.

[45] For a full account of what became known as the Gorongosa documents, discovered by Zimbabwean troops when they took RENAMO's Casa Banana base, see Al-Khaledi, 'Coercive Diplomacy'. Al-Khaledi was able to view the complete set of documents while conducting research in Mozambique.

[46] In 1987, the author met maimed survivors of this attack. They were workers at a crafts cooperative at the refugee centre. Their occupation as crafts-women of long-standing was confirmed to me by cultural officials in Lusaka.

partially so, since any study of South African foreign policy would have led him to the 1977 Defence White Paper, issued under Botha's tenure at the Ministry of Defence, which set out the strategic objective of treaties and accords between South Africa and the states of southern Africa. To offset that, it should be reiterated that the Lusaka Accord, in which Kaunda played a role, was stronger than the Nkomati Accord, in which he played no role. Was he wilful, refusing to heed the united opinion of the other frontline leaders? Yes, he was, and gained little praise from them by doing so. The grumbling this occasioned, however, has provided the foundation for the view that Kaunda was a hindrance towards the development of a unified frontline policy. This is certainly true, but it is difficult to see what that policy might have been or where else it could have led. With or without Kaunda, South African foreign policy would have followed similar lines. Even so, a circular argument is possible here: he transgressed no established policies, but he made it difficult for there to be any such policies. This leads into the further argument: there were no policies but, even if there had been, they would have made no difference. This is well and good, but misses some essential points. A Lone Ranger role against South Africa was hazardous (one could be led astray); it encouraged South Africa to think that the region could be divided (and one state played off against another); it gave South Africa international camouflage (Kaunda is proving that negotiations are possible with Pretoria, so Pretoria should be given an opportunity for peaceful change); it was misconceived (the idea of *détente* could never overcome the essential South African desire for domination); South Africa could not be trusted (not with a governing military establishment which had been set loose in the region); and it didn't work. In the end, Kaunda made no difference either. In trying to make a difference, he created difficulties for frontline unity and, perhaps in the absence of policies, unity here was important for its own sake.

All these points can be taken, and even a judgement possible that Kaunda was well-meaning but foolish – although he was probably more wilful and wishful than foolish – but none of this suggests he was a collaborator with South Africa. He had his own agenda. In parts, it coincided with South Africa's. As with the history of Angolan independence, there is circumstantial evidence to fit a pattern, but there is more than one interpretation of this evidence possible. More than one pattern can be constructed. In the end, it was Mozambique that collaborated far more with South Africa than did Zambia. Nkomati meant far more meetings between Mozambican and South African officials than Lusaka and Pretoria ever managed. Maputo expelled ANC cadres under the terms of the accord, but this was never seen as a betrayal of the frontline cause. In fact, a great deal of literature has been produced to excuse Mozambique. Its credentials of being both revolutionary and under duress have won it many friends. But one cannot make an analysis of foreign policies by preferring one state above another. Mozambique was driven into a corner. Zambia made mistakes. These are true statements.

Kaunda in the Commonwealth

Kaunda was able to use his image, acquired early, as a moral figure whenever he put forward the Zambian position in international fora. It became expected that, when he rose to speak on southern Africa, he would combine apocalyptic warnings with the theme of love. Sometimes he would ramble, as if the transition from one to the other was hard – as indeed it is – and sometimes he would cry. To be critical, as time passed much of this became his 'style'; he slipped into his performance mode easily, and even the tears could come on cue. Seasoned diplomats and international civil servants became expert at watching for whatever lay behind the style, but those meeting him late in his career would accuse him of self-righteous humbug.[47] This is unfair, although it must be said that Kaunda has always had an interest in tailoring his image. His early practice of dressing in Ghanaian style was meant to indicate a pan-Africanism and a sense of African authenticity. His insistence on wearing only safari suits, when all around him might be wearing white ties and tails, may have begun as a common man's statement in a world of glitter and deceit, but also helps Kaunda stand out in a crowd, emphasising even further his immense physical size and presence. The handkerchief he carries in his hand suggests the soft side of a muscular man and, in any case, has always compared well with the fly whisks, sceptres, and marshall's batons carried by his peers in Africa. To say he is blissfully unaware of these things is to defend his moral image too stoutly. To consciously

---

[47] Opinion of senior personnel recently recruited to the Commonwealth Secretariat, expressed to the author in 1990. Cf. the account in Carrington, *Reflect on Things Past*, pp. 254–5.

choose one's accoutrements does not dent anything about one's character. Nor should a style that has begun to seem tired and unconvincing suggest that its bearer emits only humbug. There are some things at which Kaunda is very bad, quite apart from his tendency to ramble. He cannot draft precise documents – making it very unlikely that the 1971 Commonwealth Declaration of Principles was suggested by him in the form it finally took. He has trouble editing his own documents and, whenever it is his turn to act as secretary at the meetings of frontline presidents (yes, they do take turns taking minutes), he complains afterwards that his hand hurts from too much writing.[48] He is in fact a rather bad writer, suggesting that the contribution of Colin Morris in editing his books is vital. But he is also a bad reader, not in the sense that he can't read, but that he doesn't enjoy reading lengthy briefing documents. As will be made clear in Chapter 6, he acts on the slimmest possible briefing in foreign policy and relies very heavily on intuition. It is this intuition that developed as Kaunda learnt about international relations after the independence of Zambia and UDI in Rhodesia. It is this combination of moral reputation, personal style, and intuition that Kaunda has taken into international fora.

As noted above, Kaunda has been active in the OAU, the Non-Aligned Movement, the Commonwealth, and, not always successfully, among the frontline states. He has also regularly appeared at the UN, and Zambia has both sat on the Security Council and held the presidency of the General Assembly. This multilateral activity has accomplished more for the Zambian position as an African and third world leader than has bilateral diplomacy. His meetings with South African heads of government have been controversial and have had mixed results, but have always been viewed as Kaunda's own experiments rather than Kaunda setting the pace for others. His meetings with British Prime Ministers have been variously unsuccessful: Wilson did not place Kaunda highly in his political equations; Heath thought he was unreasonable and gauche; and Thatcher, beset by Kaunda's concept of how a gentleman should behave to a lady, found him smarmy whenever she was not exasperated by his hectoring on apocalypse and love. In multilateral gatherings, however, provided Kaunda's shortcomings in precision and research can be offset by the gifts of other major figures, he can shine. Within the Commonwealth,

[48] Author's conversation with dinner companions of the president.

Kaunda found his perfect foil in the Secretary-General, Shridath Ramphal, lawyerly diplomatic on matters of detail, the practised author of documents that were, by turns and when required, completely precise and completely given to elegant obfuscation. Ramphal also liked to act on intuition, and he and Kaunda found that they could act as a duet.

The Commonwealth Secretariat's central rationale has been that it was created to provide a non-British force for the liberation of Rhodesia, and to act as a pressure-group for the ending of apartheid in South Africa. Its entire development from 1965 to the present day has sprung from this rationale.[49] In this sense, its policy history runs parallel to that of Zambia's, and the two policy lines have frequently converged. This convergence has been greatest at the 1979 Lusaka Commonwealth summit, at the Lancaster House talks that followed, and in the campaign – which reached both its highest point of intensity, and point of failure, in 1986 – on sanctions. The confluence of history, overall policy, and in the personalities of Ramphal and Kaunda, are apparent in these examples.

It is impossible, however, to speak of the Lusaka summit and Lancaster House without considering the role of Lord Carrington and, indeed, there are those who accord him the lion's share of the plaudits available.[50] Others point out the critical role played by Ramphal in keeping the talks afloat.[51] At Lusaka in any case, it should be pointed out that Carrington did indeed have a view of the way ahead, but he needed to convince a Commonwealth that was extremely sceptical of Margaret Thatcher's even-handedness that there could be a reasonable British position, and he needed to convince Thatcher herself that his and the FCO position was the one Britain should take. Thatcher's television statement in Australia, shortly after her election earlier in 1979, that she could recognise the Smith/Muzorewa

---

[49] I have written about this extensively elsewhere. See, particularly, Stephen Chan, *The Commonwealth in World Politics*, and *The Commonwealth Observer Group in Zimbabwe*, Gweru, Zimbabwe: Mambo Press, 1985.

[50] Carrington himself does nothing to discourage this and, quite clearly, viewed his role as central and unimpededly decisive. See Carrington, *Reflect on Things Past*; John Newhouse, 'Profiles – A Sense of Duty: Lord Carrington', *The New Yorker*, 14 February 1983, espec. pp. 71–80; see also the views of Davidow, *A Peace in Southern Africa*, and Lord Soames, 'From Rhodesia to Zimbabwe', *International Affairs*, Vol. 56, No. 3, 1980.

[51] Including the present author; see fn. 49 above. Colin Legum's regular reports of the Lancaster House negotiations in *The Observer*, in late 1979, certainly make this point.

Government of Rhodesia/Zimbabwe, rankled the Commonwealth membership; but it was in keeping with her desire to craft a new Britain, shorn as soon as possible of the albatrosses that weighed down the neck of the old. Carrington had to convince her that this would work through his method as much as hers, and that there would be fewer diplomatic repercussions. It was Ramphal and Kaunda that provided the environment, the arguments, and the almost gentle diplomacy that made Thatcher move towards the Carrington view which, at Lusaka, was merged into the Commonwealth position that Ramphal had devised in concert with the frontline presidents, particularly Kaunda and Nyerere, and the non-Commonwealth president, Machel of Mozambique. The reasonably easy convergence of Carrington and Commonwealth positions owed to Carrington's summer of diplomacy, in which his emissaries had travelled widely to determine what support he could muster, and what, in African outlooks, was the least he could get away with. Here, London had consulted the same people who had been consulted by Ramphal. In both exercises, Kaunda had made his contribution. But, since he was also chairman of the Commonwealth summit, Kaunda had a further contribution to make, and he did this as part of a procedural strategy mapped out by Ramphal and himself.

Aware that feelings were running high against Thatcher as a result of her Australian speech, Kaunda prevented a clash at the summit's opening session by placing the Rhodesian issue on the third day of the agenda. Some delegations had certainly come to do battle. The Nigerians had nationalised BP as a signal – though an overstated one – that Britain should not push for Smith and Muzorewa. From the first to the third day, Kaunda was sweetness and light, creating, if not a loving atmosphere, at least a positive one. Ramphal meanwhile set about his backroom work, reconciling the Commonwealth and Carrington positions, and arranging a roster of who was to say what in formal session and, more importantly, who was to make informal visits to Mrs Thatcher's conference villa, and what they were to say there. The important work was done, therefore, out of session. The carefully crafted lobby of Thatcher, during a 'retreat', a day off from the conference table, built upon the atmosphere created by Kaunda's chairmanship. That it was all successful owed much to Kaunda working in tandem with others, his role depending on his skills, but with the direction and its limits clearly scripted.

The Lancaster House talks were altogether more complicated. Carrington, in order to cut the albatross loose, was determined to steer the conference and did so brilliantly. In so doing, he sought to maintain progress and momentum and was not averse to brinkmanship and bluff. The Patriotic Front delegation, with Mugabe and Nkomo as its principals, would have been in danger of being overrun without Ramphal's assistance. Here, Ramphal was in a sensitive position. The Commonwealth Secretary-Generalship was designated a responsive post, i.e. it responded to the requests of its members as articulated by heads of government. Ramphal, being stationed in London – in fact, his headquarters of Marlborough House were the next but one palace from Lancaster House, so Mugabe and Nkomo found it easy to visit – was clearly the best suited figure to formulate and direct Commonwealth policy and strategy. Never officially admitted, that policy was, with the British and perhaps the New Zealand exceptions, sympathetic to the Patriotic Front. Smith and Muzorewa had, after all, been bombing Lusaka. Ramphal had therefore to be seen responding to the Commonwealth. He formulated policy and strategy; he advised governments by telephone what his judgement was; they arranged for their high commissioners to request particular actions of him, in line with his own judgement, and he duly responded. In this roundabout way, he became the Patriotic Front's most important adviser on negotiating strategy. This had two consequences. The Front remained at the negotiating table, so Carrington could not take a shortcut by dealing only with Muzorewa and Smith (shortly into the conference, mostly Muzorewa and the Rhodesian General Peter Walls, rather than Smith) because Mugabe and Nkomo had walked out. Secondly, it meant that the outcome was, in fact, about as fair as conditions allowed. The Front, with Ramphal's support, fought back against some of Carrington's positions and two of the results included coordinated international observation of the British governorship that replaced the Smith/Muzorewa Government, and the independence elections; and a neutral military force from outside Rhodesia to supervise the ceasefire. Carrington had originally wanted to entrust this supervision to the Rhodesian armed forces – against whom the Patriotic Front had been fighting.

In this process of negotiation, directing strategy while appearing responsive, of knowing when to back down from Carrington and when to stare back, Ramphal relied upon a small number of Commonwealth leaders for his 'telephone cabinet'. In Africa, they were Kaunda and Nyerere. Kaunda himself visited London during the negotiations to lend the weight of his presence. In this, he acted to personify the

Commonwealth concern so that, again, scripted and in concert with others, he was able to play a major role. Lancaster House led on to a period of British Governorship. Not without mishap, the governorship led on to elections, and elections led to independence. Kaunda could rightly claim some part of the success but, in the triumphalism that followed, state visits by supporters of liberation, Kaunda had to wait till last.

This did not prevent him from forging a public common front with Mugabe over the issue of sanctions against South Africa. Raised at the 1985 Commonwealth summit in Nassau, the issue continued with a mini-summit in London the following year, at the 1987 summit in Vancouver, and the 1989 summit in Kuala Lumpur.[52] It was the 1986 mini-summit, however, that saw the issue reach its highest point, and the tensions and exchanges there have even been translated into a television drama. The aim had been to shift Mrs Thatcher towards acceptance of a sanctions campaign against South Africa, and for Britain to participate in it. Thatcher, however, was obdurate in her opposition and the mini-summit failed. In maintaining her position, Hella Pick wrote, Thatcher caused Britain to lose its position in the Commonwealth as first among equals.[53] The Commonwealth Secretariat, formed to provide an alternative Commonwealth centre to Britain, was finally ceded this position by Mrs Thatcher. The ambition to shift Thatcher on sanctions, however, resulted in another bout of stage-managing on Ramphal's part. Of the select few senior leaders invited to the mini-summit, Kaunda and Mugabe were to make the early running, with Kaunda deliberately fulminating against Britain in his usual, colourful language; Canada's Mulroney was to appear conciliatory in the face of their attack; Australia's Hawke was to offer eleventh-hour worldliness; and India's Rajiv Ghandi was to apply some last minute heat. As the mini-summit began, Kaunda and Mugabe were to appear suddenly flexible and full of compromise and (wishfully) a relieved Mrs Thatcher, also under pressure from her own ministers, was meant to accept the Commonwealth position.[54] The point here is not that it didn't work, but that Kaunda was scripted

---

[52] For the author's discussion of all Commonwealth summits from 1979–91, see Stephen Chan, *Twelve Years of Commonwealth Diplomatic History: Commonwealth Summits 1979–91*, Lampeter, Wales and Lewiston, NY: Edwin Mellen, forthcoming.
[53] Hella Pick, *Guardian* (London and Manchester), 6 August 1986.
[54] Nigel Hawkes, *The Observer* (London), 3 August 1986.

into the effort to make it work. Moreover, in the script he was to utilise his well-developed and recognisable 'style'.

After the failure of the mini-summit, Kaunda became for a time pessimistic about the sanctions strategy. It had never been properly costed, even by the Commonwealth Secretariat, and depended on a projection of the political consequences for South Africa should the great powers all invoke sanctions.[55] At the 1986 Non-Aligned Movement summit in Harare, he said that sanctions could have no effect without the industrial nations of the world being full-bloodedly behind them.[56] Britain, for one, was not. What difference could the Non-Aligned's sanctions make? Kaunda also cautioned against the Non-Aligned attempting military action against South Africa, or even sending troops to safeguard southern Africa against further destabilisation. He thought they could be no match against South Africa in a conflict which Pretoria could escalate. But the Harare summit was one of thunder. Mugabe supported the idea of fighting back and Zimbabwean troops began their operations in Mozambique. The remainder of the decade, until after Cuito Cuanavale, belonged to men of arms.

A Note on Autonomy in Policy Formulation
(With L. J. Chingambo)

The execution of Zambian foreign policy and its style have been almost solely Kaunda's. What, however, of its formulation? What evidence is there that he formulates it alone? Chapter 6 provides a case example of autonomous policy formulation. Here, however, it might be suggestive at least to describe the only study that has thus far been attempted on the Zambian capacity to formulate foreign policy.[57] Outside State House, that is, outside Kaunda's executive environment, is there a wider environment of knowledge that could nurture non-presidential policy formulation? The answer is 'no'. In 1989, Chingambo interviewed a range of people in both Zambia and

---

[55] On the lack of economic costing, see Lloyd John Chingambo and Stephen Chan, 'Sanctions and South Africa: Strategies, Strangleholds and Self-Consciousness', *Paradigms*, Vol. 2, No. 2, 1988–9.

[56] *The Financial Times*, 6 September 1986.

[57] Chanda Lloyd John Chingambo, 'Destabilisation and SADCC: The Politics and Economics of Economic Integration', unpublished PhD thesis, University of Kent, 1990.

Zimbabwe, who might normally be thought interested in foreign policy. This included both government officials and non-official personnel such as journalists and academics. His findings are summarised below.

Respondents were asked if they felt knowledgeable on various key terms associated with the formulation of South African foreign policy. All these terms drew upon the recent history of South African activities in the region, and have been expounded in Chapter 3 of this book, concerned with a brief history of South African policy. An expert government official, diplomatic correspondent, or university political scientist would be expected to have a more detailed knowledge than Chapter 3 provided. These key terms included the *cordon sanitaire*; Total Strategy; the Afrikaner Broederbond; and the State Security Council.

In both countries, the majority of respondents lacked clear knowledge of these terms. The only differences were that, generally, Zimbabwean respondents fared marginally better than their Zambian counterparts and that, by specific sectors of respondent, academics were more knowledgeable than the rest. Government officials, by contrast, seemed to have no systematic knowledge of South African policy; nor did there seem to be a point of knowledge or information coordination to which they could have access. As a result, no-one possessed a detailed knowledge of what Zambian or Zimbabwean policy might be, in specific as opposed to very general terms. Chingambo contrasted this with the highly coordinated and knowledgeable South African policy apparatus, with its highly specific objectives; but it must be said that the whole thrust of Botha's State Security Council system, as described in Chapter 3, was to keep policy formulation restricted to a small presidential circle. Even so, the desert of knowledge Chingambo uncovered in Zambia and Zimbabwe has no parallel in South Africa, where knowledge is far more widely shared even if, under Botha, few could use it to help determine policy.

The parallels that existed were in the presidential commands of policy formulation. In South Africa, however, Botha formulated policy within a tight apparatus – but he had an apparatus. In Zambia, no such apparatus could be found.

* * *

Alone, and with his own style, Kaunda both formulates and executes foreign policy. Unless scripted in advance, as part of a coordinated effort with other leaders in a multilateral enterprise, his style can become erratic and stubborn, and his policy not always thought through. In all three time periods discussed in this chapter, he has made many mistakes and misjudgements, and principle has often been a placard on his sleeve rather than genuinely embedded in his thought and action. Nevertheless, it would be hard to sustain some of the charges levelled against Kaunda. The evidence is open to more than one interpretation and, sometimes, to insist upon one interpretation is to distort the evidence. This is the subject of the next chapter.

5

FOUR IMAGES OF KAUNDA

Towards an Intellectual History of Foreign Policy

The question of Kaunda's style infiltrates 33 years of reportage on his activities, beliefs, and policies – from his visit to Britain in 1957 to the Zambian riots of 1990. Even after those riots, western journalists were still prepared to accept that style at face value: the Biblical allusions, his references to himself praying, the tears, the protestations of sacrifice for liberation and peace, the still-professed humanism.[1] These components of a style still have a power, even if they are tired and on the brink of eclipse, not least because Kaunda either really believes in them or, as a lifelong actor, has played his way so often into the part that it is inseparable from him. Either way, they mark a tragic role since, whether he believes in himself or not, his style has lost its resonance among the Zambian people. Domestically, Kaunda and his UNIP have become a dead hand on development and nothing can change there until they go. In foreign policy, however, Kaunda has continued to play an active role and, in his Commonwealth part, he has at least walked the stage well under a good director. He has also had a recent success in his bilateral diplomacy when he invited President de Klerk to Zambia. This was particularly astute. At home, de Klerk used the Zambian trip to crush the lingering hold of Botha on the South African political imagination, and cast himself as a statesman in time for his national elections. For Kaunda, the rewards were calculated in the longer term, but he had committed de Klerk's first foreign policy act to a recognition of Zambia's role within the

---

[1] E.g. Andrew Rawnsley, 'African Prophet Who Could Lose Everything', *Guardian* (London and Manchester), 12 September 1990.

region – the most senior of the frontline states, the one to be consulted first – a role Kaunda would be determined to maintain in expectation of the regional brokering that will take place after majority rule arrives in South Africa, and the new state assesses its debt to its neighbours. Throughout the de Klerk visit, South African television portrayed a relentlessly reasonable, polite, and Christian Kaunda. He played his part like a trouper, and it did help de Klerk. One president began his tenure of office in debt to another. And, if he survives in his own office, or to help himself do so, Kaunda must want nothing more than to emulate Sadat's dramatic trip to Jerusalem, and to arrive out of the skies to be ticker-taped on the streets of Pretoria and Johannesburg, to give the final push towards a peaceful settlement in South Africa and be acclaimed within the economic and military powerhouse of southern Africa as the moral hegemon of the region.

In fact, shortly after the independence of Namibia, the South African Department of Foreign Affairs in March 1990 was openly floating the idea of Kaunda's coming to South Africa, to act as a 'mediator' or 'facilitator' in the opening rounds of talks between de Klerk's government and the ANC.[2] Kaunda's profile was high in South Africa. A mere two months later, however, the food uprising having taken place in Lusaka, *The Independent* newspaper in Britain was editorialising that Kaunda's moral foundation in Zambia had gone.[3] The editorials in Zimbabwe made no such judgement but, while expressing shock at the riots, nevertheless suggested that Zambian economic mismanagement was as much to blame for food price rises as any conditions for assistance set by the IMF.[4]

The inability to sustain a single judgement of himself in the space of just a few months has long been a characteristic of Kaunda's time in office. This is a caveat for what follows. Even so, four broad images of Kaunda have emerged over the years and each is now discussed in turn.

The Journalistic Image

The most recent of the British 'quality' dailies, *The Independent*, has maintained a consistently negative view of Kaunda. The longer-

---

[2] *Guardian*, 23 March 1990.
[3] Leader in *The Independent* (London), 29 June 1990.
[4] Leader in *Herald* (Harare), 29 June 1990.

established press has been slightly more volatile, with the *Guardian* tending towards a sympathetic view of him. If one were, however, to count the columns of all the qualities, then the negatives would outnumber considerably the sympathetics. On the questions of the independence campaign led by Kaunda, rail links with Rhodesia and sanctions against UDI, British aid for Zambia amidst maladministration, and Zambian defence needs, the British press has found critical questions to ask of Kaunda. After 1980, the press was less critical of Kaunda simply by commenting on him less. In part, this was due to the South African destabilisation of the region, particularly Angola and Mozambique, so that other southern African issues and figures occupied the space. Outside Angola and Mozambique, Zimbabwe's Mugabe was seen as a new major player and his policies over the years of reconciliation between white and black, of seeming persecution of Ndelebele by Shona, of intervention in Mozambique, and of favouring a one-party state, caused considerable coverage. When, by 1986, the sanctions campaign was at its height, Kaunda had to share his billing with Mugabe.

The fact that any newspaper will devote only a limited portion of its space to southern Africa has meant that Kaunda receives less attention as more actors appear. But, even in the days when he was, without doubt, the leading regional spokesman, limited space – inherent in the very act of producing a newspaper – meant that comment on Kaunda, whether negative or sympathetic, was often superficial. The options open to him, the constraints under which he laboured, and his motivations were given less attention than the often wide gulf that could be discerned between his principles and his actions. The negative image has him as a charlatan, the sympathetic image as well-meaning but inconsistent. The journalistic image of Kaunda is therefore two images united in a one-dimensional style of presentation. The good and the bad of him, however, have been treated at greater length, though not always in greater dimensions, in the industry of books.

The Hagiographic Image

The hagiographic works on Kaunda are the most plentiful but, since 1976, the least influential. In that year, scholarly writing, almost entirely in brief article, single chapter, or monograph form, introduced and sustained an image of Kaunda as a collaborator with the enemies of true liberation. In what might be called the literature of the 'comprador' image – taking the Spanish word for collaborator, since the theoretical foundation for this image was drawn from a Latin American neo-Marxism – there exists only one book on Zambian foreign policy, and that is an uneasy rendition by two authors, only one of whom worked from this foundation.[5] A more recent book which might be said to emulate such a theoretical approach treated Zambian foreign policy only in its last chapter.[6] The success, however, of this approach derived from its repetition in shorter forms – the articles and chapters mentioned above. The academic literature of the last 15 years has been dominated by such repetition – since the articles, with two major exceptions (discussed below), in fact say nothing new, but maintain the 1976 analysis. Precisely because it is an academic literature, however, precisely because it seems to have theoretical sophistication and intellectual rigour, it has had considerable influence; and it has contrasted markedly with the hagiographic literature because the books of praise had no such sophistication or rigour.

The contrast was all the more marked because they were indeed books of praise. Without theory, they were also without criticism. They not only took Kaunda's side but, plainly admiring, also Kaunda's version of events. Thus, in a single half-chapter, the reader might learn that it was Ian Smith who, having closed the Rhodesian/ Zambian border in 1973, was forced to 'rely even more heavily on South Africa', and this was because Kaunda had called Smith's bluff; that Kaunda was the true architect of *détente* in the post–1974 era; that, in his 1971 visit to Britain, Kaunda found Heath both unknowledgeable and 'so emotionally insecure that he would lose his temper under criticism'; that Kaunda was the author of the 1971 Declaration of Commonwealth Principles at Singapore, having prepared a draft well before the summit began, and that 'much of the conference' was taken up by its discussion, and that it emerged with only 'minor amendments ... as an historic witness to Kaunda's international vision'; and that the completed Tazara railway between Zambia and Dar es Salaam did indeed allow Zambia to escape

[5] Douglas Anglin and Timothy M. Shaw, *Zambia's Foreign Policy: Studies in Diplomacy and Dependency*, Boulder, Colorado: Westview, 1979.
[6] Marcia M. Burdette, *Zambia: Between Two Worlds*, Boulder, Colorado: Westview, 1988.

'dependence on the south'.[7] That these events had more than one side, or more than one dimension, is clear from my discussion in the preceding chapters, and it is unfortunate that authors have sought to write history solely from Kaunda's point of view, or have been so impressed by his person that they have accepted his own accounts – often delivered as confidences to them – uncritically. It is from this literature that the image of Kaunda, paying the high price of principles while confronting the white south, emerges.[8]

The point here is that the literature could still have been admiring – there is nothing that prohibits one from being impressed by one's subject – yet critically-informed; at least even-handed. Some articles of this sort do exist,[9] but they are a minority. As it is, no newly-authored praise-biographies of Kaunda have been published in the 1980s, although Brownrigg's effort, published from Lusaka and not readily available elsewhere, finally appeared in 1989, having however been substantially completed in 1973.[10] It, thus, really belongs to the older generation of its fellows – late 1960s and early to mid-1970s, although, frankly, their ancestor and archetype was probably Kaunda's autobiography of 1962, the Heinemann book, *Zambia Shall be Free*. For those of a newer generation who are impressed by Kaunda, I should like to suggest three possible ways forward in writing about him.

Firstly, no matter what the shortcomings of humanism might be, it can be identified as a descendant of an historical movement. Leroy Vail, among others, has put forward the argument that 'tribalism' as it is known today is not the tribalism of antiquity. Rather, there are in place those tribal ideologies that were crafted as an attempt to shore up societies facing rapid erosion at the hands of colonialism and the introduction or imposition of capitalist economies. These tribal ideologies cannot be expected to vanish easily, since the same social erosion is continuing.[11] There are elements of such arguments that can be applied to Kaunda's effort against tribalism and in favour of a

---

[7] Hatch, *Kaunda of Zambia*, the second half of Chapter 6.
[8] Even the titles leave the reader in no doubt of the author's position, e.g. Richard Hall, *The High Price of Principles: Kaunda and the White South*, London: Hodder and Stoughton, 1969.
[9] E.g. Tordoff, 'Zambia: The Politics of Disengagement'.
[10] Brownrigg, *Kenneth Kaunda*. See his preface for the provenance of the book.
[11] Leroy Vail (ed.), *The Creation of Tribalism in Southern Africa: The Political Economy of an Ideology*, Berkeley: University of California Press, 1988.

new state ideology in which, within the unified state, there lives a cooperating people. Kaunda sought, within a very short time frame, and by himself, to supersede tribal ideologies with humanism. Simultaneously, he sought to impose upon those tribal ideologies an invented history of humane communalism – so that humanism would appear a natural descendant of tribal systems while replacing them. The point I have made in Chapter 2 is that Kaunda's attempt was transparent and not deeply thought-out. The point that could be made in opposition is that his effort was grand – not grand in the sense of the language used by his admirers, leading to a new future, but grand in the sense of inventing a new past. In so doing, he became at least a postscript to the inventions of pasts in the tribal ideologies that preceded him.

Secondly, Kaunda has had charisma sufficient to bind to him a generation of foreign admirers but, to be fair, this charisma has at times successfully united the Zambian people under his leadership. As time has passed, he has relied less on charisma – while not forsaking it – and sought to shore up his position by legal and traditional forms. The 14 constitutional amendments he allowed to go forward in early 1990, discussed in Chapter 2, might be seen as an attempt to secure his authority by legal instruments. The references to himself as 'father of the nation', and the primacy of 'fatherhood' in the familial structures of humanism might be seen as attempts to establish his authority in traditional terms. In short, there is possible here a Weberian analysis of the sources of Kaunda's authority and, within this analysis, Weber's attempt to investigate charisma might prove a fascinating starting point.[12] Hassouna sought to extend Weber's work in his intellectual biography of Nasser.[13] Out of this work there appears to be a cycle of charismatic development. At first, the leader creates, almost manipulates, for himself the aura of charisma; successful overcoming of a great crisis legitimises his charisma; charisma can be so strongly perceived that, even if later crises defeat the leader, his people refuse to accept that he is diminished and, in this way, charismatic stature is conferred by them.

---

[12] Max Weber, *The Theory of Social and Economic Organization*, New York: Oxford University Press, 1947.
[13] Moustafa El Said Hassouna, 'Leadership Efficacy and Weberian Charisma: The Case of Gamal Abdel Nasser 1952–1970', unpublished Ph.D. thesis, University of Kent, 1990.

In Nasser's case, he created a charismatic aura by appearing the noble, selfless and silent force behind the free officers; Suez, which was read as a defeat of Britain and France, legitimised his charisma; and, after defeat at the hands of the Israelis, mass demonstrations in Egypt prevented his dejected resignation; whether he then wanted it or not, charismatic leadership had been conferred on him by popular wish and, perhaps, popular need. Kaunda has always craved this popular need of him. He is hurt most when his people appear ungrateful for his work on their behalf. As the 1973 rail episode revealed, he is spurred by a crisis, even if his response to it is not always adept. His constant references to God seem anxious to create an impression that Kaunda is His servant and leads by His will. Creation, crisis, and never-quite conferral would sit at the heart of any charismatic study of Kaunda. If, in the final judgement, his charisma was insufficient for his greatest purposes, there is still by this means of enquiry an intellectual biography of noble ambition.

Thirdly, more complexly, although it may seem to be more simply at first, are approaches developed by Johan Galtung, the prolific peace researcher. When Galtung writes that the task of peace research is to 'develop new peace strategies, to be imaginative, constructive and critical in additional to empirical',[14] a defender of Kaunda might say that the Zambian president has sought to apply this in practice, although his imagination has at times sought to oversoar empirical conditions. It is not that he failed, but that he tried, which makes him a man of peace in our times. Indeed, both in his practice and his writings, Kaunda has sought to fulfil the Galtungian conditions, in which mankind has 'a sort of à la carte offer, where he sets out in great detail the blueprints for a number of different worlds. . . . He should point out problems as well as solutions that others do not see, and open for new horizons.'[15] Kaunda, it might be said, certainly fulfilled the second condition, setting forth a new horizon for southern Africa, even if he was short on the first condition of detail and many alternatives. In at least seeking to fulfil such conditions, Kaunda coincided with Galtung's idea that man is mind-centred and mind-dependent, that is, he is not dependent on economic or environmental determinisms but, through his own mind, can set his own path. Man

---

[14] Johan Galtung, 'Twenty Five Years of Peace Research: Ten Challenges and Some Responses', *Journal of Peace Research*, Vol. 22, No. 2, 1985, p. 156.
[15] Idem, *Rauhantutkimus* (Peace Research), Helsinki, 1969, pp. 207–8.

is a 'culture-bearing animal',[16] and this culture is the fount of development; this development is a process which is conscious and which can change the structure of society. Thus, Kaunda's humanism acts precisely as this sort of fount for the conscious transformation of Zambia.

This much is clear, if simplified; and it is also clear that, either in Galtung's wake, or contemporaneous with him, there is a slew of modern literature which seeks to denominate all essential international relations at the level of individuals.[17] Of all this literature, however, the philosophic foundation of Galtung's is the most satisfying. It is a move from what might be described as an 'ideational' view of the world, that is, the primacy of ideas, in which – as in the Platonic world view, where all sensible things have an ideal essence – there is a world of e.g. antagonism, harmony, and nationality; there is a world indeed of race. Galtung suggests a move away from this ideation to an 'anthropocentric' conception in which all sensible things are actual-historical human beings; all things are 'man-centred' if one likes; and all instances of harmony, antagonism, nationality, and race are in fact 'human beings featured by such properties'.[18]

Obviously, these are not givens. The starting point is the discussion of the relationship between the ideational and the anthropocentric, and then any study of Kaunda must express the tension between the two found in Kaunda's career. What was his 'discourse' within himself and what discourse existed in the southern African region? Insofar, however, as Kaunda saw all things as embodied in human beings, this may provide a means for appreciating why Kaunda sought time and time again to see all solutions to problems as being possible in face-to-face meetings with Vorster, Botha, and de Klerk.

Why labour through such intellectual approaches? Precisely because one form of viewing Kaunda has been supplanted by another that claims the high ground of intellectual apparatus entirely for itself. The

[16] Idem, *Members of Two Worlds: A Development Study of Three Villages in Western Sicily*, New York, 1971, pp. 10–12.
[17] E.g. work by John Burton. See Burton, *Deviance, Terrorism and War: The Process of Solving Unsolved Social and Political Problems*, Oxford: Martin Robertson, 1979.
[18] See the excellent critique of Galtung's work, to which I am indebted, in Helena Rytovuori, 'From the Ideational to the Anthropocentric Conception', in Jukka Paastela (ed.), *Democracy in the Modern World*, Tampere: Acta Universitatis Tamperensis, Vol. 260, 1989. See also Helena Rytovuori, 'Barefoot Research and Tribune of Reason – An Analysis of Peace research in Scandinavia', Ph.D. thesis, University of Tampere, 1990.

pro-Kaunda people have not even attempted to carry the fight to their opponents, but have watched themselves marginalised from debate, still certain they and their man are right, but unable to argue their case. Perhaps this sort of case is not worth arguing because the forum for argument, a narrow segment of a narrow scholarly world, is in the 'real' world inconsequential. Well, the scholarly world is indeed narrow, and perhaps its claims to interact with the real world can be exaggerated, but not a single Zambian scholar has come to the aid of his president in a scholarly manner and this poses the question not only as to whether or not, in scholarly terms, Kaunda is defensible, but why, in the sociology of knowledge, the foreign praise-biographers have had so little local support. (No Zambian has written a praise-biography either.) For a proper debate to take place, one involving Zambian writers and scholars as well as foreign ones, a few ideas are not bad things. Kaunda's legacy should not be that his admirers are allergic to thought. This is a challenge.

There is finally the point to make that a study of Kaunda is possible on the following basis. Following from Galtung's work on the 'culture-bearing' man – man who from his mind is not solely determined by his environment, by nature – then the gap between man and nature is a volitional one, a gap achieved by acts of will. These acts of will are formulated in the mind, and it is this process of formulation which might bear investigation. I am thinking of the wishfulness in Kaunda's volition. He wishes with true sincerity for a freed southern Africa. The act of wishing is inseparable from the act of will. On this mixed and possibly flawed foundation of wish and will, Kaunda has expressed to his people the possibility of hope.

Until such investigations are made, the very broad images of Kaunda established by the hagiographic writers remain. For instance, the international pressure group, Parliamentarians Global Action, in preparing its roster of six presidents for a non-superpower initiative on nuclear disarmament, considered in the early 1980s the possibility of Kaunda becoming a member of the six. Accordingly, a brief on Kaunda was prepared which opened with the lines, 'virtually every profile, interview and statement concerning Kaunda refers to his sincerity, his humanitarianism and his spirituality'.[19] If, however, all

---

[19] *Dr. Kenneth David Kaunda*, research paper prepared by Parliamentarians Global Action. I thank Christos Frangonikolopoulos for letting me cite this paper. For a fine analysis of the PGA initiative, see Frangonikolopoulos, 'The Six-Nation

profiles of him by others have not diluted this image, then Kaunda
has, from time to time, let slip the admission that it could do with a
little dilution. Writing on the Rhodesian bombing of Zambia in 1978
and 1979, he said that 'it is important not to lose the moral advantage
of being the injured party, especially when world opinion is such an
important factor in the equation'.[20] The high price of principle is not
simply about one man's moral force. It is also about moral advantage,
and the games to be played in securing it. It is about sustaining the
image of an injured party. The hagiographies do not deal with this.
Future more enquiring works should.

The Comprador Image

The sudden emergence of a new school of thought on Kaunda in
1976 could not have provided more of a contrast to the loosely
organised thought already in existence. Whereas within the hagiographic writing Kaunda could do no wrong, he could now do no right.
The new school had predecessors. Many people were wary about the
introduction of a one-party state in 1973, and saw in it the instrument
of a Zambian élite which was determined to maintain power and
privilege for itself.[21] What the new school did, however, was to give
the notion of what an élite might be a theoretical apparatus. The élite
became a class, and this class had certain clear relationships with its
class counterparts in the rest of the world. The élite thus became part
of an international structure and, in Zambia, a local mirror of this
structure could also be found – not yet perfectly formed but sufficiently developed so that relationships between the élite class and
other classes could be identified. These were relationships of exploitation and domination, and the result was the accumulation of wealth
by the élite class. This was described as local accumulation, except
that the wealth thus accumulated did not remain entirely, or even
largely, in the pockets of the élite class. Rather, it became part of a

---

Initiative: Origins, Organisation and Policies', unpublished Ph.D. thesis, University of Kent, 1990. In the end, the PGA asked Nyerere, not Kaunda, to join their
six.

[20] *Dr. Kenneth David Kaunda*, PGA research paper, which cites a book by Kaunda
entitled, *The Riddle of Violence*, perhaps the US edition of *Kaunda on Violence*.

[21] E.g. Graham Mytton, in his review of Pettman, *African Affairs*, Vol. 74, No. 294,
1975, pp. 111–2.

global accumulation dominated by the élite ruling classes of the world's most powerful capitalist countries. Zambia, like other third world countries, was very much on the outskirts or the peripheries of these centres of class power, so it could be said that the Zambian élite class was involved in a peripheral accumulation to satisfy metropolitan class interests. Wealth was attracted to the centre of the capitalist world but, so that such a process could continue, so that a Zambian élite class would want it to continue, a portion of this accumulation was left in its hands. The process of global accumulation, therefore, depended on certain peripheral benefits. The élite class of the periphery received its percentage for collaborating with the élite class of the metropole. Thus, in Zambia, there had developed a class of collaborators or, to use the prevailing Spanish term, a comprador class.

The extreme neatness of this theory was attractive in its own right. Its compactness was also a feature since, in one theory, could be found both an explanation of international relations and an explanation for the growing gap between rich and poor within Zambia. The sensation of immediate applicability to Zambian conditions also found it many local followers. The copper mining industry, though Zambian-owned, was still dominated by expatriates. Foreign, capitalist markets determined the price of copper and, in a price slump, it was the Zambian poor who suffered. In hard times, it was never the élite who suffered. At the most general and vulgar end of thought, this was regarded as evidence for the theory. The last feature of the theory's attractiveness has something to do with the sociology of knowledge. Both vulgarian and scholar felt part of an international school of thought, and it was a school firmly identified with 'progressive' forces: it both identified class exploitation and opposed it. It allowed both a style of thinking and solidarity – solidarity with other like-minded thinkers, and solidarity the with the oppressed and exploited. In my time at the University of Zambia, I had not a single undergraduate student who did not subscribe to one form or another of this thought.

The defence of this thought begins by making claims for it. It is deeper and wider than other forms of thinking. It is deeper because it is concerned with sub-structure – what really lies behind events – and not just super-structure, or the outward appearance of events. It is wider because it combines the study of foreign policy with political economy, and it is also comparative – in that southern Africa is not

112   KAUNDA AND SOUTHERN AFRICA

taken as a separated entity, but its study is part of inter-regional comparisons. Without this depth and width, even literature that might be 'radical and relevant' will contain analysis that is 'ultimately superficial, even unsatisfactory'.[22] It claims therefore to provide a complete analysis.

The origin of this school of thought lies to an appreciable extent in the work of André Gunder Frank, who came to his conclusions through his studies of Latin America.[23] There are a number of variations of this thought among those who have accompanied or followed him, but his work remains inspirational. Frank's work, rather than that, for instance, of the Egyptian writer, Samir Amin,[24] is the animating force of those writing about southern Africa – although it must be said that no study on southern Africa has been written to compare with Frank's work on Chile and Brazil; and, in the sub-school of writing on southern African international relations, notwithstanding claims of depth and width, the total corpus of works produced is slim, not so much in numbers as in sustained and lengthy argument. If one were to take in the briefest possible form the central point of Frank's work, then it would be something like this. The third world is not in a state of undevelopment. Rather, it is underdeveloped, and this underdevelopment is an active process. It is a process maintained to secure the development of capitalism. All else is subordinate to this particular development, and everything else made dependent upon it, bonded to it. Development elsewhere is suppressed so that the extraction of wealth will benefit the development of capitalism above everything else. This denial of wealth to the third world, its redirection elsewhere, constitutes underdevelopment. Underdevelopment does not come from the survival of archaic institutions or capital shortages born of isolation.

If one adds to this the concept of the comprador class and its international class relationships mentioned above, the summary is complete. So, it is not in its outline form particularly complicated and, indeed, Nikita Khrushchev had made very similar points about

[22] Msabaha and Shaw (eds.), *Confrontation and Liberation in Southern Africa*, p. 4.
[23] André Gunder Frank, inter alia, *Capitalism, and Underdevelopment in Latin America – Historical Studies of Chile and Brazil*, New York: Monthly Review Press, 1969; *Dependent Accumulation and Underdevelopment*, London: Macmillan, 1978.
[24] Samir Amin, *Unequal Development: An Essay on the Social Formations of Peripheral Capitalism*, Hassocks: Harvester, 1976; *Imperialism and Unequal Development*, Brighton: Harvester, 1977.

underdevelopment in 1960.[25] The openness of Frank's work to summary is precisely the problem here, since the school of writers under discussion has resorted to summary and, thereby, to restatement. The foundation of their work is not original research in southern Africa, but the citation of thought based on work elsewhere. Notwithstanding the possibility of some transfer of insights, the work advertised by this school itself, that of comparison, has not been properly attempted. In what ways does southern Africa compare to Latin America? The harder question is: in what ways does it not compare? – since colonial settlement, subjugation of native peoples, independence, class formation, and peripheral position have all been differently experienced in Latin America – and this question goes unasked because the answers will pose problems and demand real research. Rather than face this, what has happened is that Frankian thought has been taken as a given and, as such, has been applied to southern Africa. Evidence did not form the theory. Theory provided the context for the evidence. Examination of work from the southern African school reveals that, even with the single book devoted to the theory of it all, lengthy quotes from other theoretical writers take up almost as much space as the author's own words.[26] The book thus attempts a validation by reference to other literature, but the question of original southern African evidence remains unanswered.

I am at pains to point out that I am not against Frank. His has been a truly exciting contribution to thought. I am simply in favour of thought that has as complete a base as possible. As it happened, Frank's own work challenged many of the Marxist orthodoxies of its time. It was excoriated by Latin American Communist Parties and, even in the freer intellectual atmosphere of the United States, Frank could give first expression to his views only in an unrefereed student journal, the established academic journals then not wishing to touch his work.[27] He was, it should be pointed out, part of a Latin American school of thought, involving writers such as Furtado,[28] and from Frank

[25] *The New York Times*, 12 February 1960.
[26] Timothy M. Shaw, *Towards a Political Economy for Africa*, London: Macmillan, 1985.
[27] These emerged in tributes to Frank, and Frank's reply to them at the session, 'Reflections on the Contributions of André Gunder Frank', at the Joint Convention of the International Studies Association and the British International Studies Association, London, 1 April 1989.
[28] Celso Monteiro Furtado, *Development and Underdevelopment*, Berkeley: University of California Press, 1966.

and this school came a neo-Marxist vocabulary. It laid an emphasis on structure and, thus, has come to be known as a structuralist school – although the structure it refers to is in fact the sub-structure of class and class relationships. Because third world countries are dependent on the capitalist metropole for any development, the theory is often known as the dependency model or, in its Latin American usage, as '*dependencia*'. This dependency is abetted by the comprador class mentioned above. Because Frank made an attempt to reveal that *dependencia* did really exist in Latin America, I feel that title should be left to him and his fellows there. People working out of his model, but without completing local empirical proofs, are certainly affiliated to *dependencia*, but are aspirants to its centrality from their own not fully developed periphery. I feel they are better described as *dependentistas* – those who believe in dependency – and this is the term I have given to the writers on southern African international relations being considered here.

Because the crux of the matter is evidence, that is what I wish to consider. Firstly, however, a brief note is in order about the process by which the southern African *dependentistas* worked in the case of Zambia. Their first task was to identify Kaunda, UNIP, and the Zambian élite as a class. Below, I suggest that they certainly attempted to identify Kaunda as a collaborator with South Africa and the US over the question of Angolan independence – but a single collaborator, if indeed he was one, is not a class. Secondly, their task should have been to identify the relationship of the Zambian élite class with other Zambian classes. This was problematic, as the question of class formation in Zambia is unsettled, and even the question of class identification – what shall we call those classes that are not the élite class? – uncertain. What was done, therefore, was to assert the existence and operation of an élite class, and that it operated with classes outside Zambia, but, beyond generalities, nothing satisfactory was ever written about internal class relationships. The literature thus presents a head without a body, a ruling élite atop a conceptual vacuum. Again, I wish to say more on Zambian class formation below. Thirdly, if Kaunda did collaborate with South Africa, this should represent a Zambian ruling class acting as a comprador for a South African ruling class, or perhaps there were two comprador classes, one in each country, working for a metropolitan class elsewhere. The distinction has never been properly made. But, if there was any sort of class collaboration, the question arises as to which South African class was involved? What was the South African ruling class? Was it denominated solely by its economic command, or could it be differentiated according to the distinctions I have made in Chapter 3? Did Kaunda (and his class) collaborate with the Afrikaner Broederbond, the more-integrated (English and Afrikaner) constitutional government, the secretive military establishment and the eventually central State Security Council, the multi-national companies in South Africa, or some amalgamation of all of them? Just as the question of class formation is problematic in Zambia, so it is also in South Africa, even ignoring the question of how class is meant to have greater primacy than race. The matter of which class Kaunda collaborated with has never been properly considered. Classes, including the South African ruling class, have been put forward as homogenous categories, and their heterogenous compositions dealt with briefly. On the subject of heterogeneity, some recent work has suggested that there are 'three distinguishable capitalist sub-classes in South Africa, which broadly correlate with the main white political groupings'.[29] The process of forming a *dependentista* analysis of Zambian foreign policy was thus an incomplete one, and remains so to this day.

The first of the *dependentista* publications on Zambian foreign policy appeared in 1976.[30] A distinction should be made as to who said what in this monograph. Kaunda had, as described above, supported UNITA in the Angolan civil war until late in the day, and he had also paid a visit to the US – where it was thought he had held discussions with the Americans on the UNITA question. This was taken as evidence by the editors of the monograph series that Kaunda was a collaborator with the US, and they said so in their preface. The monograph's author, the Canadian scholar, Timothy M. Shaw, was far more restrained and laid out, in one of the most extensive elaborations he has attempted on this subject, the foundations of Zambian dependency. Both a trend and a conclusion were started here. The editors' accusation was adopted by many others, so a certain prefatory conclusion had a great deal of influence. And Shaw himself

---

[29] Reginald H. Green and Carol B. Thompson, 'Political Economies in Conflict: SADCC, South Africa and Sanctions', in Phyllis Johnson and David Martin (eds.), *Destructive Engagement: Southern Africa at War*, Harare: Zimbabwe Publishing House, 1986, pp. 259–60.

[30] Timothy M. Shaw, *Dependence and Underdevelopment: The Development and Foreign Policies of Zambia*, Athens, Ohio: Ohio University Center for International Studies, 1976.

ensured there was a trend, simply by continuing to write in the same vein as his monograph. In 1976 alone, two journal articles on Zambia appeared, essentially mined from his monograph.[31] In 1979, much of this material was restated in his joint-authorship of the only book thus far published on Zambian foreign policy.[32] In 1979 also, he began writing about dependency outside southern Africa.[33] To all this work, the same theoretical apparatus applied, and my discussion of it appears above.

But Shaw became a most extraordinarily prolific publisher of articles, chapters, and edited collections. The solely authored books are few indeed, and this means that his work has been primarily in association with others. As his editing skills grew, so did his ability to attract conference grants. Growing conferences and contacts resulted in a growing number of edited collections. This meant two things. Firstly, and very much to the good, it meant a huge number of African scholars owe Shaw their first real visibility in the western academic press. A great debt is in fact involved; Shaw could, if he wished, lay claim to being the progenitor of a contemporary awareness of African opinion on international relations. Secondly, however, it meant that many African scholars, seeking visibility, were only too pleased to write as Shaw did. He has thus created a huge literature which all says the same thing, and which all says it briefly – in arguments that are exactly chapter-sized. He has become, therefore, both a giant figure and one who is cynically used. This usage is no way to repay a debt. The entire phenomenon is, ironically, a by-product of a north American style of academia, in which not to publish is to perish, and publishing much is, for the commercial publishing houses anyway, preferable to publishing excellent books rarely. The numbers game is important for tenure, promotion, a university's reputation, and the health of the book publishing industry which, in the late twentieth century, works on the supermarket principle of vast turnover. The writers of the third world periphery, therefore, benefit the publishers of the metropole. This is barely a digression. The entire system has meant that one school can dominate thought by repetition, by a form

---

[31] Idem, 'Zambia: Dependence and Underdevelopment', *Canadian Journal of African Studies*, Vol. X, No. 1, 1976; 'The Foreign Policy of Zambia: Ideology and Interests', *The Journal of Modern African Studies*, Vol. 14, No. 1, 1976.

[32] Anglin and Shaw, *Zambia's Foreign Policy*.

[33] Timothy M. Shaw and Kenneth A. Heard (eds.), *The Politics of Africa: Dependence and Development*, London: Longman, 1979.

of rote. I am for much of what Timothy Shaw has done, but I am against this. What is required is evidence and, in my mind, the evidence has yet to be properly presented in the following seventeen areas.

i. Conceptual Objections

1. Third world states participate in an international capitalist economy. In this economic system, relationships are unequal, and third world states have a dependent relationship with richer ones. There is no argument against the existence of inequality and dependency. The argument is over how they got there. Inequality and dependency are not proofs that a victimisation has taken place, or that, in *dependencia* terms, there has been immiseration. As Norman Etherington points out, there is not necessarily any direct causal link between political control and immiseration. 'There was an obvious circularity in argumentation. Victims of underdevelopment were identified by their relative poverty which in turn was taken as proof of victimisation.'[34]

2. The *dependencia* school, with its analysis of a comprador class, has had both champions and defectors. In defecting, scholars give a number of conceptual and practical objections to the school's approach. In 1975, in what was considered a pioneering study of Kenya, Colin Leys wrote of the 'replacement of direct colonial administration by "independent" governments representing local strata and classes with an interest in sustaining the colonial economic relationships'.[35] In 1977, however, he wrote that 'it is becoming clear that underdevelopment and dependency theory are no longer serviceable and must now be transcended'.[36] One of the most noticeable rethinks of *dependencia* came from André Gunder Frank himself, who, in the wake of the world economic crisis of the 1970s, wrote that the school was partial and parochial, and hence 'invalid and inapplicable'. The flaw of the school was that the idea that there was 'some sort of "independent" alternative for the Third World . . . never existed'.[37] In

---

[34] Norman Etherington, 'Theories of Imperialism in South Africa Revisited', *African Affairs*, Vol. 81, No. 324, 1982, p. 404.

[35] Colin Leys, *Underdevelopment in Kenya: The Political Economy of Neo-colonialism, 1964–1971*, London: Heinemann, 1975, p. 9.

[36] Idem, 'Underdevelopment and Dependency: Critical Notes', *Journal of Contemporary Asia*, Vol. 7, No. 1, 1977.

[37] André Gunder Frank, *Reflections on the World Economic Crisis*, New York: Monthly Review Press, 1981, p. 27.

a world system that functions as a whole, there cannot be exemptions from the world system. What are third world states meant to do if they are not involved with international capital?

3. Involvement with international capital is neither one-dimensional nor uni-directional. The picture painted by *dependencia* is flat, in that the compradors do not resist but merely serve the capitalist centre. There have been, however, efforts in Zambia to reschedule debt and repay debt on its own terms and, even though such efforts have not been very successful, neither the effort nor the failure differ substantially in their orientation or objectives from those made by Jamaica, Peru, and Tanzania – countries with different governments and sub-structures to Zambia's. This reinforces the point above, that there are no exemptions from the international system, but introduces the point that governments and sub-structures of all stripes nevertheless seek exemptions. Dependency means that certain things are unavoidable; it does not mean that certain things are commanded. The danger in insisting upon a sub-structure that has a determined function in the international system is one of caricature.

4. There is a fundamental objection to *dependencia* in Africa, and that revolves around the question of class formation. Has class formation reached the stage where there can be said to be a class system with a ruling class? *Dependentistas* have sought to identify a ruling class, but not within a class system. If there is no class system, is the ruling élite a class? An élite is differentiated from those who do not possess its privileges, gifts, and responsibilities. A class is identified by its relationships with all other classes, since an entire sub-structure is involved, not a partial one. If there is only a partial class structure, is it sufficient to sustain the view that the sub-structure has greater importance than the state, both as the unit of analysis and of action? If only a partial sub-structure can be defined, then there is nothing complete that can be said about the dynamics of the class system, and no dialectical thought is possible about the class struggle.

5. The question of class formation poses several complicated problems yet to be resolved, quite apart from the general doubt as to how far it can be said to be proceeding at all, a doubt that has reached even radical scholarly journals.[38] Among the problems is the fundamental one of classification. If, in the industrialised world, a wage-

---

[38] E.g. Joshua B. Forrest, 'The Contemporary African State: A "Ruling Class"?', *Review of African Political Economy*, No. 38, 1987.

earner might, in very broad terms for this argument, be classified as a 'worker' and, again in very broad terms, an employer be classified as 'petty-bourgeois', these classifications are at least resonant enough for a discussion on class to begin. In Zambia, where there are very few wage-earners indeed, there being a small and shrinking formal sector, income is more and more dependent on activities in the informal sector. People are self-employed in what is often the most precarious of senses. Yet, at least from time to time, their business enterprises succeed and they have employees. Are such people informal sector workers, or informal sector petty-bourgeoisie? Since, in Zambia, any working class is subject to this debate – and the debate must differentiate in turn between urban and rural, large industrial and small commercial, and state and private enterprise – then the debate can only proceed according to a vocabulary of 'sections', 'fractions', and 'elements'.[39] These terms are borrowed from the late Greek Marxist thinker, Nicos Poulantzas.[40] But, precisely because Poulantzas was writing primarily of contemporary industrialised society, the usage of these terms in Zambia is far from agreed.[41]

When it comes to how the ruling class might be defined, similar problems arise. James Scarritt has asked the question as to which is the dominant class in Zambia? Is it the bureaucratic bourgeoisie or is it the indigenous capitalists? What are the social bases of these groups?[42] Of all scholars on this subject, Scarritt has at least attempted to give illustrative measures of political change and class formation in Zambia but, on his own admission, his data is incomplete, his analyses incomplete, his conclusions tentative, and his respondents limited in number.[43] Yet, his question is a pertinent one since most formal production and exchange in Zambia is state-controlled. The bureaucratic bourgeoisie therefore control production, but are not necessarily

---

[39] See the work of Gilbert N. Mudenda: 'Class Formation and Class Struggle in Contemporary Zambia', *Contemporary Marxism*, No. 6, 1983; 'The Process of Class Formation in Contemporary Zambia', in Klaas Woldring (ed.), *Beyond Political Independence*, London: Mouton, 1984.

[40] Nicos Poulantzas, *Classes in Contemporary Capitalism*, London: Verso, 1978.

[41] See Pempelani Mufune, 'The Formation of Dominant Classes in Zambia: Critical Notes', *Africa Today*, Vol. 35, No. 2, 1988.

[42] James R. Scarritt, 'The Analysis of Social Class, Political Participation and Public Policy in Zambia', *Africa Today*, Vol. 30, No. 3, 1983.

[43] See idem, 'Measuring and Explaining Changes in Regime Structure in Zambia, 1973–1985', paper delivered at the Joint Annual Convention of the International Studies Association and the British International Studies Association, London, 28 March–1 April 1989.

enriched by it. Indeed, as employees of the state, they are a working fraction if not the dominant working class, as well as possibly the dominant group within the ruling class. However, they do not, by and large, have the same status as some indigenous capitalists, and this raises the question of how status may be a determining factor in class formation or, at least, class consciousness.

To complicate matters further there is, within the working class, a labour aristocracy, a term coined by Lenin,[44] and used more colloquially in Zambia to refer to the mine workers, who, as industrially-trained employees in the nation's only significant export-production sector, differ markedly from other workers and, comparatively very well-paid, cannot be counted upon for any class solidarity, when and if a working class is identified and, more importantly, becomes conscious of itself. This helps to complete a circle of problems since, in the international capitalist system, there is no guarantee that industrialised working classes of the west could feel any solidarity with the workers of Africa. Arghiri Emmanuel has written that the western working class would scarcely contemplate a dilution in its hard-won privileges and income in the cause of any international redistribution of wealth.[45] And Paul Baran has said that the interests of whole working classes in different countries could be radically opposed.[46] If working-class relationships, both within Zambia and the international system, can be so variegated, what is there really that demonstrates that ruling-class relationships and compositions could not be variegated? To what extent, therefore, does general talk of a sub-structure disguise an unwillingness to consider the world's pluralism?

6. Finally, in this section, there is the question of tribalism. There are in excess of 73 distinct tribal groups in Zambia, and Kaunda's expertise in at least balancing them in his political appointments has been well remarked. In what way has class superseded tribe in the Zambian political economy? The question of tribal affiliation is as difficult for the *dependentistas* as it has been, in practice, for Kaunda. If the true sub-structure of the state is something for which western class theory is unprepared, then it is a mild grotesquerie to assert a

[44] V. I. Lenin, *Imperialism*, Section VIII in his *Selected Works*, Moscow: Progress Publishers, 1968.
[45] Arghiri Emmanuel, quoted in Michael Harrington, *The Vast Majority*, New York: Simon and Schuster, 1977, pp. 121–4.
[46] Paul Baran, *The Political Economy of Growth*, Harmondsworth: Penguin, 1973.

sub-structure in its place. The avoidance of this question is perhaps a lingering intellectual neo-colonialism of its own.

* * *

There are, therefore, six conceptual objections to the approach of the *dependentistas* – six areas in which their evidence is incomplete. Evidence is required to demonstrate a historical process of immiseration; that there were alternatives to involvement with the international capitalist system; and that there was no resistance on the part of African governments to the international capitalist system. Evidence is also required to complete a view of national sub-structure, rather than relying on the partial sub-structure that emerges from most writing; to demonstrate the primacy of classes over and above those pluralisms that exist at least within classes, if not in place of them; and to demonstrate that primacy of class above tribe in the sub-structure. After providing evidence for the concept of class, however, comes the work of meeting certain historical objections.

ii. Historical Objections

7. The question arises as to how the comprador class might have been established. In the former British colonies of southern Africa, the time available for this process was short. Up to the very eve of World War II, the British did not foresee or plan for independence except in the very long term. Indeed, British investment in the administration of its colonies was meagre and, in the words of Kirk-Greene, was accomplished through a 'thin white line' of expatriate civil servants,[47] the imperturbable district commissioners of yore. Malcolm Macdonald, at the Colonial Office, set in train the idea that independence might come very much sooner than anticipated but, during the war, British resources were channelled into the fight against Hitler and, after the war, into a costly reconstruction. These strained resources had from 1945 to 1957 to turn Nkrumah and the Ghanaian élite into a comprador class, and to 1964 to do the same with Kaunda and the Zambian élite – which, as noted above, was comprised of teachers and clerks; and not a few in Kaunda's cabinets and central committees were badly educated and had been, in

---

[47] A. H. M. Kirk-Greene, 'The Thin White Line: The Size of the British Colonial Service in Africa', *African Affairs*, Vol. 79, No. 314, 1980.

Zambian colloquial terms (but also literally), 'kitchen boys'. These were short periods in themselves, but particularly for class formation or even class creation. (How actually does one 'create' a class anyway?) Given that the British also took some time to reconcile themselves to nationalist leaders like Kaunda, and only managed to do so very shortly before independence, the creation of class, class interest, comprador leadership, and the assurance of comprador reliability in a neo-colonial order was compressed.

8. This raises the natural observation, one which relies on a judgement of human nature rather than something that can be evidenced, that people who struggled and suffered for independence were hardly likely to embrace overnight a clandestine contract with neo-colonialism. Even the most bourgeois nationalist had some capacity for sincerity.

9. If it is difficult to appreciate the creation of a comprador relationship with British neo-colonialism and, through it, with international capital at large, it is more difficult to locate the time and process which developed a comprador relationship between bourgeois southern African states and South Africa.

iii. International Objections

10. If it becomes possible to demonstrate some form of comprador relationship with South Africa, it is then necessary to demonstrate that South Africa is a recruiting agent for an indispensable mechanism of international capital. It is part of this capital and acts for it in the region. It is a problematic rather than clear-cut relationship, however, as Merle Lipton has indicated.[48] In the brief space here, it should be pointed out that the western capitalist world does rely on South Africa for many of its economic materials and benefits. It would be inconvenient to make other arrangements. But it is possible to make other arrangements – otherwise the sanctions lobby would have had no case. It has been argued, for example, that with judicious planning the US can certainly live without South Africa's economic output – despite South Africa's production of various strategic minerals.[49] If South Africa's link with international capital is convenient rather than indispensable, it is not certain that its regional role is fundamentally to serve and recruit for this capital.

[48] Merle Lipton, *Capitalism and Apartheid*, Aldershot: Gower, 1985.
[49] Larry Bowman, 'The Strategic Importance of South Africa to the United States'.

11. Nor is South Africa necessarily an agent for international imperialism. Despite great efforts to implicate itself formally into the western defensive alliance, South Africa has never been welcomed as a member. Its post-war history of attempting to secure western blessing for a SATO (South Atlantic Treaty Organisation) with itself as the leading power and its concurrent attempts to install itself as an auxiliary member of NATO have failed.[50] In terms of South Africa's economic and military behaviour, it might be better to seek – as I have in Chapter 3 – regional rather than conspiratorial international explanations.

12. Although countries like Zambia are located within unequal relationships in the international economic system, so also are Angola and Mozambique. Where is the alternative, let alone a socialist alternative? Moreover, although South Africa has attacked militarily Angola and Mozambique, it is not as if bourgeois states like Botswana and Lesotho have been immune. Again, the level of analysis might best be regional rather than international.

iv. Regional Objections

13. A bourgeois country like Zambia has spent much time and effort campaigning against racism and supporting independence struggles. Notwithstanding its search for negotiation wherever possible (and even when it is really impossible), all the region's revolutionary states owe much to Zambia for assistance in military struggle and diplomatic manoeuvring. It may be complicit with South Africa in a desire for negotiated settlements and, through them, a predictable region, but for reasons very different from South Africa's. Kaunda, aware of South Africa's agenda for the region, was against it and supported others who were against it. I return to this theme below.

14. Growing out of this, there are common regional aims and resistance among the southern African states. The leaders of Zambia, Angola, and Mozambique meet in summit as allies. They do not meet as a consortium of fundamentally differentiated revolutionaries and compradors.

15. For the sake of completeness, an earlier point may be restated

---

[50] Christopher Coker, 'South Africa and the Western Alliance, 1949–88: A History of Illusions', *Royal United Services Institute Journal for Defence Studies*, Vol. 127, No. 2, 1982.

124 KAUNDA AND SOUTHERN AFRICA

in this list. With whom in South Africa are the ruling classes of bourgeois southern African countries complicit? Which part of the Zambian ruling class collaborates with which part of the South African ruling class? Is there an indigenous capitalist class fraction that deals with a military class fraction? There is no real assurance that, within South Africa itself, local capitalists get on particularly well with the military leaders; moreover, there is a very real history of Afrikaner nationalism's resistance to domination by foreign capital,[51] so even if there was a demonstrable collaboration between indigenous capitalists in both countries, this would not necessarily be evidence of an international sub-structure at work, but a peculiarly regional one.

v. Public Administration Objections

16. As noted above, in Zambia there is very little way in which any group outside the president's own circle, and this would include the bulk of the bureaucratic élite and indigenous capitalists, can organise a foreign policy view, let alone an input. As Chingambo suggested, there is not much by way even of foreign policy knowledge. How then does a class dominate a nation's foreign policy under such circumstances? How does the sub-structure work without an infrastructure?

17. Precisely because the number of people dealing with foreign policy is small, and the number with foreign policy knowledge is small, can there be said to be a comprador class involved? Is there merely a comprador president? A comprador cabal? Perhaps this is the case, but then class analysis has little to do with it.

* * *

The idea of class collaboration must surely turn, in the end, after all the other arguments have been exhausted, on the question of choice. If there are compradors, what choice did they have but to collaborate? As André Gunder Frank himself said, there were no alternatives for them. This is because there is an international structure, a world system, they cannot escape. The idea of structure is truly based, but the idea of volitional class collaboration is full of problems. The wish to escape the world system, to be exempt from it, leads likewise to

---

[51] For a radical statement of this see Archie Mafeje, 'South Africa: The Dynamics of a Beleaguered State', in Bernard Magubane and Ibbo Mandaza (eds.), *Whither South Africa?*, Trenton, New Jersey: Africa World Press, 1988.

problems, since there is nowhere one can go. The rewarding thought on structure, on the world system, originates more from Immanuel Wallerstein than Frank and the *dependencia* school, and the various *dependentistas*. The world system is not something anyone can do much immediately about, third world countries least of all. This does not mean that there are not contradictions in the capitalist world system, or that there should be no struggle against it, but there will be no changes in the short term. None has been possible from the independence of African countries to the present day.[52]

The problem with accepting Wallerstein's 'world system' approach is that one gives up the ability readily to identify with or against particular national classes. A reordering of the forces in the equation is necessary and this reordering makes it harder for a scholar also to be a class warrior on the international conference circuit. One might support various forces for change, but these forces cannot be as neatly arranged as before. The image of being a class warrior on the circuit is a cheeky one, but there is emerging in southern Africa itself a significantly more radical form of neo-Marxist analysis than many *dependentistas* managed. Nowhere is this more apparent than in Zimbabwe, and, here, among the more restrained assessments would be that by Brian Raftopoulos: 'It is tempting to reach for slogans, acts of faith, restatements of orthodoxies. It is less attractive to confront a set of radical tenets without the foreclosure of absolute success, a "Marxism without guarantees".'[53] Among the less restrained is an attack, disguised as a book review, against the 'radical white paternalists . . . self-appointed specialists on Southern Africa in England who have for long deceived themselves that their neo-classical polemics couched in Marxist terminology would somehow influence history'.[54]

Here is not the place to discuss the rights or wrongs of scholarship on the left; nor whether scholarship on the right has anything 'progressive' to contribute. What I have sought to say is that the current *dependentista* apparatus for viewing Zambian foreign policy is limited, wrong. One does not have to be a hagiographer of Kaunda,

---

[52] Immanuel Wallerstein, 'The Rise and Future Demise of the World Capitalist System: Concepts for Comparative Analysis', *Comparative Studies in Society and History*, Vol. 16, No. 4, 1974.

[53] Brian Raftopoulos, *The Left and Crisis in Africa*, Harare: Zimbabwe Institute of Development Studies Discussion Papers I, 1989, p. 8.

[54] T. D. Mashanda-Shopo, 'Of Radical Pessimism and Polemics', *Pan African Liberation Platform*, Vol. 1, No. 2/3, 1989, p. 7.

or a man of the right, to say that a structural analysis of southern
Africa requires greater evidence and fewer preconceptions than has
been the case. In the *dependentista* view of Zambia, the comprador
image of Kaunda arose through a process peculiar to the exigencies of
modern professional life in the western universities, and has restated
conclusions never fully demonstrated by the examination of evidence.
It is still, however, the dominant image of Kaunda.

I should not wish to leave this section without at least a word for a
way ahead, and this should not just be a flourish in the direction of
Wallerstein, because there is something quite apart from structure,
whether seen in terms of an international relations of classes or in
terms of a world system. Iliffe, among others, distinguishes between
structural poverty and conjunctural poverty. The first is an outgrowth
of particular systems that originated in colonial times. The second is
the poverty that stems from war and famine, but which may be
exacerbated by the deficiencies in structure. It gives rise to the poorest
of the poor. Iliffe has taken great pains to point out that, historically,
there was always a distinction in Africa between the poor and the
destitute. That distinction is still present today except that, in the
twentieth century, the destitute, the poorest, are the very old, the sick,
and the very young.

Yet is was rarely understood. Men of the left commonly misconceived it as a recent phenomenon due to colonial and capitalist
exploitation. Men of the right misconceived it as a recent
phenomenon due to the weather or population growth or the
incompetence of African governments. Few realised that conjunctural poverty had changed its nature during the twentieth
century. Fewer still realised how much of structural poverty had
not changed at all.[55]

The question, 'what is the structure?', should not obscure the fact that
great structural poverty exists and that conjunctural poverty, which
cannot so easily be laid at the hands of the capitalist system, is making
the most poor out of the most vulnerable. Fewer villains here, more
numerous victims. A way ahead is to recall the end-result of both
structure and the more enigmatic conjunctions of history, and to

[55] Iliffe, *The African Poor*, p. 259.

publish a literature that not only blames but seeks to help: a humane if not a humanist literature.

The Image of Impediment

This last image is very recent and grows out of the preceding one. It is the work mainly of one scholar, Kenneth Good, who has taught at several third world universities including that of Zambia, who was expelled from a teaching position at the University of Rhodesia by the Smith regime, and who has propounded his position in two articles that startled his former colleagues in Zambia because of the audacity of his attacks on Kaunda.[56] Not that it restated the view of the *dependentistas*, rather it went three steps further. Firstly, it brought up to date a catalogue of data testifying to Zambia's economic decline. Good identified this decline firmly with, not merely the avarice of the élite, but its incompetence and inability to plan. Secondly, it made the point, not far removed from Iliffe's, that those who had been abandoned most by élite avarice and incompetence were the rural poor. They were the poorest of the poor and their parlous condition also left them most open to calamity. Thirdly, moving to the field of international relations, Kaunda's efforts to launch dialogue with the South Africans, including his summits with South African presidents, were seen by his frontline peers as an impediment to a unified frontline position on liberation and how to go about it.

This shifts the ground of the *dependentista* critique a little. A Zambian élite still exploits the poor. The central charge of collaboration, however, has changed. It is not so much that Kaunda collaborates with the South Africans by meeting them but, in meeting them, he impedes the frontline states. If Kaunda retains any honour abroad, he retains it least closest to home, as the frontline presidents are annoyed by his adventurism in dialogue. Of all the images of Kaunda, this fascinated me most, since there is some real evidence for it. At the same time, there remains more than one interpretation of this evidence. This image provided a starting point for my investigations of the next two chapters. They lead to a fifth image of Kaunda, one which opens on to, I feel, a particular reality.

[56] Kenneth Good, 'Debt and the One Party State in Zambia', *Journal of Modern African Studies*, Vol. 27, No. 2, 1989; 'Zambia and the Liberation of South Africa', *Journal of Modern Africa Studies*, Vol. 25, No. 3, 1987.

6
THE FIFTH IMAGE: KAUNDA AS MEDIATOR

When, in March 1990, the South African Department of Foreign Affairs floated the idea that Kaunda might be an ideal 'mediator' or 'facilitator' – the honest broker or third party – in opening talks between de Klerk's government and the ANC,[1] it was using the language of a new and growing discipline. The same language had been used in government circles around the world, including the State Department in Washington, and reached as far as the ANC and Nelson Mandela himself. In South Africa, this language had been pioneered by Professor Hendrik van der Merwe of the University of Cape Town's Centre for Intergroup Studies.[2] Van der Merwe had been more than a scholar, over the years actively involved in mediation and, as noted in Chapter 4, he had personally inaugurated the informal diplomacy between Pretoria and Lusaka in 1984. He had not, however, acted on the basis only of his own ideas, although he was the pioneer in seeking to apply international thought to the South African situation. This thought has been given various labels, but 'conflict and mediation studies' would summarise them. A summary label does not, however, disguise pronounced differences among schools of thought in this area, but emphasis on 'facilitation' would usually be drawn from the school of 'conflict resolution', pioneered by the Australian

---

[1] *Guardian* (London and Manchester), 23 March 1990.
[2] Hendrik Van der Merwe and Sue Williams, 'Pressure and Cooperation: Complementary Aspects of the Process of Communication Between Conflicting Parties in South Africa', *Paradigms*, Vol. 1, No. 1, 1987; Van der Merwe, 'Principles and Practice of Facilitation and Mediation in South Africa', in Stephen Chan and Vivienne Jabri (eds.), *Mediation in Southern Africa*, London: Macmillan, forthcoming.

diplomat and scholar, John Burton.[3] The language and theoretical approaches of these schools, particularly the Burtonian school, help to elucidate the image of Kaunda as mediator – a role often claimed for him and one which he has done his best to fill.

There are certain problems to such an examination of Kaunda's work, not the least of which is that it would be seeking to impose a structure of which Kaunda himself was unaware. Kaunda as mediator in practice is older than the schools of mediation in theory. He was not originally inspired by them, may perhaps have learnt of them as they grew (but they are still growing and any agreed bodies of thought have gained agreement only recently), but, more than likely, Kaunda made his role up as he went along. This is not to say that he was unaware of the broad idea of mediation. It is still perfectly possible, even in the scholarly community, to publish quite good books on mediation that mention theory not at all, or only in passing.[4] And, if the idea of disciplined thought on international relations is felt to be very old, in the west dating back to Thucydides and his comments that campaign objectives and strategic strength have a relationship, as do objectives and their systematic environment,[5] then the image of persons intervening between armies and demanding peace is also at least as old. Lysistrata and the women of Athens preventing their husbands from going to war, the Sabine women throwing themselves between their husbands and fathers, the mother of Coriolanus leading an embassy to her son – these are all images of western culture that say that war can be prevented and that there are higher values than those of conflict. The Judaeo-Christian tradition is centred around the idea that one man might intervene between his fellows and the wrath of God. Abraham did not merely intervene, but he negotiated with God over the safety of Sodom and Gomorrah; his opening position being that God would surely not destroy these cities if there could be found in them fifty righteous men and, having established a principle, pleading all the way down the line to the safety of the cities for the sake of ten righteous men. The image established by Abraham

---

[3] Burton had an extraordinary career. He was the youngest Permanent Secretary of External Affairs in Australia, played a key role in the San Francisco conference that established the United Nations, became an ambassador and then a distinguished professor on both sides of the Atlantic. See A. J. R. Groom's tribute to him in Michael Banks (ed.), *Conflict in World Society*, Brighton: Wheatsheaf, 1984.

[4] E.g. Ramesh Thakur, *International Conflict Resolution*, Boulder, Colorado: Westview, 1988.

[5] Thucydides, *The Peloponnesian War*, Harmondsworth: Penguin, 1954.

was resolved by Jesus, who, as the Son of Man, established man's redemption in the sight of God. The general idea of a certain kind of mediator therefore, the moral third party who comes between opposing forces, who comes not merely from a moral tradition but a Christian, perhaps a holy, one, would certainly have been known by Kaunda.

The second problem in imposing a structure on Kaunda is that one has to search the literature to find one that really fits. The best-known literature on mediation has carved out a pretty clear idea of what a mediator is. He or she is very much a third party, someone not involved in the dispute at hand. Yet, like the Athenian women with their husbands, the Sabine women with their husbands and fathers, Volumnia with her son Coriolanus, even Abraham with his relatives in the condemned cities, Kaunda has his own position and interests in southern Africa. Indeed, as a supporter and host of liberation groups, he is a party to the dispute. Similarly, by his campaigns to launch sanctions upon South Africa, and diplomatically to isolate Pretoria, he is not a true third party, cannot be a disinterested mediator.

The third problem is that any attempt to bring structure to Kaunda's work is difficult not only on theoretical grounds, but on the grounds of Kaunda's own operational method. His tendency towards sudden decisions may truly fulfil his little-known African name – Buchizya, One Who Was Unexpected – but means the discernment of thoughtfulness is difficult simply by virtue of there having been no thought. There has been, as I shall argue later in this chapter, a particular form of intuitive foreign policy, with very little researched foundation.

Yet Kaunda has retained the image of mediator. He, himself, constantly talks of morality, Christianity, and how he has sought to prevent violence; and the public information, at least, is that Zambia has not lifted a military hand against any other state. The journalist, Colin Legum, has written that 'few have done more than Kaunda to play the role of mediator between blacks and whites'.[6] The continuing evidence of attempted mediation is the strongest card in the deck left to the hagiographers of Kaunda. For the protagonists of the comprador school, there has been a hidden agenda of collaboration in Kaunda's mediation. Likewise, the charge that his attempts at mediation have impeded the development of a unified policy by the frontline states points to the centrality of mediation in forming an assessment

[6] Cited in *Dr. Kenneth David Kaunda*, PGA research paper.

of Kaunda. The issue of mediation, in short, must be dealt with. The first step in this is to see what the literature on mediation actually says.

Thought on Mediation
(With Christos Frangonikolopoulos and Abiodun Onadipe)

Mediation contributes to negotiation and cannot always be relied upon to change the course of negotiation. A tendency in the literature is to regard mediation as an autonomous action, whereas it should properly be linked firmly to negotiation. The only time when a third party might reliably bind negotiating parties to its own decisions is when the negotiating parties have agreed to accept arbitration or judicial settlement – in short, when they have sought legal means to end their dispute. Otherwise, negotiation influences mediation – the state of negotiations, the gains and losses involved, the relative power and resources of the parties, determine the entry point and scope for mediation – and it is less often the case that mediation, without its own power and resources, influences negotiation. When mediating third parties do have their own power and resources – as, for instance, the United States in mediating between Israel and Egypt – then mediation may influence negotiation; except that the Camp David talks between Carter, Begin, and Sadat were as much a trilateral negotiation as a case of bilateral negotiations with third party mediation. I say more on this below.

Negotiations may be held with one side intending to 'win', to extract as much as possible from a weaker opponent. Mediation in this case may be able only to soften the blow, but not to alter the situation of victory and (possibly cushioned) defeat. Mediation may help in the settlement of conflict, that is, in the reduction or suspension of violence, the signing of treaties or other agreements, the promise from both sides to hold further negotiations or to send regular 'confidence-building' signals to each other. This is to secure at least temporary good behaviour from the disputing or conflicting parties – to remove or reduce their bad behaviour – but stops short of resolving the fundamental causes of conflict. After winning, and settlement, comes the most ambitious of three broad levels of mediation, and that is conflict resolution. The mediator has resolution in mind. The causes of conflict are removed or resolved. Two things should be said about this third level immediately. It is the level which has generated most of the recent literature on mediation: it is an academic growth-discipline; its language at least has permeated governments; it is, therefore, conceptually influential. Having said that, the second point is that there is no empirical evidence whatsoever that any international conflict has ever been resolved, or could be resolved. They might be settled, but resolution is a different matter.

For instance, majority rule may come to South Africa. There may be a constitutional settlement. Both sides may compromise to achieve a settlement. The causes of conflict between black and white, however, will not disappear with the settlement. Racial prejudice, economic stratification, and accumulated generations of thought – a culture of regarding the other as different, if not opposed – will linger, and will do so for the foreseeable future, no matter what 'politics of reconciliation' there might be. The same might be said about conflict between Palestinians and Israelis, between Turkish- and Greek-Cypriots, between Tamils and Sinhalese. All of this would seem sensible and obvious, but the literature is more ambitious than that. Moreover, in the case of Kaunda, his language is the language of resolution: prayer and love overcome everything; in his vision, all men live in peace; the causes of their hatred are removed; Kaunda does not talk about a contemporary social contract by which men might coexist in a legislated manner.

What is the literature? There is firstly a distinction between what is endogenous and what is exogenous – by which is simply meant that endogenous efforts are undertaken by the parties to a dispute, they negotiate; whereas exogenous efforts come from an ousider, so that a true third party is exogenous, not a party to the dispute, and mediates between those who are.[7] The second distinction is between mediation that is supportive and that which is directive. Supportive mediation involves the use of good offices to conciliate opposing parties and to facilitate negotiations. It is this sort of mediation that the South African Department of Foreign Affairs probably had in mind for Kaunda. Directive mediation is when the third party actually participates in a negotiation between the disputants; he or she may seek to make suggestions regarding the substance of the conflict; bargain with one or both disputants to extract changes in stance and concessions. It is this sort of mediation that Kaunda has probably had in mind

---

[7] Jacob Bercovitch, *Social Conflicts and Third Parties*, Boulder, Colorado: Westview, 1984, p. 11.

since the 1970s. To locate Kaunda as mediator, therefore, is first to untangle him from his mixture of mediatory roles.

Supportive mediation, conciliation, and facilitation concern the changing of attitudes within the negotiating parties, removing misperceptions, and improving understanding by placing the dispute in its wider context.[8] One of the ways in which this is done is by means of what are called 'problem-solving workshops' (which are in turn meant to be a form of 'facilitative conflict resolution'), which provide a setting in which disputing parties participate equally, and usually unrestricted by a negotiating agenda, in finding solutions that are self-sustaining and self-supporting.[9] They are, therefore, settings outside those normally provided in the legal and diplomatic traditions.[10] They have special value in removing misperceptions since, in a non-legal, non-diplomatic setting, the old emphases on winning or losing are relegated in favour of the expression of basic needs which may be mutual.[11] Here, however, there is a conceptual problem, and this concerns whether or not there are basic needs which can be so readily expressed. Burton has argued that these are needs of identity, participation, control, recognition, and security.[12] Others, however, question the possibility of being able to identify universal basic needs,[13] and there is of course the argument that, even if such needs exist, they will be seen through particular historical, cultural, and political perspectives. These perspectives may lie behind certain conflicts and, although the grosser, propagandistic misperceptions that one side has of another might be dispelled, a problem-solving workshop cannot undo the work of history. Such an ambition is presumptuous or simply naïve.

Nevertheless, even a fragile integration of the perceptions of

[8] See Georgios Kostakos, 'Third Party Management of Disputes. The Role of the U.N.: A Case Study of the Cyprus Problem', unpublished MA dissertation, University of Kent, 1987.

[9] A. J. R. Groom, 'No Compromise: Problem-Solving in a Theoretical Perspective', *International Social Science Journal*, No. 127, 1991.

[10] J. W. Burton, *Conflict and Communication*, London: Macmillan, 1969.

[11] See A. J. R. Groom, 'Problem-Solving in International Relations', in John W. Burton and Edward Azar (eds.), *International Conflict Resolution: Theory and Practice*, Brighton: Wheatsheaf, 1986.

[12] For the most succinct summary, see J. W. Burton, 'World Society and Human Needs', in Margot Light and A. J. R. Groom (eds.), *International Relations: A Handbook of Current Theory*, London: Pinter, 1985.

[13] C. J. Brown, 'International Theory: New Directions', *Review of International Studies*, Vol. 7, No. 3, 1981.

disputants is often a victory, although this may take a series of meetings or workshops,[14] so the problem-solving workshops can't be written off, although some of the grand claims made for them should be seasoned with a grain of salt – or common sense. But the methodology suggested for the workshops does involve procedures which seem widely contradictory. On the one hand, the mediator or facilitator is merely a channel, a conduit for a process which only the parties to the dispute can undertake.[15] On the other hand, the facilitator aims to transform the very grounds of the dispute, resolving goal incompatibilities so that the disputants can realise the wider context of their relationship.[16] But how is he or she to do something so fundamental while still remaining a channel or conduit? It is hard to see how the grand phraseology is not merely a cover for a form of professional manipulation. The mediator's most important knowledge is in conflict theory, rather than in the particular conflict at hand,[17] an emphasis which, if taken to an extreme, will see (has seen) a multitude of professional mediators crossing the globe, confident in their theory of conflict while handing out racial insults, making cultural *faux pas*, and failing to appreciate what has led opposed groups to a bloody history. No conflict can be subordinated to a series of techniques to do with group interaction and the capacity to appear non-judgemental. So the methodology remains in question, the ambition over-reaching, and the idea of workshops might best be summarised as a useful preliminary in seeking to get formal negotiations off to the best possible start.[18] There is always the danger that an unsuccessful workshop will get negotiations off to the worst possible start.

There is, however, a particular virtue of the workshop idea, and that is neither its participants nor the facilitator need be drawn from the official sector. Burton argues that the closer participants are to official policy-makers the better,[19] while Kelman argues that partici-

---

14 Margot Light, 'Problem-Solving Workshops: The Role of Scholars in Conflict Resolution', in Banks (ed.), *Conflict in World Society*, p. 115.
15 A. J. R. Groom and Keith Webb, 'Injustice, Empowerment, and Facilitation in Conflict', *International Interactions*, Vol. 13, No. 3, 1987, p. 276.
16 C. R. Mitchell, *Peacemaking and the Consultant's Role*, New York: Nicholas, 1981, pp. 106–8.
17 John W. Burton, 'Procedures of Conflict Resolution', in Burton and Azar (eds.), *International Conflict Resolution*, p. 95.
18 As seen by Herbert C. Kelman and Stephen P. Cohen, 'Reduction of International Conflict', in W. G. Austin and S. Worchel (eds.), *The Social Psychology of Intergroup Relations*, Monterey: Brooke/Cole, 1979, pp. 288–304.
19 Burton, 'Procedures of Conflict Resolution', p. 108.

pants far from the centres of power will more likely be open-minded.[20]
The further away from the centres of power a participant is, the greater
will be his or her 're-entry' problem, having new beliefs or perceptions
accepted outside the supportive and enlightening workshop environment. Insofar as more and more people from outside the official sector
become involved in mediation exercises, then the greater is the growth
of what might be called 'track two' diplomacy. Burton sees track two
as an alternative to official power politics and, by extension, its normal
'track one' diplomacy,[21] but it might be best to view track two as
preparatory to official negotiations,[22] if for no other reason than the
fact that track two cannot change the world without, at some point,
dove-tailing with track one. What can be taken as Burton's hatred for
state governments should not obscure the fact that they remain the
principal actors in at least the international relations of state conflicts.

The discussion has a relevance to southern Africa, however. The
visit of van der Merwe and Muller to Lusaka in 1984 was an example
of track two paving a way for track one (with the full knowledge and
agreement of those in official positions), as were the subsequent
meetings between South African businessmen and the ANC
(although, at the time in public, these did not receive official sanction).
The manner of the meetings held between Kaunda and South African
leaders is also of interest. Of his 1982 meeting with Botha, Kaunda
said that it would 'enable us to analyse the situation in a cool and
honest manner'.[23] The objective, at least partially, was to overcome
misperceptions. Without an agenda, the nature of the meeting was
remarkably in the workshop mould. There are insights available here
through the use of the academic literature. Before summarising them,
however, a comment is in order on the sort of mediation Kaunda
probably sought above the others, and that is directive mediation.

Directive mediation is where the third party not only makes
suggestions on the substance of the conflict and suggests compro-
mises, but becomes involved in negotiations with the disputant parties,

[20] Herbert C. Kelman, 'The Problem-Solving Workshop in Conflict Resolution', in R.
L. Merritt (ed.), *Communication in International Politics*, Urbana: University of Illinois
Press, 1972, pp. 195–200.
[21] John W. Burton, 'Track Two: An Alternative to Power Politics', in John W.
Macdonald and Dianne B. Bendahmane (eds.), *Conflict Resolution: Track Two
Diplomacy*, Washington DC: Foreign Service Institute, 1987, p. 65.
[22] Maureen R. Berman and Joseph E. Johnson (eds.), *Unofficial Diplomats*, New York:
Columbia University Press, 1977, p. 5.
[23] *Herald* (Harare), 29 April 1982.

bargaining with them, in an attempt to have them alter their stances. He or she seeks to reformulate the issues in dispute or, to use the jargon, to modify the issue structure; in redefining the issues, to become involved in 'substitute proposing'; and to find a formula for progress or 'de-committing'.[24] What might have begun as a bilateral negotiation becomes a trilateral one; and, just as the two original parties have their own constituencies to consider, so also has the third party.[25] The existence of constituencies means also the existence of interests so that, in what has become a trilateral negotiation, costs may be incurred (and benefits gained) by all three. These are what might be called relationships of influence and, above all, exchange. The third party must have his or her own power and resources in order to participate fully in this process. This need not be power and resources in the same terms as those of the original negotiators. Indeed, the third party might seek to avoid comparability with them, projecting instead – having his or her constituency confer – both national and international status and approval. With this sort of support, the third party might even use exaggerations and threats, itemise rewards, even project calamity, distort information, in order to drive the original parties onwards to agreement.[26]

The third party, *in extremis*, might even create a 'hurting stalemate' by strengthening the weaker of the two disputants.[27] This is a form of coercive mediation, but the coercion need not be a military or economic one. It might be 'both subtle and simple . . . used either to make the present situation unpleasant or to make the future situation of a mediated peace more pleasant for the parties'.[28]

To coin a phrase, these are the 'power politics of mediation' and, clearly, they involve a dangerous game in which a third party, in entering mediation, stands to lose as well as gain; may be drawn into the conflict itself, or drawn far more deeply than its original interests thought proper. It means that a third party may have to posture, as

---

[24] Saadia Touval (ed.), *The Peace Brokers: Mediators in the Arab-Conflict, 1948–1979*, Princeton: Princeton University Press, 1982, p. 4; Saadia Touval and I. William Zartman (eds.), *International Mediation in Theory and Practice*, Boulder, Colorado: Westview, 1985, p. 7.

[25] Touval (ed.), *The Peace Brokers*, p. 6.

[26] James A. Wall, 'Mediation: An Analysis, Review and Proposed Research', *Journal of Conflict Resolution*, Vol. 25, No. 1, 1981, pp. 167–9.

[27] I. William Zartman, 'Ripening Conflict, Ripe Moment, Formula and Mediation', in Macdonald and Bendahmane (eds.), *Conflict Resolution: Track Two Diplomacy*, p. 225.

[28] Touval and Zartman (eds.), *International Mediation in Theory and Practice*, p. 13.

well as imposture, in order to sustain a position of mediatory strength
– tell lies, sell people out, collaborate.

Those who have supported Kaunda have pointed to a mediation
that is itself supportive – conciliatory, facilitative, aimed at conflict
resolution in the names of love and God. Much of Kaunda's mediation
has in fact been an attempt to be directive. Neither the techniques nor
the objectives of such mediation are concerned primarily with conflict
resolution, but at compromise, settlement, and the preservation of
interests. It is a process of politics, not of humanism. Humanism
might have underlain the impetus towards mediation but, in the
contemporary history of southern Africa, it has been the processes of
issuing threat and receiving threat, of seeking to reduce, balance, or
nullify threat, that have consumed energy and lives. In this process,
certain mediatory images have been used. The reality of mediation
has been different.

The Reality of Mediation

The components of Kaunda's mediation are as follows:

1. He is an endogenous actor using the language of an exogenous
   mediator.
2. This language, premised on the resolution of conflict, makes
   him appear a supportive mediator concerned with conciliation
   and mediation.
3. The language camouflages the fundamental point that Kaunda
   and Zambia are party to the southern African conflict so that,
   if he mediates at all, he must sometimes mediate between his
   frontline colleagues on the one hand and South Africa on the
   other. This creates the tension of self-appointed leadership
   and distance from the frontline as a whole.
4. Nevertheless, the language he uses has won him an international reputation as a moral person or, at least, as a moralist;
   and the backdrop of his philosophy of humanism – however
   flawed in the formal sense – has certainly helped this reputation. This reputation, or image, has been a resource for Kaunda
   in dealing with South Africa.
5. It has not, however, been his only or even major resource.
   South African intelligence is keen enough to discern an image
   that has a frayed credibility in international capitals, for instance

in London, but South Africa is keen also to exploit what is left of the image – to be seen talking to the man who has epitomised decency in the region.

6. What the image affords, therefore, is a moral cloak – under which, far from anything to do with third party mediation, Zambia and South Africa seek to achieve a framework for negotiation as the region's two principal powers; certainly as its two principal negotiators.

7. This is resisted by the frontline to the extent that Kaunda has never received any formal authority from it to act as spokesman or representative – so that Kaunda's constituency is problematically divided. Internationally, his image survives but is tired. With the frontline region, he is active but an unguided missile. He has a constituency in South Africa which, at times encouraged by the South African Government, has viewed Kaunda as the reasonable face of the frontline. And he has a domestic Zambian constituency which is essentially uninvolved in his efforts at negotiation and mediation, except to give official endorsement to the philosophy of humanism.

8. The uncertainty of his real influence, the limits to his actual and mobilisable resources, have always made Pretoria wary of how much and how often to deal with Kaunda. But, insofar as Kaunda has made no significant military threat to South Africa, but has suffered under the threat of military action from it, Pretoria regards him as both a predictable (stubbornly pacific) and a safe (non-military) negotiating partner whenever public negotiations have seemed useful.

9. Kaunda has sought to maximise his own resources and power as much as possible – the sanctions strategy, the hosting of liberation movements and his good offices with them, the seniority that is his with regard to some sort of support for liberation, something that cannot be denied by the frontline – in order to bargain with Pretoria. His use of threat in the general rather than specific sense, in the apocalyptic rather than military sense, has been an attempt to strengthen his bargaining hand. Counterpointed with his sermons on love, he is simultaneously, in one person, both the 'hard man' and 'soft man' of a negotiating team.

10. Under these conditions and limitations, what has been negoti-

ated is not love and resolution, but the sort of region that both Lusaka and Pretoria could live with.

11. Notwithstanding any of these points, however, the use of a 'problem-solving workship' format in meetings between South African leaders and Kaunda has lent the possibility of something unstructured slipping through an almost ritualistic net – so surprises are still possible at these summit meetings.

12. The image and language of mediation are invaluable and necessary for Kaunda, in that he must appear concerned for the region as a whole, and not just for the region as suitable to Lusaka and Pretoria. He cannot afford too much distance between himself and the remainder of the frontline.

These dozen points summarise the reality of Kaunda's mediation, and are a little removed from the image – yet combine attributes from different parts of the literature on mediation. He is, in short, a peculiar type. These points might be tested by reference to the latest case study constructed by Kaunda and de Klerk, and this concerns their summit meeting in Livingstone, on the Zambian side of the Victoria Falls (no straddling of the border this time), in 1989.

The Meeting Between Kaunda and de Klerk

Prime Minister Botha had prepared himself for his 1982 meeting with Kaunda in Botswana. He asked Kaunda to open the meeting with prayer, spoke warmly of Kaunda's writing on humanism, and even affirmed the principles of human dignity in the Lusaka Manifesto.[29] The same was true of Vorster in 1975. He came to the Victoria Falls summit with a full package to offer: a transformed region based on *détente*, with movement towards majority rule in Rhodesia, anchored on a *modus vivendi* between Pretoria and Lusaka. The same could be expected of de Klerk's preparations, not so much by way of a package to offer this time as a thorough knowledge of the personality and inclinations of the Zambian President. The first issue that I wish to address here, however, is how much Kaunda knew of de Klerk.

Lloyd John Chingambo (at that time my Ph.D. student) and I were both in Lusaka in August 1989, throughout the period of de Klerk's visit to Zambia. Two weeks before the visit, Chingambo could find no

---

[29] According to Brownrigg, *Kenneth Kaunda*, p. 131.

person within the Zambian Ministry of Foreign Affairs who knew anything about de Klerk, or who could say that any file existed on him. The same was true within the UNIP's research department. For my part, I concentrated my interviews on the de Klerk question upon ministers who had held responsibilities for foreign affairs – it having been impossible to interview the current minister, Luke Mwanan-shiku, since he had gone to Wellington, New Zealand, during both the build-up to de Klerk's visit and the announcement that it was actually to take place. At that time, a visit by de Klerk had been the subject of speculation, but none of it had been confirmed. Moreover, de Klerk was preparing for elections in South Africa, and no-one knew with what mandate he might emerge. All my interviewees knew these things from the media, and had no other sources of information, despite in some cases still holding cabinet or even UNIP Central Committee positions. Kaunda attended a meeting of the frontline presidents two weeks before his summit with de Klerk, and no-one I spoke to had any information on what links there might have been between the two.

One minister spoke of the desirability of Kaunda's meeting de Klerk. He did not, however, foresee any such meeting until after de Klerk's election, 'to assess just what the National Party can deliver in terms of a mandate.'[30] Another minister would not comment directly on the possibility of a summit between Kaunda and de Klerk, but viewed South African foreign policy initiatives with 'great scepticism'. He did imply a parallel, however, with a meeting between Botha and Mandela (this was some time before Mandela's release and no-one knew what the South African agenda or sense of timing then was), and stressed the enigmatic nature of that meeting. Had it been for true domestic purposes, or merely for party-political advantages? He seemed to be suggesting, like his colleague, that any meeting with de Klerk should be after the South African elections, to prevent its being used for party-political purposes.[31] A further minister spoke of a desirable Zambian policy of 'utter caution'. South African initiatives required 'constant monitoring'. This minister expressed great distrust of South Africa in the wake of its duplicity over the Nkomati Accord.

---

[30] See Appendix 1 for a note on the difficulties of research in third world countries, and the reasons for inexact attribution. Author's interview with minister with former responsibilities for foreign affairs and defence, Lusaka, August 1989.

[31] Author's interview with another minister with former responsibilities for foreign affairs, Lusaka, August 1989.

'We once thought Botha was straight, but we came in the end not to trust him.' On a possible meeting between Kaunda and de Klerk, he said that Kaunda should meet the South African leader only if it was deemed helpful to 'the situation'. President Kaunda had not made a statement of policy in expressing his willingness to meet de Klerk. 'It was a statement of principle, since the president is a man of negotiation and dialogue.' Accordingly, it could not be concluded necessarily, just because Kaunda was willing in principle to meet de Klerk, that any meeting had been planned or was about to go ahead.[32]

Outside the ministerial circle, a senior party official said that he would advise meeting de Klerk only after the elections and a scrutiny of how much he commanded the Nationalist vote and how much 'he can deliver'. But he added the general comment, 'you wouldn't believe the amount of traffic and coming-and-going between Lusaka and other African capitals in his [Kaunda's] attempt to have these nego-tiations lead somewhere'. The implication was that any meeting with de Klerk should be viewed as part of a process and not an aberration.[33] Two government officials with permanent secretary rank also expressed their views. One cautioned only 'conditional acceptance' of South African sincerity: 'We should keep a club in the other hand.'[34] The other was the only interviewee at any level, including those later contacted at the University of Zambia, who made the pertinent point of a global context: 'If the Americans and Soviets are serious about the de-escalation of global tension and, as part of that, the winding down of regional conflicts, then the South Africans have to be serious about negotiations.' But he wouldn't commit himself to whether or not the Americans and Soviets were indeed serious.[35]

At the University of Zambia, I could find no-one with whom to discuss seriously such issues. Conversation inevitably and speedily turned to accounts of poor pay, poor conditions, poor morale, and how difficult it increasingly became to resist offers of salubrious employment at the bantustan universities. There was, I concluded, no academic input to any policy discussions of whether and when to meet de Klerk.

The question of any input from any sector soon became a serious

[32] Author's interview with a further minister with former responsibilities for foreign affairs, Lusaka, August 1989.
[33] Author's interview with senior party official, Lusaka, August 1989.
[34] Author's interview with senior civil servant, August 1989.
[35] Author's interview with another senior civil servant, August 1989.

one. De Klerk's visit duly came, and surprised everyone I had talked to. The Minister of Foreign Affairs had been abroad. His predecessors would have counselled a meeting after de Klerk's elections had they been asked, but they weren't. Senior echelons of both the party and the civil service were not asked, and academic experts certainly weren't. I could extract no comment from the staff at State House, except that the President had been very busy but, some weeks later, I spoke to a former State House aide and asked him what course and what consultations, in his time, a presidential decision would have taken. He immediately divined my intentions and talked of the meeting with de Klerk. 'There is no minister who is not a junior minister before the president. [The Foreign Minister] Mwananshiku would have known nothing about it [plans to meet de Klerk]. That was the president acting alone.' When I pressed him on the question of Kaunda's consultations among his own ministers and advisers, he replied: 'It was de Klerk who was briefed by teams of advisers for weeks, on the hour, in preparation for that meeting. No one briefed KK.'[36]

The summit for which Kaunda had received no briefing had a stormy genesis. A change in South African leadership had seemed inevitable after President Botha had suffered a stroke in January 1989 and, in due course, F. W. de Klerk was named his heir-apparent, and was to become president after elections in September. In June 1989, Kaunda made what his minister called 'a statement of principle' and said he was 'quite happy to meet de Klerk and hear his views'.[37] It wasn't until the second week of August that the news was released that de Klerk and Kaunda would meet on the 28th of that month. The news was released by Kaunda and seemed almost calculated to throw the ruling National Party in South Africa into disarray. President Botha immediately made a terse and angry statement: 'I am not aware, in terms of the rules covering overseas journeys by ministers, of the discussions to be held on 28 August as announced by Dr Kaunda.'[38] He flatly contradicted a conciliatory statement by the Foreign Minister, Pik Botha, that the proposed summit was a continuation of discussions with Kaunda initiated by President Botha himself in 1982 and, in the opinion of commentators, 'for Mr de Klerk, events of the past few days

[36] Author's interview with former senior special assistant in State House to President Kaunda, October 1989.
[37] *Guardian* (London and Manchester), 14 June, 1989.
[38] *The Independent* (London), 12 August 1989.

represent the realisation of a deep dread: contradiction at a critical stage in the election campaign by an "irascible and unpredictable" President Botha.'[39] 'Unprecedented in 41 years of National party rule, the row has set the president and his successor-elect, F.W. de Klerk, at each other's throats little more than three weeks before a crucial general election . . . [whereas] the party would far prefer him [Botha] to hang on until after the September 6 election.'[40] De Klerk summoned the cabinet to him and extracted from all the ministers their loyalty. What was at stake were the party fortunes in an election predicted to be close. 'Mr de Klerk has had to invest considerable effort in portraying himself to the electorate as a strong and trustworthy leader.'[41] The decision to go to Lusaka had been part of that process of self-portrayal, designed to add a statesmanlike lustre to his other qualities. Now, de Klerk had no choice but to face down the president or find himself portrayed instead as weak and able to be dominated. In the event, the cabinet sided with him and, in a pique that he never sought to disguise, Botha resigned, still of the opinion 'that it is inopportune to meet with President Kaunda at this stage',[42] and the cabinet swore in de Klerk as acting-president. It was, thus, as head of government and state that de Klerk met Kaunda. The crisis had been precipitated by Kaunda's announcement before the South Africans had had time to deal with their own internal consultations and mollifications. Now, with the meeting just over a week before his elections, de Klerk had to look good in his summit with Kaunda.

Kaunda acted to smooth de Klerk's way. The press was leaked a story about the ANC having been ordered by Kaunda to quit Lusaka.[43] This was subsequently denied by the ANC, which, at the same time, ostentatiously stepped up its preparations for negotiations rather than military confrontation with Pretoria.[44] The principles for future conduct were being established, and a threat from the past was tentatively being withdrawn.

---

[39] Patrick Laurence, 'De Klerk Under Fire Over Kaunda Talks', *Guardian*, 12 August 1989.

[40] Peter Godwin, 'Botha Set to Plunge Party into Turmoil', *The Sunday Times* (London), 13 August 1989.

[41] John Carlin, 'Cabinet to Tell Botha to Shut Up', *The Independent*, 14 August 1989.

[42] Idem, 'Botha Resigns After Cabinet Showdown', *The Independent*, 15 August 1989.

[43] Richard Dowden, 'Kaunda Orders the ANC out of Zambia' *The Independent*, 19 August 1989.

[44] Andrew Meldrum, 'ANC Seeks African Backing for Talks Plan, *Guardian*, 21 August 1989.

De Klerk, however, anxious not to appear within the initiative of
the Zambian President, paid a surprise visit first to President Mobutu
of Zaïre on 24 August, and a joint communiqué was released which
sought to convey a positive mood on Angola.[45]

When, finally, de Klerk and Kaunda met on 28 August, everything
was calculated on both sides, down to the beauteous backdrop and
almost platitudinous soundbites. Held at Livingstone, the television
cameras were treated to panoramas of the Victoria Falls – against
which, surrounded by green trees, the two leaders, if not holding
hands, from time to time touched each other on the arms to point out
yet another cascade of water, yet another roller bird wheeling out over
a rainbow. Amidst the peacefulness of it all, the official versions of the
talks said that de Klerk had given Kaunda a 'positive vision' of the
future South Africa, in which it would 'break out of the cycle of
conflict and mistrust', in which dialogue would be the order of the
day. Kaunda made no criticism of apartheid. The release of Nelson
Mandela was said not to have been discussed, nor the question of
dialogue and negotiation specifically with the ANC.[46] Yet it is
inconceivable that, under the public face – which did indeed help de
Klerk appear statesmanlike and which did indeed enhance his electa-
bility – something more specific was not discussed. The ANC had
certainly been expecting Kaunda to convey its negotiating proposals to
de Klerk.[47] Kaunda would have given de Klerk at least a general
impression of the opinion of the other frontline leaders, which he
himself had received a fortnight ago. De Klerk would have spoken
about Angola and the mood of Mobutu in Zaïre. And, if the future of
South Africa was to be one of dialogue, it seems difficult to imagine
the name and release of Nelson Mandela not intruding into the
conversation. The independence of Namibia would also have been in
the discussion, since it represented part of the process of change in
the region and the breaking-out of the cycle of conflict. So the public
version of the talks should not be fully trusted. At the same time, the
discussion was certainly unstructured. There was no order paper or
agenda, no minute takers, no large staffs on either side. It was at least

[45] Kin-Kiey Mulumba, 'De Kerk and Mobutu "Positive" on Angola', *The Independent*,
26 August 1989.
[46] Phillip van Niekerk and David Beresford, 'Kaunda and De Klerk Strive for Peace',
Guardian, 29 August 1989.
[47] Shaun Johnson and Richard Dowden, 'ANC Taking Initiative on Talking to
Pretoria', *The Independent*, 11 August 1989.

in part a 'getting to know you' session and, as mentioned above, Kaunda's giving de Klerk such an easy ride in front of the cameras was a way of placing the South African President in his debt. Having created a crisis for de Klerk by the suddenness of his announcement that he would meet him, Kaunda now helped him win the election. The public version of the talks was, therefore, a campaign advertisement.

A Method of Work

If Kaunda had received no briefings from his ministers or party researchers, if he had not even informed them let alone consulted them about his meeting with de Klerk, how did he prepare himself? The stakes were quite high. De Klerk's visit could have been viewed in South Africa as having backfired if even minor discord had arisen. His election majority might have been reduced and, in the future, he might have had only a very slim mandate for both domestic and regional reform. There could have been less of a president for Kaunda to talk to if these first talks went wrong. If no-one briefed Kaunda, even about the type of man de Klerk was, it seems a monumental trust in instinct or intuition for Kaunda to have set about the meeting unprepared in anything except perhaps in the spiritual or psychological sense. Since he had no apparent helpers, except perhaps in State House, and since none of the normally responsible ministries prepared paperwork for him, there is nothing to extract from the record. There isn't a record of how he did it. What is available is the revealing comment I received from a former State House aide to Kaunda, but even this is a speculation – based, however, on a knowledge of Kaunda's previous working habits.

> State House advisers are, by and large, discriminating conduits of advice from ministries to the president.... The president, however, is willing to act alone if he feels the situation demands it, even if afterwards it all falls apart like a pack of cards.... And this is because KK is a political adventurer. He is a confrontationalist. He likes to precipitate a crisis. He works through crisis and trusts his instinct. If there is no crisis, he will precipitate one. He cannot work without crisis.[48]

---

[48] Author's interview with former senior special assistant in State House to President Kaunda, October 1989.

He works best when the stakes are highest – a crisis manager who cannot manage the mundane, someone who likes to work dangerously. De Klerk in a difficult position would have appealed to this Kaunda, not because it was gratifying to see a South African President under stress, but because Kaunda could work at his best. Such a view provides some sort of explanation for Kaunda's sudden policies in the 1973 rail dispute with Ian Smith, making a crisis out of a confrontation that could have been managed. It helps explain Kaunda's flair for the dramatic gesture, setting up situations in the hope that something can then be engineered from them. In footballing terms, he is the master of the long ball, hoping for mistakes from the opposing defence and scoring from the secondary play; the Wimbledon of southern Africa – not a Real Madrid, not even Spurs – doing without the cultured midfield players of advisers and ministers, of man-to-man markers who know exactly the capabilities of those they are marking, doing without a sweeper at the back to clean up any mess that slips through. Kaunda is the goal-keeper who takes the long kick and who then races up the field to be the lone striker.[49]

This sort of image of Kaunda is illuminating without necessarily being reliable. Some parallel at least is required to sustain the image. If Kaunda does not consult his own ministers, does he consult the other frontline presidents? Kaunda announced that he would meet de Klerk on 11 August, immediately after a frontline summit in Lusaka. He had not consulted de Klerk about the timing of his announcement, nor did he consult his fellow presidents about the wisdom of the meeting. I spoke to an official who had been present at the frontline summit. 'Right at the end of the agenda, under General Business, Kaunda simply announced he was going to meet de Klerk shortly in his capacity as President of Zambia. He did not say he would do this as Chairman of the frontline states.'[50] I received a slightly different version, not from an eye-witness, but from a senior western diplomat in Harare with long experience in political reporting and, in other southern African countries, with intelligence gathering. 'Mugabe

---

[49] Apologies to North American readers. Kaunda is a soccer fan, given to taking the ritual kick-off at the start of every season. He always kicks the ball long and hard and has yet to be seen passing it. Wimbledon is an English team that kicks the ball long, hard, and high. Real Madrid, the perennial Spanish champion, plays a cultured passing game, as does London's top team, Tottenham Hotspur. The next soccer World Cup is in the US, at which time the arcane imagery should be made clear.
[50] Author's interview with senior Zimbabwean Ministry of Foreign Affairs official, Harare, September 1989.

vetoed the idea that Kaunda could represent the frontline states in his meeting with de Klerk. Kaunda, therefore, met him only in his capacity as President of Zambia, not as Chairman of the frontline states.'[51] This version says that Kaunda did indeed raise the issue earlier in the agenda, but it was then that Mugabe, with support from the others, vetoed the idea. Undeterred, Kaunda raised the issue again under Any Other Business, and simply said that he would still meet de Klerk, but as President of Zambia. At neither instance did Kaunda seek advice and the meeting gave him none, except that he could not represent the frontline. There was little that could be done to stop Kaunda going ahead with the meeting as President of Zambia and, although there was a minor drawing in of breath, there was no dissent either. In a way, the presidents were themselves curious about de Klerk (although I found that the Zimbabweans seemed to know far more about him than the Zambians did) and, as a senior Commonwealth diplomat in Harare said to me, the frontline presidents 'were mindful that a new era could be opening, so they were prepared to give Kaunda his head. They would wait and see.'[52]

Once Kaunda had made up his mind to meet de Klerk, without advice from his own ministers, he was determined to do so and was not going to take 'no' as an answer from the other frontline presidents. Unadvised domestically, he was also unadvised regionally. His ministers, who weren't asked, would have preferred a meeting at a later date. His frontline colleagues, who were informed but not asked or consulted, would have preferred no meeting but would not stand in the way of a strictly bilateral piece of diplomacy. That it was all, without any major breakthroughs being announced, quite successful leads to some observations about Kaunda's method. He is at his best in two types of situation – either tightly scripted and briefed, as in the Commonwealth initiatives under Ramphal discussed earlier; or unscripted and not briefed at all, in an unstructured, agenda-free face-to-face, confident of his intuition and his charisma at close quarters, confident in short of his technique. This is very like the unstructured problem-solving workshops advocated by some scholars of mediation. This does not mean that Kaunda works out of an unstructured process, however. He has always been committed to

---

[51] Author's interview with western ambassador, Harare, September 1989.
[52] Author's interview with Commonwealth High Commissioner, Harare, September 1989.

negotiation and dialogue. Within this process there have been, from time to time, sudden instinctual decisions that have alarmed others. I deal with the Zimbabwean discomfiture over Kaunda's mediation in the next chapter. Here, it might be instructive to recapitulate the twelve points I made earlier on the reality of Kaunda's mediation, in the light of the case study on de Klerk.

1. Kaunda, although a party to the conflict in southern Africa, met with de Klerk in the guise of a mediator, having first caused de Klerk considerable embarrassment by the announcement of their meeting but, during the meeting itself, going out of his way to assist de Klerk in the projection of a statesmanlike image. In short, he was a protagonist of Zambia's position, creating first danger for his opposite number and then imposing a debt upon him. The entire episode was far from disinterested from Kaunda's point of view.

2. Nevertheless, Kaunda used supportive language outside the meeting, never publicly chastising de Klerk or seeking to extract promises, timetables, or even specific pledges from him – content with generalised statements of good intent.

3. However, Kaunda was having to meet de Klerk as President of Zambia, unable to represent the frontline states in any official capacity. Indeed, he had not consulted his frontline colleagues, at least one of whom, discussed in the next chapter, was concerned about Kaunda's decision. The episode added to a tension in particular between Lusaka and Harare.

4. Despite this, the meeting was widely regarded in the international media as a step forward in the reduction of regional tensions and as a possible step towards regional peace. It coincided with Kaunda's reputation for peaceableness and dialogue.

5. For their part, it was exactly this reputation that the South Africans sought to exploit. De Klerk would look statesmanlike and himself a conciliatory figure alongside another so regarded.

6. Whether the two presidents discussed matters of substance or not, they emerged from their meeting with general statements to do with positive visions and breaking out of a cycle of violence. The impression sought was of a morally acceptable South Africa in the near future. If there had been discussion and bargaining over matters of substance, and I tend to believe

there was, then it was shrouded by this 'moral cloak'. What had been established, however, was that Kaunda and de Klerk were capable of talking to each other. It was a precedent for a future meeting and, indeed, the South African Department of Foreign Affairs later toyed publicly with the idea that Kaunda should act as a supportive mediator or facilitator in talks between de Klerk's government and the ANC. Kaunda thus staked out a position or relationship with Pretoria that none of the other frontline presidents achieved.

7. None of this is necessarily impressive in the eyes of the frontline presidents and, should detailed negotiations between the frontline and South Africa ever develop, then it would be most unlikely that Kaunda would be permitted to represent the frontline alone. Domestically, Kaunda's political stock is very low and a popular mood might be discerned that questions Kaunda's energy in international affairs when it might be better spent in solving problems at home.[53] Apart from his reputation and good offices based on that reputation, Kaunda may have nothing more to offer the South Africans.

8. Accordingly, the South Africans might well play Kaunda for whatever he is worth in terms of his image, then bypass him as soon as negotiations reach a particular stage. They might then wish to meet somebody with a hard bargaining edge to him, who can deliver the frontline, such as Mugabe. Until then, Kaunda is a useful resource because of his image and reputation and because (although his frontline colleagues do not find him so, nor his own ministers) of his predictability. He can be counted upon to stick at the theme of dialogue and thus be available whenever the South Africans feel the need to be seen talking.

9. Having said that, the South Africans cannot use him too cynically or abandon him too abruptly. Kaunda still operates sufficiently well in international circles outside the frontline to make life difficult for South Africa. In his meeting with

---

[53] It is politically impossible to conduct formal opinion surveys in Zambia. The author conducts an informal version by attempting to drink people under the table at a succession of Zambian bars. Usually unsuccessful, he might nevertheless sample the opinion of some 40 persons on the same topic in any one week. The notion that Kaunda spends too much time on international affairs was, in this context, a very common one.

de Klerk, it would have been against form if he had not alternated at least a low-key sermon on apocalypse with one on love. If de Klerk had indeed been briefed 'on the hour' about Kaunda, he would have been ready for that.

10. More likely, however, the time was spent in discussions on the future of South Africa and the future of the region. What sort of South Africa could the region live with? What sort of region would be suitable to both Lusaka and Pretoria?

11. The meeting was unstructured and agenda-free and both men got to know each other. It was a confidence-building meeting, creating positive perceptions of each other, and seeking to establish a mutuality of needs within the region.

12. Kaunda's public performance was, however, generalised enough to reassure the frontline that nothing had been given away.

Kaunda's mediation, in summary, has been a much more calculated affair than talk of love and war suggests. His mediation is a political act, seeking political gains and capable of political losses, not simply a humanistic urge. Having said that, there are highly spontaneous moments to it, particularly when he intuits that a situation could be exploited. Once the decision to exploit a situation is made, there appears to be no turning back and, as importantly, no consultation with those who could help him or raise difficulties. As a mediator he has a curiously existential isolation from all else around him. He is in this sense a peculiarity in southern Africa and this, as much as anything else, helps to explain the different perceptions of him and the different images that surround him. Kaunda is not easily a conformist. It helps to explain also the distrust of him, both by scholars and by his regional peers. There is, however, a last word on his behalf, as said to me by his former aide after he had explained Kaunda's method. 'KK is a brave man in a complex situation. When you write your book, address this problematic. It is hard to do what he has tried to do and, often, he has failed.'[54] Calculating and opportunistic, a politician in the guise of a mediator, but brave, yes. What Kaunda does takes courage. It also carries risk. Neither the political motivation, nor the courage, nor the risk appear well-founded to Zambia's neighbour and rival in the region, Zimbabwe.

[54] Author's interview with former special assistant in State House to President Kaunda, October 1989.

7

THE COMPARATIVE DIMENSION: KAUNDA AND MUGABE

When Kaunda met de Klerk the Harare press maintained a studious though not impolite scepticism about the value of it all. The editorial of a glossy new addition to Zimbabwe's output of political journals labelled de Klerk's visit as posturing and posing and that, while 'playing to the international tune of negotiations . . . it would be erroneous to believe that the Pretoria regime is anywhere near being ready for serious negotiations'.[1] Its feature article on the summit said that, as with his two other meetings with South African leaders, 'Kaunda had little to show for the affair', and later described one of Kaunda's comments as 'seemingly endorsing de Klerk's election campaign.[2]

Unlike the publishing scene in Zambia, books and periodicals thrive in Zimbabwe. Relative plenty has meant none of the shortages of equipment, paper, and ink that bedevil Zambia; and defiant courage in the face of the Smith regime has meant a pedigree for at least one journal which the current government cannot question, despite often searching criticism from it.[3] All of the independent press, however,

---

[1] 'Editorial: The Negotiations Shuffle', *Africa South*, No. 1, September/October 1989, p. 4.
[2] Govin Reddy, 'ANC Moves First, Waits for Pretoria', ibid., p. 6.
[3] *Moto*, the church-based journal. Others include the weekly *Financial Gazette*, the new *Africa South*, *Parade* – once a pictures and light entertainment magazine, but now including political articles – and *Southern African Political & Economic Monthly*, a combination of an academic journal and one concerned with current affairs. Publishing houses include the Mambo Press, Martin and Johnson's Zimbabwe Publishing House, and Mandaza's SAPES Trust. They are the most visible and active of many others.

together with the government-controlled papers, adopted a politely sceptical line on the meeting between Kaunda and de Klerk.

Again, unlike Zambia, there thrive in Zimbabwe independent research institutes; the university is quite actively engaged in research and publication; and there are a number of research inputs into the government machine. If the Zimbabwean president is to become as isolated from the thought of his citizens as his Zambian counterpart, then he will have to work harder at it. He has much more to ignore. I visited Harare one month after the meeting with de Klerk, and spent some time in discussion with scholars in a research institute, a 'think-tank' that was part of the President's Office. There, I encountered two approaches. The first, with studious politeness again, maintained that Kaunda was respected throughout the region as an elder states-man – but not for his attempts as a mediator and negotiator.[4] The second was reminiscent of the approach adopted by those who saw in Kaunda's work the image of a comprador. The question at the heart of it was, 'who pressurises Kaunda to negotiate, since it is not his cabinet and it is not the frontline states?' The information behind the question was certainly correct, since Kaunda had paid very little attention indeed to his cabinet and had been willing to adopt his own path outside the frontline; but the suggested answer was the vague reference to international capital as his inspirational force. When I sought a pragmatic reason for the frontline's caution over Kaunda, the reply was clear: 'If negotiations proceed, then for what should one negotiate, and what should one concede? These questions exercise the frontline whenever Kaunda negotiates.'[5] The frontline, it was argued, feared a concession too far. But, in addition to a *dependentista* view of Kaunda, and a more pragmatic distrust of his diplomacy, there was also a parochial consideration. 'Why don't you examine the history of Kaunda's relations with liberation groups? He always supported the wrong group. UNITA in Angola. ZAPU in Zimbabwe.'[6]

I decided to investigate further the distrust of Kaunda based on the fact that Zambia had supported Joshua Nkomo's ZAPU during the Zimbabwean war of liberation. Throughout the early 1980s, whenever I had visited Harare, I had been astounded by the hostility that ZANU

---

[4] Author's interview with research fellow in the Zimbabwe Institute of Development Studies, Harare, September 1989.
[5] Author's interview with research section head in the Zimbabwe Institute of Development Studies, Harare, September 1989.
[6] Ibid.

supporters had directed towards ZAPU. In 1982, during one of my visits, the first of the ZAPU arms caches was uncovered, leading to speculation that ZAPU had always been prepared to relaunch a war if the coalition government, in which it had played a part, did not fulfil its expectations. This was the start of the disintegration of relations between Mugabe and Nkomo, the prelude to the security crackdown in the Matabelelands, involving later the infamous Fifth Brigade,[7] and the arrests of several ZAPU officials during the 1985 election campaign.[8] In 1982, employing a favoured research technique of drinking in as many beerhalls as possible (in what are now called 'high-density' suburbs but which were, in the Smith days, called 'African townships'), the hostility I encountered towards ZAPU was matched only by the hostility towards Kaunda which emerged in scathing and dismissive tones whenever it was discovered that I lived in Zambia. Now, years later, I was meeting something like the same reactions in completely sober official circles.

Here, there was not so much evidence in what was said, but how. A tone of dismissiveness, of sarcasm, infiltrated many comments. Even so, officials took pains to mouth diplomatic words. A senior figure in the Ministry of Foreign Affairs said that, 'despite Zambia's having backed the wrong party, there had been a very quick adjustment' after independence. 'Kaunda was very much respected as an elder states-man', he said, and shrugged off any suggestion of a regional rivalry between Kaunda and Mugabe.[9] Another official from the same ministry said that, after the death of Samora Machel in 1986, Mugabe and Kaunda had no alternative but to become closer. Machel had been Mugabe's closest confidant and Mugabe had, after Machel's death, drawn Kaunda deeper into his confidence as the only possible replacement. He gave an illustration of recent consideration from

[7] North Korean-trained in a mixture of crude Tae Kwon Do (Korean martial art) and brutal anti-terrorist techniques centred around population control, the Fifth Brigade later wilted when sent to Mozambique in 1986 – as soon as a group it attacked fired back.

[8] I made a point of talking to several of these former inmates during my visit to Zimbabwe in June and July 1990, and, although their comments form part of a future book I am preparing on African dissidence and democracy, tentatively entitled *The Just Rebellion in Commonwealth Africa*, it should be noted here that, by 1990, there did seem to be a more genuine working relationship between former ZAPU and ZANU cadres than before. If there was some suggestion of national reconciliation, however, the ZANU antagonism towards Kaunda remained strong.

[9] Author's interview with senior Zimbabwean Ministry of Foreign Affairs official, Harare, September 1989.

Mugabe towards Kaunda. The Zimbabweans considered they had evidence of cross-border ivory poaching by Zambian officials but, when a Zimbabwean minister said so in public, Kaunda had become indignant. Mugabe immediately issued a 'no offence to Kaunda' notice to his cabinet, and the matter died.[10] It seemed an inappropriate illustration of true cooperation between the two leaders but, since officials did not raise any others, I took the matter of elephants to senior diplomatic personnel in Harare. One Commonwealth High Commissioner recalled the poaching issue as having given the Zimbabwean side 'considerably greater annoyance before Mugabe gave his "all quiet" notice'. He said that, despite some close cooperation between the Ministers of Foreign Affairs of both countries, 'at the highest level, between presidents, there was some friction'. On the meeting between Kaunda and de Klerk, he said that the Zimbabweans were wary 'in case Kaunda ever went too far and made too many concessions'.[11]

Another western ambassador was of the same opinion, but extended his comment beyond the two presidents. 'Mugabe and Kaunda definitely do not like each other and do not as a rule cooperate. This runs all the way down almost all political and economic relations between the two.'[12] Accordingly, I sought out the opinions of officials further down the line. A former aide to Kaunda had told me that there had indeed been 'tremendous misunderstanding' but 'now I feel Mugabe has exorcised that ghost of Kaunda supporting Nkomo, but those under him haven't'.[13] They certainly have not. Officials in the Office of the President, when questioned on the naming of a Harare street after Kaunda, and why it had been a dusty road by the railway station instead of a broad boulevard, repeated the justification that it helped to make up a grid, but could not restrain themselves from bursting into laughter as they did so. I mentioned to them that a senior UNIP official in Lusaka had suggested to me that, perhaps, 'in ten to fifteen years time, Zimbabwe might be in a position to challenge Zambia's regional leadership role'.[14] Their response was enigmatic

[10] Author's interview with further Zimbabwean Ministry of Foreign Affairs official, Harare, September 1989.

[11] Author's interview with Commonwealth High Commissioner, Harare, September 1989.

[12] Author's interview with western ambassador, Harare, September 1989.

[13] Author's interview with former senior special assistant in State House to President Kaunda, October 1989.

[14] Author's interview with senior UNIP official, Lusaka, August, 1989.

but dismissive. 'Zambians have had a complex about needing to be pre-eminent . . . it was an understandable complex.'[15]

If a word had to be found to describe the attitude of Zimbabwean officialdom towards Zambia, it would be patronising, and I do not think that the Zambians appreciate the low esteem in which they are held or, if they do, why. I tested the idea of no love lost between Kaunda and Mugabe in non-official circles. The consensus of foreign correspondents I talked to was, 'Mugabe can't stand Kaunda'.[16] It occurred to me, however, that Mugabe might not be able to stand a lot of people, and that his dislike of Kaunda was simply symptomatic of a more general sense of disdain. I quickly abandoned this line of enquiry, since it began rapidly to assume the style of a psychological portrait of Mugabe which could not be tested. Before abandonment, however, some interesting comments emerged. A witness to a meeting between Mugabe and Nyerere in Dar es Salaam in 1978 said that, 'before 1980, the Zambians simply hadn't understood Zimbabwean politics and were wrong to have favoured Nkomo so heavily'. The depth of antipathy from Mugabe towards Nkomo was witnessed by this person as Nyerere, meeting Nkomo and Mugabe separately, one after the other in his office, in an attempt to foster unity between the two factions, saw out Nkomo and ushered in Mugabe, offering him a seat as he did so. 'Mugabe refused to sit in that chair and said point-blank to Nyerere, 'if you think I will fight alongside that thing, that fat thing that just sat here – well, I will never do so!', and, you know, Nyerere was very, we were all very startled.'[17] There has been at least a consistency in Mugabe's disdain. It has been directed against those who sought to rival him or who did not support him.

In October 1989, Mugabe closed the University of Zimbabwe after student protests against what they saw as the unresponsiveness and corruption of his government. One particular pamphlet was said to have incensed him, saying that his government was no better than de Klerk's. Even so, the protests had been largely confined to the campus, had been loud but peaceful, and had continued a tradition of raucous complaint. The only other time the university had been closed was

[15] Author's interview with officials in the Office of the President, Harare, September 1989.
[16] Author's conversation with foreign correspondents visiting Associated Press, Harare, September 1989.
[17] Author's interview with former senior special assistant in State House to President Kaunda, October 1989.

when it was the University of Rhodesia and Ian Smith had expelled several students and staff for opposition to his regime. Many highly-placed individuals in the Zimbabwean Government were veterans of that first closure and reacted, in private, strongly against the second. It seemed a rerun of Smith's authoritarian action. And it set up several dinner-time conversations about the nature of Mugabe's style and psychology. As noted above, such comments cannot be anything other than opinion but, in September and October 1989, and June and July 1990, I heard many such opinions tending towards a view of Mugabe as himself isolated, proud, and needing to feel centre-stage in Zimbabwe – unchallenged – and, here some relevance to the present study, centre-stage also within the region.

A western ambassador gave me his opinion of how Mugabe works: 'Kaunda is a true pragmatist under the rhetoric. Mugabe is not. He has more than once been isolated within his own cabinet on the sanctions issue.' Yet, despite commitment to principle, 'Mugabe can be often strangely inactive. He did very little as Non-Aligned chairman in 1986–9.' What he does or does not do is done largely alone. 'Mugabe is not advised by his Ministry of Foreign Affairs. . . . Mugabe may, from time to time, get his advice from the Central Intelligence Organisation.'[18] This comment poses a novel comparison. Both Mugabe and Kaunda do not use their ministries of foreign affairs for advice but, of the two, Mugabe is the man of principle. Kaunda is the pragmatist. Officials in the Ministry of Foreign Affairs were, under-standably, more concerned to comment on the question of advice rather than principle. 'It might be true in current institutional terms that the CIO provides more information than the ministry but, at the highest level, the Minister of Foreign Affairs is considerably more influential than the minister in charge of security.'[19] This may well be true; yet, just as the Zambian Minister of Foreign Affairs, Luke Mwananshiku, was in Wellington, New Zealand, for talks on the Commonwealth Games, at the time of Kaunda's decision to meet with de Klerk, so also was his Zimbabwean counterpart, Nathan Shamu-yarira. The input to determine Zambabwe's response to this decision was, therefore, not one from the appropriate minister. 'Essentially, Mugabe's is an executive foreign policy formulation.'[20] Mugabe, like

[18] Author's interview with western ambassador, Harare, September 1989.
[19] Author's interview with Ministry of Foreign Affairs official, Harare, September 1989.
[20] Author's interview with western ambassador, Harare, September 1989.

Kaunda, formulates his own foreign policy. What does he want from it?

'There are two underlying causes for the distance between Kaunda and Mugabe. First, Zambia's having supported the wrong side in the liberation war and, second, because Kaunda occupies the role of regional elder statesman which Mugabe, with a real economy and a real military force, covets.'[21] 'Mugabe wants very much that sort of central role . . . mediation, negotiation.'[22] Whether this is what Mugabe really does want or not cannot be demonstrated. A considerably more private man than Kaunda, he has committed less of his beliefs and aspirations to paper. He may seek to practise mediation, but it cannot be said that he, like Kaunda, professes it – since he has not professed it. He has professed very little indeed, and an intellectual history of Mugabe's policy would be considerably more problematic than the present exercise. Yet, if there is no clarity about what he wants, there are some clear observations about the style in which he wishes to get it. Like Kaunda, Mugabe has been prepared to put himself under the discipline of Shridath Ramphal's Commonwealth initiatives. At the Lancaster House talks in 1979, Mugabe worked with Nkomo under Ramphal's strategic direction. In 1986, in the wake of the report of the Commonwealth Group of Eminent Persons, Mugabe worked with Kaunda under Ramphal's orchestration of pressures against Mrs Thatcher on the sanctions issue. Mugabe wants the frontline to work in a similar way. Whether or not he wishes to be the Ramphal of the frontline, he wants a clear strategy agreed upon and not deviated from. 'Mugabe is a consensus man and wants all frontline action agreed and rehearsed.' Kaunda will not accept that sort of discipline. 'Kaunda, however, is willing to act alone if he feels the situation demands it, even if afterwards it all falls apart like a pack of cards.'[23] There is a clash of styles here, and this was evident in the meeting of the frontline presidents in which Mugabe objected to Kaunda's meeting de Klerk as chairman of the frontline. Kaunda went ahead anyway, but as President of Zambia, trusting to his instinct and his cunning.

But a clash of styles does not mean that Kaunda is an impediment to the policy of the frontline. For what exactly is this policy? What has

---

[21] Ibid.
[22] Author's interview with former military adviser to Zimbabwe, October 1989.
[23] Author's interview with former senior special assistant in State House to President Kaunda, October 1989.

Kaunda breached? His was a departure from strategy, which was that the frontline should apply pressure and that the ANC should negotiate, but he did not compromise the ANC and may well have placed pressure on de Klerk. Essential policy remained intact. It is not a question of who formulates policy for the frontline, for the frontline's policy has always been loosely centred around a small number of central points and has always been fluid, accommodating Mozambique's signing of the Nkomati Accord, and the inability of frontline members to impose sanctions on South Africa despite their championing of the sanctions cause at international fora. However, even a question of who formulates strategy is an important one and, here, larger considerations are indeed involved that go beyond strategy and style and have something to do with power.

In 1975, it was possible to consider a bipolar region. Zimbabwe was not yet independent. Angola and Mozambique were just becoming so. Botswana was sufficiently tied to South Africa to be unable to exercise any true leverage on Pretoria. Tanzania was too far away. Zambia and South Africa were the obvious candidates to establish and sustain a *détente*. As the 1980s progressed, the possibility of such bipolarity declined. Zimbabwe grew in regional stature. Even so, neither Zambia nor Zimbabwe could guarantee the safety of the region from South African destabilisation. The Zimbabwean decision to send troops to Mozambique in 1986, however, staked a claim for Zimbabwean pre-eminence in the region on the basis that some degree of protection against South Africa was possible through Zimbabwean strength. By that time also, Zimbabwe was the region's most economically-diversified nation and its agricultural production had more than once helped to make up shortfalls in other parts of the frontline, such as Zambia. Harare rivalled Lusaka as a diplomatic centre and had hosted the Non-Aligned summit. Mugabe had projected well beyond the region an image of himself as capable and strong. By contrast, Zambia, Lusaka, and Kaunda seemed tired and tarnished. Economic woes were mounting and the Zambian President seemed to have little by way of new ideas in reserve. The first major food riots in Zambia occurred in 1986, and the Zambian attempt to live without the IMF seemed doomed to failure. Even with some residual Zambian strength, the southern African region could no longer be bipolar. There was at least a tripolar system at work, involving Pretoria, Harare, and Lusaka; and, in view of the South African commitment against Angola, and the MPLA and Cuban resistance to South African invasion, Luanda would also have to be included in the list of the region's politically and diplomatically significant capitals. The problem in all this is whether Kaunda recognised what multipolarity meant. For his insistence on talking alone, on sequestering together the Zambian and South African Presidents, suggested a mode of thinking that had not progressed beyond 1975. He did not ignore the frontline, was mindful of not creating too large a gap between it and Zambia, but behaved all the same as if Zambia meant something special within the grouping. Whether or not Mugabe as an individual had his own aspirations, self-centredness, or vanity, Zimbabwe should have been incensed at Zambia's behaviour.

There were, therefore, questions of personal style, group strategy, and regional multipolarity. Offence may have been given but, still, nothing was actually impeded. The image of Kaunda as impediment cannot be sustained, but the image of Kaunda as determined to go ahead with his own particular brand of mediation can be. But, here, another point is introduced; for it would be incorrect to view Kaunda as a politician seeking political advantages from negotiation on the one hand, and Mugabe as a self-centred and austere man ready to commit his armed forces to the region on the other. This might be an attractive distinction, but what if the images were reversed, and Mugabe became the man of mediation, and Kaunda the man of force?

Towards a Coercive Mediation

The Zimbabwean decision to send troops to Mozambique was a bold one. This was particularly so given Zimbabwe's military profile in 1986. The army, integrated after liberation, and with a high command largely drawn from guerilla ranks, had not since been tested. What experience the high command had was in irregular warfare, yet there would be more conventional demands in Mozambique, particularly in defending the Beira rail corridor. Many parts of the junior officer corps, non-commissioned officers, and rank and file had received British training after independence and, while this training was of a high calibre, given the limited extent of British investment in this aid project, it was both selective and brief.[24] Sabotage had destroyed the

---

[24] Over a period of years I met several of these British military trainers and advisers. Their task had been to make the Zimbabwean army a credible regular force – not to ensure it became a top-class fighting machine. There is a difference here.

Zimbabwean airforce one night in 1982, as it was lined up on the runway. South African agents spent the night, undetected, attaching explosives to each plane, and the airforce was destroyed at dawn. The airforce had never completed its recovery from this sabotage, so the Zimbabwean soldiers who entered Mozambique did so without air cover. In sending troops to Mozambique, Zimbabwe was making a direct challenge against RENAMO, the guerilla organisation which was destabilising the Mozambican Government, and was therefore indirectly challenging Pretoria, whose proxy RENAMO had been. The Zimbabwean move risked a more direct intervention from Pretoria itself. In the event, however, Pretoria assessed the cost of Zimbabwe's operation and settled down to watch the country economically bleed itself to death.[25]

The Zimbabweans were meant to guard the Beira rail corridor so that Zimbabwe, in the same quest as Zambia before it, might have access to the sea that did not run through South African territory. They soon found that the corridor could not be secured defensively and were drawn into attacking RENAMO positions. One such attack led to the capture of the 'Gorongosa Documents', RENAMO field diaries which described the extent of South African assistance to the RENAMO enterprise.[26] This had been despite the provisions of the 1984 Nkomati Accord, a mutual non-aggression pact which South Africa, or an extremely clever and powerful military faction in South Africa at least, was flouting. RENAMO destabilisation of Mozambique had been so severe that the soldiers of the FRELIMO Government had become spiritless. The Zimbabweans, with the railway in their minds, nevertheless found that they had entered a vacuum of resistance on the part of FRELIMO. RENAMO was dictating the military terms in that country.

In 1989, three years after the Zimbabwean entry into Mozambique, the Beira rail corridor had been largely secured, and the Zimbabwean force which had begun with some ten thousand men was now only three thousand strong.[27] However, RENAMO was still grouped around the Beira corridor, and around the two other shorter rail routes, and the guerillas could coordinate their operations nationally

---

[25] Michael Evans in Colin Stoneman (ed.), *Zimbabwe's Prospects*.

[26] These were made available to Al-Khaledi in Mozambique and are described in detail in Al-Khaledi, 'Coercive Diplomacy', Chapter 5.

[27] Estimates provided to the author in interviews with a Commonwealth High Commissioner, Harare, September 1989; and with a former military adviser to Zimbabwe, October 1989.

by means of a 'superb radio communications network'. There were then some twenty thousand RENAMO troops under arms, many under press-gang conscript. 'These conscripts are blooded as soon as possible, made to take part in some atrocity, so they can't easily go back again. They could as easily have been fighting for FRELIMO, who also press-gang porters.' As for the FRELIMO troops, 'they can't fight. They are simply terrible'.

Right now, the war is a series of ritualised contacts. RENAMO sends a FRELIMO garrison written notice of its imminent attack. FRELIMO withdraws; RENAMO attacks; RENAMO withdraws; FRELIMO reoccupies. RENAMO don't send written notices to the Zimbabweans. They won't withdraw. But this means that FRELIMO can't win.[28]

Other opinion in Harare considered FRELIMO lack-lustre in the extreme. 'They are cowardly, incompetent, lazy and badly-officered. The Zimbabweans don't even coordinate with FRELIMO forces. The Zimbabweans run their own show in Mozambique.'[29] But, if the Zimbabweans were better soldiers than both FRELIMO and RENAMO, there was a poignant postscript to it all.

Recently, a Zimbabwean force received one of the RENAMO warnings of attack and decided to hold its ground. RENAMO clearly thought it was a FRELIMO group it was attacking. The Zimbabweans held the attack, then countered. Then spent hours weeping over the boy soldiers they had killed. It's come to the slaughter of children now.[30]

The letters home had not been about victories. For the Zimbabweans, the risks of entering Mozambique had paid off. The letters were about the tragedy of Mozambique and were acknowledgement that, although a railway could be secured, the war could not be won. FRELIMO had lost the will to fight. RENAMO, in its press-ganging, sent children into the attack. I saw one of these letters. 'I feel disgusting', it said.

[28] Author's interview with former military adviser to Zimbabwe, October 1989.
[29] Author's interviews with western ambassador, Harare, September 1989; and former Zimbabwean senior army officer, Harare, October 1989.
[30] Author's interview with Ministry of Foreign Affairs official, Harare, October 1989.

162   KAUNDA AND SOUTHERN AFRICA

What entry into the Mozambican war did was to concentrate Zimbabwean minds on alternative ways forward. Even the left-wing Zimbabwean intelligentsia began advancing new critiques of the Mozambican parties. RENAMO had always been seen as a bandit organisation, one-dimensional proxy of Pretoria, concerned only with destabilisation and without its own political programme. Now, suggestions were made that RENAMO, after all, as with UNITA in Angola, did have a political platform and that its political thought and aspirations could not be ignored.[31] Western diplomats in Harare noted that 'Mugabe has sought to mediate in Mozambique', but so has Kenya (problematically, since allegations have been made that Kenya has provided base facilities for RENAMO)[32]. Mugabe has also sought to mediate in Angola, 'advising the MPLA that, as in the Zimbabwean experience in seeking to establish a one-party state, the future can only operate with an accommodation and incorporation, not just of individuals but of all UNITA. The detail of these mediatory initiatives has never been made public.'[33] But President Mobutu of Zaïre has also sought to mediate in Angola as, of course, has Kaunda. The problem of mediation in southern Africa is that everybody wants to be the mediator. Everybody seeks the prestige it might bring if their mediation is successful, and everybody has their national interests at least partially in mind when seeking to steer disputants towards particular forms of settlement. In the case of Mozambique, some felt that Mozambican President Chissano was the essential pivot. 'Chissano has been trying to persuade his senior ministers that FRELIMO cannot win. Thus, the current suit for peace. It's Chissano, not Mugabe, who is the man of the hour. Chissano is seeking mediators and using negotiation. There's great international sympathy for him. But Mugabe wants very much that sort of central role.'[34]

The asset that Zimbabwe has that other states in the region do not have is an economic and military base. It is the majority-ruled region's economic leader, and its military intervention in Mozambique was seen as daring and principled before it became also successful. Its military effort did not over-expose its economy. It did not bleed to death. If anyone sought to revive the idea of bipolarity in the region,

[31] E.g. Lloyd M. Sachikonye, 'UNITA and RENAMO: "Bandit" Social Movements?'
[32] Denied by the Kenyan Government. But see Karl Maier, 'Kenya Gives Backing to Mozambique Guerillas', *The Independent* (London), 28 August 1990.
[33] Author's interview with western ambassador, Harare, September 1989.
[34] Author's interview with former military adviser to Zimbabwe, October 1989.

then Zimbabwe would be the candidate to balance South Africa, not Zambia. In that sense, Mugabe might feel he deserves the central role, but this feeling is juxtaposed with a commitment to discipline and joint-rehearsal of strategy and initiatives on the part of the frontline. Having seen Kaunda move like an unguided missile, he would not wish to do the same. Yet, like Kaunda, he is tenacious, stubborn, and enjoys the feeling of centrality. Unlike Kaunda, there is more steel in his government apparatus – he is willing to deliver force – and, unlike Kaunda again, he is the region's man of principle. Kaunda has the reputation of principle, makes sudden intuitive decisions, but is at base comfortable with the requirements of political dealing and compromise. Mugabe says little, is disciplined rather than intuitive, but can be prised from the direct pursuit of his beliefs only by the unified might of his cabinet and politburo.[35] He would make a formidable negotiator and mediator, though not necessarily a successful one. He might seek to be a form of coercive mediator. Unlike Kaunda, who can only threaten general apocalypse, and none of that from his own resources, Mugabe can use his economic and military base in specific threats.

Having said that, it is not that Zambians have shied clear of any military action at all. When Zimbabwean troops first entered Mozambique, RENAMO press releases insisted that dead soldiers had been found with Zambian identity papers. This was denied in Lusaka but, since the late 1970s, Lusaka has been a capital which has been periodically given over to rumours of Zambian military action. During the war against Rhodesia, when Kaunda ordered no Zambian soldier to return fire against either Rhodesian aircraft or commandos without his own specific orders, rumours of mutinous resistance grew. One senior airforce officer was said to have armed his aircraft and to have flown off towards the border. There, he was intercepted by Rhodesian jets and, after making a show of surrender, was escorted to a military runway. He came in as if to land but, instead of doing so, flew the length of the runway dropping delayed-fuse bombs and smoke bombs as he went. The runway was destroyed and he escaped under cover of smoke and flew home. This story is either untrue or very much exaggerated for the simple reason that the officer's exploits are

---

[35] By his cabinet over the issue of applying sanctions against South Africa as Mugabe wished in 1987; by the politburo over the issue of the one-party state which Mugabe wished in 1990. The author's future work, see fn. 8, will contain some detailed accounts of these occasions.

technically impossible, given the nature of Zambian airframes and armaments, and the cover that is possible from smoke bombs. Nevertheless, it would seem that there was a limited defiance of the president's orders, even if the actions were glamorised in the recounting afterwards.

The three following stories, however, were told me personally in 1981–2 by individuals who insisted that they had participated in what they recounted, and each story came with technical details which would at least have required research to uncover. In the extreme west of Zambia, a corridor had long been used by South African columns as they cut across this part of Zambia to outflank SWAPO guerillas in Angola. That the area was militarily sensitive was confirmed to me by international aid agencies which had been denied access to the province concerned, despite rampant malnutrition amongst the population there.[36] A 'phoney war' was in the process of being conducted, with South African and Zambian patrols deliberately failing to find each other. In 1981, however, a Zambian camp of conscripted National Service youngsters had not been told of this agreement and, upon detecting a South African unit, attacked it with great ferocity. The South African military, hitherto disdainful of the Zambian army, was said to have professed slightly greater respect for the Zambia National Service in the wake of the incident. In the same year, Zambian special forces were said to have entered Namibia to assist a particular SWAPO operation. Here, the technical detail was to do with the sorts of amphetamine used by South African troops to maintain alertness and combat spirit. By contrast, the Zambians were issued with mustard which, when ingested undiluted and in quantity, causes both alertness and fury. I tried this afterwards and can report that bloodlust was indeed induced. The third story relates to the entry of Tanzanian forces and Ugandan partisans into Uganda in 1980, and the subsequent overthrow of Amin. I was told that Zambian soldiers were also present. In 1982, I retraced the Tanzanian invasion route town by town, and it accorded with the account I had been presented. There is no other evidence as such for these stories. All that can reasonably be extracted from them is some coincidence and a consistent belief among Zambians that, at times, Zambia is not the

[36] Author's interview with International Committee of the Red Cross official, Lusaka, June 1981. The ICRC subsequently left Lusaka in protest against this lack of access, since people were in its opinion clearly in need of relief, and relocated to Harare.

doggedly pacific country portrayed by its president. If, however, some of these operations did take place, then it would seem that the president must have known. Authorisation for actions such as the incursions into Namibia and Uganda could only have come from State House. Whatever its faults, the Zambian military does have a tight command structure. In fact, this is responsible for one of its greatest faults – the absence of initiative and improvisation. It has special units of high quality but, generally, it is an under-funded, under-equipped defence force which operates militarily from a textbook. Departures from the text are possible on the command of the president. I wish to return to this story below. At this point it is worth pointing out that there has been publicly acknowledged military action against RENAMO. Since Zambia and Mozambique share a border, RENAMO elements often cross into Zambia and, by the doctrine of hot pursuit, Zambian forces have crossed into Mozambique. This hot pursuit received official approval in 1988.

Zambia's policy of pursuing RENAMO bandits into Mozambique has been approved by that country's President, Joaquim Chissano. President Kaunda said that he had sought permission from his counterpart [Chissano] to cross the border in pursuit of bandits who had murdered, looted and destroyed Zambian property.[37]

Reports of further RENAMO activity in Zambia brought the following press comment in 1989: 'Zambian soldiers have often mounted cross-border raids after attacks by Mozambican bandits . . . scores of bandits have been reported killed in these operations.'[38] And a recent report in 1990 described how Zambian forces killed seven RENAMO members, close to a RENAMO camp within Zambia's Eastern Province. Others were wounded and captured, and local collaborators were arrested. The information of this operation came from the Zambian Minister of Defence.[39] If that were the extent of Zambian military involvement in the Mozambique conflict, it would appear both modest and reasonable. In 1989, however, during a visit to Zambia, I was approached by a delegation of military personnel and given the following extraordinary story.

[37] *Herald* (Harare), 2 May 1988.
[38] *Herald* (Harare), 27 September 1989.
[39] *Daily Mail* (Lusaka), 19 October 1990.

Zambian Military Action in Mozambique and Namibia

Theirs was a surprise visit, unsolicited, lasting two hours, and made for no discernible reason. The personnel involved had been long known to me, trusted by me, and had no reason to lie to me. Nor did they know the subject of my research; nor had I pressed any of my interviewees before them on military questions. Their account was developed logically if, by the end, emotionally, and it was sustained under questioning.

The information given seemed not to have been possessed by any of my other interviewees, friends, or usual contacts in Zambia; yet I could hardly believe that some account of the actions described would not have entered the rumour mills, but none had. Moreover, if this information had been known to the South Africans, and I could scarcely believe it would have escaped them, if true, then they would have had excuses to delay the independence of Namibia, and cause embarrassment to the frontline – unless they had made a conscious decision not to release and use it. Accordingly, I proposed to check the information with other sources, but thought it safest to attempt this outside security-conscious Zambia. But I thought also that the information, presented as an account from participants and survivors, deserved reporting.

1. Quite apart from instances of hot pursuit, Zambia has a military presence in Mozambique. (RENAMO has long claimed this.) This is primarily an intelligence gathering exercise conducted by groups of two, disguised as peasants, unarmed, and fluent in Portuguese. These operate in enemy zones.

2. Zambia has long been involved in training SWAPO forces in unarmed combat. (This is probably true, but the Zambians would not have been the exclusive trainers. East Europeans, particularly East Germans, were also involved and probably more prominently. Under a similar division of duties, Zambian personnel would also have trained ANC forces.)

(These two categories of information, elaborated as first-hand accounts, are credible. The second is probably true, and the story could have derived from common enough knowledge. The first is at least possible. The real difficulty comes with the third category of information which, again, claims to be a first-hand account.)

3. On the occasion of the SWAPO crossover into Namibia in April 1989, SWAPO forces were met by terrible South African fire, and a

great number of SWAPO soldiers died. (This has been widely viewed as a tactical blunder by the SWAPO high command, and some have suggested that the objective of crossing the border was to have a sign of strength in place, inside the country, as an electoral device for SWAPO. The presence of returned guerillas in assembly camps during the Zimbabwe independence elections in 1980 created a potent electoral image: the victors have returned for these elections. Some thought, therefore, that SWAPO had acted under advice from Mugabe. The crossover, however, may simply have been a SWAPO misunderstanding of the agreements negotiated among the US, South Africa, Angola, Cuba, and Britain. SWAPO was never invited to the ten formal sessions of negotiation, held in the second part of 1988, on the future of Namibia; was never a party to the agreements that emerged.[40] The fact that there was terrible slaughter of the SWAPO soldiers who crossed over has never been denied. The question has turned upon whether the South Africans used grossly excessive force, and on the tardiness of United Nations control of the situation. The SWAPO units concerned certainly did not seem to be in battle disposition, or to have any battle plans, although carrying light arms.)

3(a). However, accompanying the SWAPO troops in their crossover were different units drawn from different frontline countries. These units were not integrated. Each frontline unit kept to itself. All the frontline units, to disguise their identities, wore SWAPO uniforms. Each frontline unit ranged from 20 to 40 men. The Zambian unit comprised 38 men. (There is an immediate difficulty here, as these are unusual configurations.) The frontline units were to act as monitors of the crossover.

3(b). But they met the same fate as the SWAPO troops. Unprepared for South African attack, let alone the ferocity of the attack, tremendous casualties were incurred. Of the Zambian unit of 38, three survived to tell the tale, which they were telling to me. The bodies of those killed were not recoverable. The survivors spoke of funeral ceremonies in the Zambian countryside where empty coffins were buried. 'They were symbolic, but we buried no-one like that. Imagine the grief of not being able to bury someone properly.' (This, however, is a point against the story. Zambian funerals are immensely social occasions. How could word of how and why these soldiers died be repressed?)

---

[40] See Berridge, 'Diplomacy and the Angola/Namibia Accords'.

(The major implications of this account which, on the day, was augmented by detailed descriptions of fire fights with the South Africans, death and escape, are two-fold. Firstly, the SWAPO decision to enter Namibia was not a SWAPO blunder alone, nor an action simply upon Zimbabwean advice, but an action taken under much wider advice and with wide collaboration from the frontline. Secondly, it reveals a Zambian readiness to be militarily involved in certain regional actions, despite the pacific reputation and image. Because the story was told me with great sincerity, by men who seemed to be unburdening themselves of a terrible experience, my first reaction was to believe it. I was very moved by it.)

Checking the Story

I checked the story with sources in Zimbabwe. On the question of Zambians operating in Mozambique, one diplomat was sceptical, particularly in the light of reference to Zambian soldiers 'fluent in Portuguese'. He referred to the use of native Mozambican tongues and to the extensive use of Shona.[41] Zimbabwean sources, however, did not doubt the use of Portuguese as a pervasive language. 'Everybody speaks Portuguese. Everyone wants to be a polite Lisboner.'[42] 'Mozambicans have aspirations about the Portuguese language and culture. They were effectively deculturised by the Portuguese and their indigenous social systems have gone. But they don't make particularly good ersatz Portuguese either – yet they try to speak the language.'[43] Some caution is in order here. Mozambique may or may not have been 'deculturised', but there has certainly been resistance to deculturisation by the Portuguese in Angola, as David Birmingham's fascinating account of dance festivals and carnival shows.[44] Yet, even with indigenous cultural traditions, what is striking is 'the entrenched position of the Portuguese language. During the liberation struggle Portuguese had been one unifying factor which held the MPLA together. . . . After independence the political significance of the Portuguese language became even more crucial to Angola. . . . Language became a central feature of political rivalry, of ideological

[41] Author's interview with Commonwealth High Commissioner, Harare, September 1989.
[42] Author's interview with Ministry of Foreign Affairs official, September 1989.
[43] Author's interview with multinational consultancy officer, just returned from Mozambique, Harare, September 1989.
[44] David Birmingham, 'Carnival at Luanda', *Journal of African History*, Vol. 29, 1988.

confrontation, of regional factionalism, of rural discontent, of class confrontation, and of neo-colonial interference.'[45] Portuguese, in short, was the language of political debate, ideology, and confrontation. In Mozambique, whether with culture or not, Portuguese would occupy a similar position. It is the language of politics in Maputo, and the language used in captured RENAMO documents. In short, the idea of Zambian soldiers fluent in Portuguese is fitting with the image of Zambian operations in Mozambique.

Although some military experts were sceptical of any 'large-scale informal Zambian presence in Mozambique',[46] others did not discount the idea of 'small-scale Zambian intelligence gathering in Mozambique, but this would not be coordinated with Zimbabwean military dispositions and plans'.[47] So the idea of intelligence patrols of two men, trained in Portuguese, is at least a feasible one. Yet, the latter comment is telling: any Zambian presence is not coordinated with the much larger Zimbabwean effort and, in fact, 'there has never ever been any SADCC military coordination, not even Zambian and Zimbabwean coordination. I don't think SADCC could coordinate a military presence amongst the SWAPO troops without making mistakes and becoming visible.'[48] Nobody I spoke to in Zimbabwe, in diplomatic, government, or military circles, gave much credibility to the story of frontline units accompanying SWAPO into Namibia. 'It's extremely unlikely. If they had been, South Africa would have had a propaganda coup.'[49] 'We deny any Zimbabwean involvement absolutely.'[50] However, few were prepared to discount the possibility entirely. 'Strange things can happen in this region', was a common rejoinder. I wrote finally to a member of the seven-person Commonwealth Observer Group on Namibia, which visited Namibia to monitor preparations for the independence elections.[51]

---

[45] Idem, 'Angola Revisited', *Journal of Southern African Studies*, Vol. 15, No. 1, 1988, p. 43.
[46] Author's interview with former military adviser to Zimbabwe, October 1989.
[47] Author's interview with western ambassador, Harare, September 1989.
[48] Ibid.
[49] Author's interview with Commonwealth High Commissioner, Harare, September 1989.
[50] Author's interview with officials in the Office of the President, Harare, September 1989.
[51] For their report, see *Preparing for a Free Namibia: Elections, Transition and Independence – The Report of the Commonwealth Observer Group on Namibia*, London: Commonwealth Secretariat, 1989.

In regard to the SWAPO incursions into the Northern part of
Namibia on 1st April 1989, it would appear to me that your letter
is the first intimation that members of the SADCC countries
were involved in that and that they had sent their own army
personnel to join PLAN (SWAPO) fighters and dressed them
appropriately in SWAPO fighting fatigues. No such claims were
made during our visit to Namibia; even by the most ardent critics
of SWAPO. Indeed, had there been any suspicion of this, the
frontline observer group in Namibia would have lost its credibility
and South Africa would not have wasted time in seizing on such
an opportunity to condemn the frontliners and this would have
made world newsworthy condemnation by members of the International Community.[52]

In summary, I was unable to substantiate the story of frontline units
crossing into Namibia with SWAPO. The only supportive comments
came, in the end, from other Zambians living outside Zambia. Their
feeling was that it would have been most unusual for lies of this sort
to be told, particularly by people well known to me. This was in part a
cultural defence: Zambians don't lie. And it was perhaps to be
expected from persons living far from home and who had gotten used
to defending their point of origin. Even so, as they carefully indicated,
the story fits a long line of stories about Zambian military endeavours
– some of which I have recounted above – so that, at the least, within
Zambia, there exists an internal image of Kaunda as not purely a man
of peace and negotiation. Everything else about grains of truth in parts
of the story is speculation. Why then tell the story at all in the first
place?

The Construction of an Image

Firstly, it is worthwhile suggesting that internal images of Kaunda
exist, then counterposing them with the received images from his
biographers and critics.

Secondly, there is the matter of demonstrating how research works,
and what must be investigated before being accepted. Related to the
story above is Kaunda's relationship with Nujoma. Kaunda and

---

[52] Letter to the author from Dr Rodger M. A. Chongwe, member of the Commonwealth Observer Group on Namibia, 13 March 1990.

Zambia hosted SWAPO in Lusaka during its years of exile. If the
Zimbabweans were not the ones who advised SWAPO to cross into
Namibia in April 1989, then perhaps the Zambians did, and afterwards
sent Zambian units to accompany the crossover, making it a unilateral
Zambian exercise, not a SADCC or frontline one. All here is
speculation. Although some feel 'it was probably true' that Zimbabwe
had advised SWAPO to enter Namibia,[53] and that 'there have been
persistent reports that SWAPO's breach of the UN plan followed
unofficial advice from Zimbabwe, with an eye to influencing the
election',[54] these suggestions were staunchly denied in Harare itself.
A curious postscript to one such denial, however, was the suggestion
that SWAPO crossed the border on ANC advice in Lusaka.[55] There
is very little support for this, and the suggestion may simply have been
a gratuitous swipe at the ANC by Zimbabweans who supported the
PAC. General consensus seems to be that it was 'a typically silly
SWAPO mistake',[56] a feeling held not only in diplomatic circles but in
the press corps as well.[57] Yet, SWAPO's Nujoma and Kaunda were
reasonably close and, in this instance, Nujoma certainly demonstrated
how a bad decision can be reached without proper research or wide
enough soundings, and without a prepared fallback position – not
unlike Kaunda on the question of rail links in 1973. But this hardly
provides evidence for any Zambian involvement in the SWAPO
decision. All there is here are the Lusaka rumours and, given their
lack of consistency or even real interest in this issue, it would be best
to declare the case unproven.

   Thirdly, and more profitably, is the entire question of how images
are constructed. Present enough circumstantial evidence long enough,
provide a consistent interpretation of it throughout, and eventually it
will attract believers. The desire to believe something good, or bad,
about a person can know no bounds. The glowing notices Mugabe
received in the early 1980s reflected a desire to give glowing notices,
to believe that a victorious man was also good; and was a rerun of the

---

[53] Author's interview with Commonwealth High Commissioner, Harare, September
   1989.
[54] Roger Hearing, 'Frontline States Dangle Summit Carrot', *The Observer* (London),
   23 April 1989.
[55] Author's interview with officials in the Office of the President, Harare, September
   1989.
[56] Author's interview with western ambassador, Harare, September 1989.
[57] E.g. John Carlin, 'Responsibility for Namibia Violence Placed on Nujoma', *The
   Independent* (London), 6 April 1989.

desire to give glowing notices to Kaunda in the late 1960s and early 1970s, to believe that an embattled man was good – to have it both ways in Kaunda's case: that he was embattled because he was good, and that he was good because he was embattled. The evidence had a circularity to it which knocked all the rough corners and edges off the image of Kaunda that emerged. Conversely, to believe he is bad requires very little more in the way of effort and imagination. To take a middle path, however, and to suggest that he is an intuitive politician, of good intentions but able to compromise, a man of genuine contradictions but also opportunistic, sentimental, and frequently out of his depth, is much harder. It raises the question among his supporters and opponents: is this a book for Kaunda or against him? Thus far, it is neither; but, thus far again, it is open to the reception of unorthodox, even extraordinary, images of Kaunda. The point here is that to have a fixed image of him is to leave oneself open to surprise. All images should be investigated.

To compare him to Mugabe is, therefore, a difficult exercise, since Mugabe's image needs also to be investigated. The possibility is that neither man is quite what he seems, and this possibility has been the subject of this chapter. One thing that has emerged, however, is that Mugabe does not like Kaunda, and this has a little to do with Mugabe's close-range perception of him and consequent ability to distinguish image and reality. A very great part of that image has become tired and unconvincing, yet Kaunda persists with it. Perhaps there is no choice now, as the final chapter to this book suggests, but the magic he worked with earlier generations of, sometimes, otherwise quite worldly figures is not being repeated. I recently met a senior member of the Commonwealth Secretariat, recruited only after Kaunda's contribution to the sanctions debate when it was at its height in 1986. He had come from a diplomatic background entirely unconcerned with Africa, and had read nothing on Kaunda. His reaction after their first meeting, volunteered and unsolicited by me, was 'humbug. That man is nothing but moral claptrap and humbug.' This, I feel, is untrue, and it would be a pity for Kaunda's political epitaph to reflect only the shredding of a tired image, to say that it was all posturing and posing; to reflect the dismissiveness of him found in Harare official circles. What would be a judgement based on reality?

8
MORALITY, POWER AND THE TWISTING PATH

By any standards Kenneth Kaunda has had a remarkable career. He came to Britain in 1957 as a naïve young man, but impressed many in the Labour Party with his dignity and idealism. He made lifelong friends and supporters. He became the leader of Zambia and, despite rebellion to the south and white minority rule in Rhodesia, Mozambique, Angola, and South Africa, published the most hopeful of philosophies. He emerged as a leader of the southern African states and as a spokesman for the continent. He has played a major role in the movement towards liberation, and has been an idiosyncratic thorn in the sides of successive British Prime Ministers. He has been a major actor in the Commonwealth. Despite a poor education, he has authored many books and had academic honours piled upon him from universities in North America, Europe, Asia, and Africa. But, throughout his career, he has attracted controversy; many judgements of him are harsh; very distinct and differing images of him have grown; and, as the last decade of the twentieth century gets under way, his leadership and that of the UNIP are under heavy challenge. The pages are turning for Kaunda. The second part of this chapter describes the events that have placed his future in jeopardy. This first part seeks to assess his past.

The arguments of this book have sought to construct a real Kaunda, rather than an image, and the chapters have covered the following ground. Firstly, Kaunda acts alone in Zambian foreign policy formulation. In theoretical terms, he personifies Allison's Rational Actor Model – he narrows the model to himself. He reduces the state to what he says it is and what he says it believes in, and what he says it wants to do. Secondly, in order to give an intellectual framework to this intense narrowing, he has advanced a personal philosophy as the state philosophy, and has argued that it derives from the national culture. This last point, however, is untrue and, as a philosophy, humanism is trivial – although it should be said that its ambition to establish new norms of behaviour was very great indeed. Thirdly, the personalisation of policy and thought was meant to provide Kaunda with some means of facing South Africa's regional policy, and to create for him some reservoir of moral strength. South African policy, however, in both its guises as *cordon sanitaire* and Total Strategy, but particularly the latter, was ruthless, coercive, and bent on regional domination. Through negotiation, Kaunda might have been able to lessen some of the ruthlessness and coercion, but would have left unchanged the essential fact of domination – whereas many who believed in armed struggle thought that the domination itself was the issue, not interim mercies. Fourthly, in putting forward his foreign policy, Kaunda was sometimes impetuous and self-damaging, as in the case of rail links in 1973. He was sometimes naïve about the underlying agenda of South African policy, as in the South African thrust towards a series of treaties and accords from 1980–4. Yet, he was also sometimes genuinely instrumental in initiatives against South Africa, particularly when these were scripted and coordinated in a Commonwealth framework. Fifthly, because of his lack of consistency, he has attracted a number of differing images of himself and his work. The hagiographic image has lost much of its early resonance, but the dominant comprador image contains the basic flaw indicated by André Gunder Frank himself; third world nations have no alternative but to cooperate with the international system that exists; they cannot escape dependency. The image Kaunda has of himself seems to be that he is a man engaged in a volitional act; that, if he could sustain wishing as if wishing were an act of will, then he could will southern Africa towards a new dawn. Simultaneously, will and wish are made on the basis of constructing an image of Zambia as injured party. This is also the party of God. It is injured and suffers, and Kaunda represents this suffering. This is, to be harsh, often little more than daydreaming and theatre – a tawdry and confused metaphysic. Sixthly, however, he is still capable from time to time of quite successful political calculation. His mediation style is based on such calculation and he himself is best motivated towards mediation and negotiation if there is a crisis afoot – even if he has to create that crisis himself. Seventhly, because he indulges himself in creating crisis, because he is given to sudden intuitive gestures, the frontline can be wary of his actions. He is simply disliked by Mugabe. Nevertheless, it is possible to see more similarities between Kaunda and Mugabe than first meet the eye. Mugabe is also interested in mediation and has the means to issue specific threats in a directive form of mediation, including military threats. There have been many rumours in Zambia, over a number of years, that Kaunda also has not been averse to military actions – although these have not been sustained, prolonged, or even very successful manoeuvres. There is at least an internal image of Kaunda as not always the man of peace.

In short, Kaunda is a man of contradictions. These are certainly rich. They cohabit sufficiently within him to make hazardous any attempt to untangle or reconcile them. There is one observation, however, that is immediately possible. Once Kaunda has learnt one way of doing things, he is not likely to change. Thus, there is a curiously antique quality to many of his actions. Once he had learnt, by 1971, a way of dealing with British Prime Ministers, he kept dealing with them in this way. Heath, Wilson, and Thatcher, if ever they lingered over Kaunda in their memoirs, would have exactly the same complaints of him. Once he had achieved a summit with a South African leader in 1975, he saw the summit process as the way ahead, and has repeated it twice. All his summits have attracted criticism. His view of them, however, tends to ignore present day realities. In 1975, Kaunda could plausibly speak for southern Africa. In 1989, almost one and a half decades later, the political map of southern Africa had changed. The possibility of a *détente* between Zambia and South Africa stabilising the region ignores a decade of South Africa doing exactly the opposite – destabilising the region – and ignores also the emergence of a multipolar region, in particular the strength of Zimbabwe. But Kaunda still acts as though he and Zambia have the regional primacy of old. The language of his foreign policy has not changed. It is still apocalypse on the one hand and love on the other. And this means that some aspects of his mediation style have not changed. The preliminary exchanges at least between him and a South African leader must include this combination of sermon and transparent hard man/soft man, stick and carrot approach. The most comprehensive attempt to give shape to Kaunda, to differentiate his contradictions, and to annotate his style, may be this book – but it is more likely to have been the briefing file de Klerk received in preparing himself to meet Kaunda. The South Africans have researched the man. It is not so much that he collaborates with them, but that most aspects of him are visible to them.

Even so, he is capable of surprising them, and may consciously delight in doing so. The timing of his announcement that he would meet de Klerk prompted a constitutional crisis in Pretoria and a final showdown between Botha and the National Party Cabinet. He is capable also of some fundamental differentiations. He will pursue RENAMO intruders into Zambia, but not UNITA ones. This may well be because he remains sympathetic to UNITA, but it also derives from a sense of proportion. Taking on UNITA is a different proposition from taking on RENAMO.

That he is sometimes calculating, and sometimes intuitive, means that although most aspects of him are visible to the South Africans, the combination of those aspects may change from situation to situation, and what that combination may be is not predictable. To an extent, consciously or unconsciously, Kaunda picks and chooses from among his images. That the South Africans choose to deal with him is not because Kaunda can any longer deliver the frontline, but that he is an entry-point for them to international respectability. They calculate too. The basis of this calculation is that, to a remarkable degree, the hagiographic image of Kaunda retains some potency. To be seen talking to a man of peace and negotiation means credit by association: they also must be interested in peace and negotiation. For the South Africans, the risk in exploiting this image is that Kaunda's combination of images at any one moment in time may be unpredictable. For them, as for the frontline, he is an unguided missile, talking in the same consistent moral fables, but following a twisting path. Thus, although there is an antique quality to Kaunda's actions, the feeling of repetition of modes of behaviour he found either successful or comfortable some time ago, the outcome of that behaviour can still be surprising.

He is therefore neither consistently praise-worthy nor consistently blame-worthy but is extraordinary and enigmatic; neither always rational or irrational but extrarational – outside the bounds of normal rationality, rational to himself.

Kaunda has held power in Zambia since 1964 and faces multi-party elections in 1991. That will be 27 years. It is not simply his longevity that is remarkable, but the fact that, for most of it, he has presided over a one-party state in a presidency of very centralised powers. In gradually coming to view himself, the presidency, his philosophy, and the state as one, Kaunda invited comparison with de Gaulle and has certainly expressed his belief that, without him in his presidential place, there would be deluge. The remarkable thing is that he has held it all together for so long, with himself not deviating from his belief that he should be in the centre of power.

A Future Without Kaunda

In June 1990, there was an uprising in Lusaka.[1] It began at Munali, at a shop on a crossroads. Across the road is Munali Secondary School, where several of Kaunda's contemporaries were educated. Because so many of its graduates went on to positions of power it has been called the 'Eton of Zambia'. Behind the shop begins the sprawl of the University of Zambia. Customers buying maize meal at the shop were stoned by protesters who sought a boycott in reaction to its 120 per cent rise in price. The university students joined the protest and, from Munali, the riots spread to the neighbouring suburbs of Mutendere and Kalingalinga. The last of these suburbs is adjacent to the Mass Media Complex of radio and television studios. The three suburbs, the university, and the media complex, all to the east of Lusaka, became the centre of the uprising. To the north of the city, the suburb of George rose up and, slightly to the south, residents of Kanyama – a suburb regularly flooded by rains, and regularly pilfered of its relief monies – joined in. There are no suburbs west of Lusaka, the three long streets of the commercial centre run parallel to nothingness. From east, north, and south, citizens came towards Cairo Road in the commercial centre, and ransacked it end to end.

The government imposed a 24-hour curfew around Cairo Road, but the police regarded it merely as a dusk to dawn restriction. The breakdown in communications and command structure in the uniformed services became graphically clear in the incident at the media complex where, by official accounts, a deranged signals lieutenant from the city of Kabwe single-handedly took over the radio station and broadcast for hours to the nation that Kaunda had fallen. It is impossible, however, for one person to seize control of the radio station. It is part of a complex that is very large and is technically very sophisticated. One person could not have held the station, continued

---

[1] The following account, which differs from official accounts, is based on the testimony of several civilian and military eye-witnesses given to the author.

to broadcast, and technically kept himself on the air for any time at all. It is clear that a greater number of army personnel was involved and other soldiers cruised the streets of Mutendere and Kalingalinga, inviting the residents to rejoice at the fall of Kaunda, which they did. Witnesses reported to me that the firefight to retake the station left 19 dead, but these casualties have never been officially acknowledged, and the death toll in total was probably very much higher than the 23 admitted.

Unable to rely upon his own army, Kaunda sought help from his frontline neighbours. Here, despite distrust or wariness of Kaunda, they responded. Tanzanian soldiers ringed the University of Zambia campus, while the Zambian para-military rounded up the students and arrested their leaders – with customary para-military brutality. It was rumoured that Kenyan troops were also seen in the city. In a show of symbolic solidarity, Zimbabwean jets flew into Lusaka. This was to bolster the position of the Zambian Air Commander who was loyal to Kaunda. The Air Commander was promptly named Minister of Defence, but this meant that Kaunda was down to his last security reserves. Within the army, rumours of a large-scale coup plot spread rapidly. This time, the rumous said, it would be done right. Tanks would simply line up outside State House and blast their way in. Kaunda rapidly shuffled his generals and began talking of a referendum on the issue of a multi-party state, to be held on 17 October 1990. He had acted decisively but the pressure against him increased. He announced that the referendum would not be held but that multi-party elections would go ahead in October 1991. In conceding the principle of political pluralism, he caught his own UNIP by surprise, not having consulted it.

Kaunda made the announcement about multi-party elections on 24 September 1990, at the opening of the 25th UNIP National Council. It was an extraordinary speech, beginning with prayer, silence to mourn the passing of various UNIP luminaries, a note on the uprisings in eastern Europe, a defence of UNIP achievements and the value of humanism, and a reference to the Zambian uprising of June. Then he went on to deride the irresponsibility of the multi-party advocates: 'I believe too that as a developing nation we cannot afford the luxury of political debate for its own sake which will only delay development.' The introduction of such debate by the multi-partyists was 'not addressing itself to the core issue of the referendum', would only encourage 'divisions in the nation that can end up in bloodshed', and was seeking to win over 'the poorest of the poor in our society who have become the target group of the Multiparty Party advocates'.[2]

Let us make these people who are now hiding behind empty multi-party slogans, who are shielding behind false accusations of oppression by UNIP sit down and think what it is like to run a real political party. . . . Let us take them on comrades. Personally, I am more than ready to lead UNIP in an election against any party or parties in this country . . .

[The Central Committee decided to] recommend to you that we do not carry on with the referendum which was an excellent idea if everybody was prepared to behave in a civilised fashion but which has now been turned into an instrument for creating anarchy in the nation by some individuals and organisations not known for their democratic values, principles and practices.[3]

Kaunda therefore came out fighting, and sought to carry the fight to his opponents. The remainder of his speech was devoted to the revitalisation and democratisation of UNIP itself. Since then, however, UNIP has not itself behaved in the most civilised of manners. The largest daily, the *Times of Zambia*, has been told by Kaunda to 'project the policies of UNIP', and the pages of the paper are 'no longer for everybody'. Kaunda has banned all parastatal and government bodies from advertising in the independent, church-owned weekly, the *National Mirror*, which has supported the multi-party movement. He said that UNIP would publish 'terms of reference' to govern the media, including broadcasting.[4] In the city of Ndola, the Senior Governor announced that 'no one will live in a council house, ride on UBZ buses or enter the market without a UNIP card'. And UNIP officials instructed the Lusaka Governor 'to make it practically impossible for non-UNIP supporters to live in their areas'.[5] Kaunda also reshuffled his cabinet, sacking one minister outright and sending

---

[2] *Address by His Excellency the President Comrade Dr Kenneth David Kaunda at the Opening of the 25th National Council of the United National Independence Party at Mulungushi International Conference Centre, September 24–29 1990.* See Appendix 3.
[3] Ibid.
[4] *Times of Zambia*, 1 and 2 November 1990.
[5] See *Times of Zambia*, 4, 9, 11 November 1990. A court injunction was later gained against the Governor of Ndola.

two to the foreign service.[6] Harassment of multi-party figures began, with some emphasis on the union leader, Frederick Chiluba, who was charged with illegal assembly in October,[7] and removed from the board of a leading parastatal in November.[8] Although Kaunda had called for a new UNIP, 'totally eradicating the paternalism of the past',[9] and which had to 'develop a brand new approach to the electorate,[10] the Senior Governor of Ndola, continuing the theme of making life difficult for non-members of UNIP, reported above, said that it was 'time to revert to the old tactics'. If Kaunda spoke of divisiveness being engendered over a referendum on the multi-party issue, then the year-long countdown to actual multi-party elections seemed set to eclipse his own projections, with himself in the thick of things, in the centre of a crisis, laying about himself with swings and hooks.

The students responded with vitriolic satire that was peculiarly Zambian. Posters were pasted up depicting Kaunda with genitals growing from his head. Slightly more subtly, but its meaning not lost on passers-by, an immaculately scrubbed dog was tethered in Cairo Road.[11] But the true scale of protest against Kaunda was seen in the street demonstrations. In the small city of Kabwe, 40,000 marched for a multi-party state; and, if the television producers could ever think that Kabwe had the same resonance as Prague or Gdansk, then their crews would film something no less amazing, the dusty African streets thronged with the desire for pluralism and democracy. But Kaunda gave himself a long time, twelve months, in which to campaign. Many of the leaders of the multi-party movement have their own murky pasts. Condoned or forgiven by Kaunda before, details of their lives are now being dragged into the public eye. It will be a dirty campaign and the central issue has to be Kaunda and UNIP's rule. Kaunda's electoral image must be that he is better and wiser than his opponents. It cannot be that there is or will be a better and cleaner UNIP, since UNIP activists and militants are those being used to 'revert to the old tactics'.

What a Zambia without Kaunda might be is a depressing vision.

---

[6] *Times of Zambia*, 2 November 1990.
[7] *Daily Mail* (Lusaka), 18 October 1990.
[8] *Times of Zambia*, 2 November 1990.
[9] See his speech reproduced in Appendix 3.
[10] Ibid.
[11] That is, no matter how clean an image the president tries to present, he is still a dog.

Not because Kaunda could have been any better than his successors, but because the Zambian economy cannot easily recover. It is one thing to point out the misrule of UNIP, and the ossification of public administration under a one-party state; to point out Kaunda's own ineptitude at economic affairs; but it is another thing to suggest remedies. Decline may be halted. A bad economy might be handled more efficiently. But it is unlikely that the economy will improve. Politically, if Kaunda is defeated at the polls, then a new era of pluralism will have become enshrined. This will be a great shift in Zambia's constitutional history. There is nothing to suggest the multi-party movement has any tribal affiliation, so the justification of UNIP, that it alone could foster unity in the face of tribalism, is being proven false. Political pluralism will mean a political maturity within the electorate – that Zambia the state is also Zambia the nation. But political maturity does not feed the nation, does not by itself and immediately transform the agricultural sector; does not repay international debt; does not staff schools and equip clinics; does not even do something simple like ensure that the largest hospital in Lusaka has access to treated water – or any water at all. If Kaunda wins, it is hard to anticipate that there will not be a period of UNIP triumphalism, in which all the 'old tactics' are seen as vindicated and healthily entrenched. If Kaunda wins by rigging the poll, then the tanks will, one fine Lusaka morning, line up outside State House; and, if indeed Zambian soldiers accompanied the Tanzanian march into Uganda, they will have learnt from the Tanzanians how groups of six tanks, directing their fire at allocated corners of a building, can bring it down.[12] To ensure that victory by whichever side is accepted, Kaunda might do well to invite UN or Commonwealth observer groups to monitor the final months of campaigning, the days of polling, and the count. Essentially, however, Zambia cannot win. If Kaunda remains, political pluralism will not flower. If he goes, the economy cannot flower. Kaunda cannot really win either. If he stays in power, it is inconceivable that the Zambian people will ever unify around him again. If he loses power, he loses that centrality of action and thought which he has cherished. What Zambians will be voting for is not so

---

[12] Favourite Tanzanian tactic when confronted by one of Amin's sniper nests. Heavy-handed, wasteful of ammunition, but it wiped out the sniper nests that were meant to delay them, and Amin never had time to regroup. The author retraced the Tanzanian invasion route in 1982 and saw the ruination such a tactic left in its wake.

much the prospect of great economic improvement, but the possibility of political change made possible by political choice.

Southern Africa Without Kaunda

When Lusaka rose up in June 1990, and the army moved clumsily and ineptly towards a coup, neighbouring countries sent their own soldiers to bolster Kaunda's position. This has never been officially admitted, but eye-witnesses insist it was the case. Unlike the story of Zambian soldiers wearing SWAPO uniforms in Namibia, these soldiers retained their national uniforms, insignia and languages. Elements of the Zimbabwean airforce were reported among the foreign services involved. Why, if Mugabe dislikes Kaunda, did he come to his aid? Kaunda is unpredictable, but a coup in Zambia would have meant even greater unpredictability. Who would suddenly have emerged as the new leader? Would he have had any knowledge of foreign affairs? The answer to this second question is almost certainly no, since Kaunda had monopolised important foreign policy decisions and, as Chingambo found, even basic foreign policy information is rare. Would he have fitted well into the coterie of frontline presidents? For, even though Kaunda was the lone ranger of the group, his personality was known, accommodated and, in the chemistry of it all, he was probably good company. Some group loyalty would therefore have been involved. Of all these considerations, that of greater unpredictability was probably the most important. The last thing southern Africa needed was instability of its own creation. As change in South Africa began to appear possible, the frontline needed to remain intact, to devise hopefully a united strategy for greeting change. Kaunda could not be guaranteed to keep within this strategy, but he was at least a known quantity.

This was a reaction to the possibility of a coup and the sudden change of leadership. This would not necessarily be the case if change came by electoral campaign and victory. Over a twelve month period, the frontline will be able to assess the emergence of possible alternatives to Kaunda, and prepare itself for his possible replacement.

Mugabe might welcome a change in Zambian leadership under these conditions. The question facing the region is a simple one. If South Africa gains majority rule, who will bargain for the frontline? For South Africa owes the frontline a debt. Years of destabilisation cannot be wiped away in a ticker-tape parade for President Mandela, or whoever heads the first majority government. It is not just that the frontline assisted liberation, but that it paid a price to do so. Now, it will seek recompense; but a black South African President must also give recompense to all who have suffered in his own country. Even the resources of South Africa are finite. There might not be much left over for the frontline. Beneath the euphoria, there will be hard, calculating, and ruthless bargaining. The frontline might want then truly to rehearse its position. The free-wheeling, non-technocratic, broad-brush-stroke, no-details Kaunda might be a liability here. Because in the future he might be an impediment, the frontline might welcome Kaunda's replacement by someone slowly emerging in the visible Zambian electoral process. If Kaunda wishes, like Sadat in Jerusalem, to march in triumph through Pretoria, he should do so soon; and, indeed, might do so. De Klerk might want to help his election campaign, just as Kaunda helped with his own.

Mugabe of Zimbabwe

The 1990s should see completed what began in the 1980s. With the independence of Zimbabwe, a new focus was given to views of southern Africa. Zimbabwe replaced Zambia and Mugabe replaced Kaunda in the immediate judgements of many. Some embassies and international agencies relocated to Harare; many of those that remained in Lusaka were scaled down and became the poorer cousins of larger missions in Harare. Countries such as New Zealand, opening missions for the first time in southern Africa, opted to open them in Harare. It was not always that Zimbabwe seemed fresh or more important, but that Zambia seemed spent and, even in the early 1980s, untrustworthy with development assistance, and ruled with a stale hand.[13] Generally, however, the dynamic promise of Mugabe, variously seen as a man of reconciliation because of his election-night reassurances to the white community and subsequent non-racialist measures, as an intellectual because of his five university degrees – earned rather than honorific – and as an ascetic because he had acquired most of them while imprisoned, hence seen as uncorrupted and incorruptible, was attractive to many members of the international community. Even in 1990, seasoned diplomats in Harare, many of

---

[13] Author's interviews with New Zealand Foreign Affairs officials and the Special Assistant to the Prime Minister for Commonwealth and African Affairs, Lusaka, November 1984 and April 1985.

them with long lists of faults and dishonesties in the Zimbabwean Government, still viewed Mugabe as 'ascetic and so intense; there is almost a spiritual aura about him'.[14] Also, because of Zimbabwe's economic base, it was possible to view it as the region's powerhouse. Southern African drought in the early 1980s, with only Zimbabwe able to produce maize surpluses, and therefore able to rescue its neighbours, added to this image.

The rise in the regional economic importance of Zimbabwe did indeed coincide with the economic decline of Zambia. But the rise in the stature of Mugabe did not mean a dimunition of Kaunda's activity. This has been discussed in earlier chapters. Nor did it necessarily mean a dimunition of Kaunda's importance. What it did was to feature two statesmen in the region rather than one. Both were important, Kaunda for instance continuing to host both the ANC and SWAPO in Lusaka. There was tension between the two, and it did mean that Kaunda's domestic foundation was more fragile economically than Mugabe's. 'Mugabe could come to dominate the region in time just by force of economic movement. Or, he might dominate it because Kaunda is no longer there.'[15] As the 1980s have progressed, not only has Kaunda's economic foundation become more fragile, but his political foundation also. If Kaunda loses the 1991 election, Mugabe will lead southern Africa. The completion of a change in leadership will have taken somewhat longer than expected in 1980. The rush to make Harare a diplomatic capital was not a complete success. Mugabe took until 1986 to consolidate his domestic position. Only then did he move decisively in regional relations with the Zimbabwean entry into Mozambique. Until then, Kaunda remained very visible indeed.

But, if Kaunda's domestic foundation is slipping, Mugabe's is, though currently assured, somewhat problematic. The 26-member Zimbabwean Politburo decisively rejected Mugabe's plans for a one-party state in August 1990.[16] This followed earlier rejections on 29 June 1990, by the Central Committee of Mugabe's ZANU Party and, on 30 June, by the National Consultative Assembly – the joint Central Committees of both ZANU and Nkomo's ZAPU. Although the results of the June meetings were never made public,[17] it meant that Mugabe had only one last chance to secure approval for his plans before some

---

[14] Author's interview with western ambassador, Harare, September 1989.
[15] Ibid.
[16] *Guardian* (London and Manchester), 18 August 1990.
[17] The author learned of them through sources who were present at the meetings.

public announcement had to be made. When the Politburo outvoted him, his defeat within his own councils could no longer be hidden.

Although Mugabe won the 1990 Zimbabwean elections handsomely, the build-up to those elections included intense politicking within his own ZANU party, with some senior members on the verge of forming an electoral pact with Edgar Tekere's opposition ZUM (Zimbabwe Unity Movement), and having their disaffections mollified by senior appointments in the government and ZANU apparatus.[18] Moreover, after the elections were over, senior ZAPU officials privately refused to predict the longevity of Nkomo's current coalition with Mugabe and ZANU. They indicated strains within ZAPU itself, which could turn to fissures after Nkomo's death or retirement. And they related that the disaffection within ZANU, bought off just before the last elections, had not necessarily disappeared.[19] When questioned on the reasons for the Zimbabwean attachment to a multi-party system, these same officials gave three international reasons: 'There are the events of eastern Europe. Secondly, there is the influence of Julius Nyerere, who has come out against a future of one-party states.' This was indeed the case. On the day of the 29 June ZANU Central Committee meeting, Nyerere was reported as saying that parties should be judged by their efficiency and effectiveness. 'Now, how can we be led by a party that is not sure of itself. What it means is that the party is sick and it is not good for a country to be led by an ailing party. It should give a chance to other parties which can.'[20] The ZAPU officials reckoned that Nyerere's timing had not been accidental, but that he was sending out a regional message, that pluralism had to come not only to Tanzania but to the region; that Nyerere saw the importance of Zimbabwe for the future, so his message was timed primarily for Zimbabwe's benefit. 'Thirdly, after all this, we have the example of Kaunda – and Kaunda is under threat.'[21]

Even the Zimbabwean government-owned press had run lengthy features on the demerits of single-party states.[22] In them, the example

---

[18] Author's interviews with aides to those concerned, Harare, September and October 1989.
[19] Author's interviews with senior ZAPU officials, Harare, June 1990, and Bulawayo, July 1990.
[20] *Herald* (Harare), 29 June 1990.
[21] As fn. 19 above.
[22] Charles Samupindi, 'One Party System has Failed in Africa', *Herald* (Harare), 26 June 1990, and idem, 'The One-Party State and Some Economic Effects', *Herald*, 27 June 1990.

of Zambia was again raised. The message was that the single-party had failed Zambia.

Zimbabwe remains a multi-party state and the example of Zambia has played a small role in keeping it so. While it remains pluralistic, opposition to Mugabe remains possible outside ZANU. But opposition to him remains also within ZANU and within the ZANU/ZAPU coalition. He may speak for southern Africa, but he should not necessarily be viewed as another Kaunda. He may seek centrality, but he is not Zimbabwe. Kaunda, however, made a fair fist of fusing state and president together, and his foreign policy was the foreign policy of Zambia. Mugabe also tends towards the formulation of foreign policy alone but, for him, it is a business with the greater possibility of dissent.

* * *

Kenneth Kaunda has contributed to the history of southern Africa. It was at times a noble contribution. He always sought to make it seem moral. He was not always convincing. He is a greatly emotional man,[23] and he is not least emotionally moved by his own effort. When asked about the June 1990 riots, when his little old house in Chilenje suburb, maintained as a national monument, was despoiled by an angry mob, his eyes were 'glistening with tears and flickering with incomprehension at their ingratitude'.[24] Many have sought to explain Kaunda's behaviour by his emotionalism, but this is unsatisfactory precisely because it was, at least at times, calculated to give greatest effect. The man who carries a handkerchief ready in his hand because he knows he is going to cry is replaying an old and trusted trick. Once learnt, it has never been forgotten – or its continuing merit and effectiveness questioned.

As the multi-party movement swung into gear and Zambians defected from UNIP to it, Kaunda and his lieutenants would go down the list of names who had abandoned his ship. 'What did we ever do to this person that he should leave us now?' 'Perhaps he was insulted once when we refused him permission to . . .'[25] The trick Kaunda always knew, from the earliest days of his rule, was how to exchange items of value. That was how he balanced all the competing demands

[23] See Joshua Nkomo's testimony to this effect in Charlton, *The Last Colony in Africa*, p. 54.
[24] Andrew Rawnsley, 'African Prophet Who Could Lose Everything' *Guardian*, 12 September 1990.
[25] Author's conversation with an eye-witness at such a meeting.

within Zambia. He did this extremely well. Now, in his dark days, he recast his eyes over what value had been given and asked why nothing had come in return. In State House, the President of Zambia calculated his support, calculated those who had left. When asking why they had left, he did not mention principle. Finally, back to the wall, the twisting path to the retention of power reaches the boundary of the moral and the amoral.

9

A POSTSCRIPT:
THE END OF IT ALL*

Nothing in his life
Became him like the leaving it.

Unlike Shakespeare's Thane, Kaunda did not die. At the elections of
31 October 1991, however, he was comprehensively defeated. In his
televised concession speech at 10am on 2 November he was at great
pains to appear dignified, forceful and generous. He did not cry into
his handkerchief, spoke briefly and to the point, indulged himself in
his rhetorical habit of repeating sentences only mildly, made only one
statement that could be interpreted as sour grapes, and generally
appeared the statesman used to the swings and roundabouts of a
democratic culture. Only when he left the television studio and came
to his limousine did he betray his feelings. Personally detaching the
presidential pennant from his car, he wept as he handed it to his
driver, climbed in and moved away. It was in a sense a reprise of the
Kaunda of old, a Kaunda who had faded away since Zimbabwean
independence, becoming only the echo of what his early biographers
saw in him.

This image of departure will perhaps linger for some time. The rains
that had begun early in the season had cleared away for the elections.
People queued all over Zambia from 5am on the day of voting. Bright
sunshine accompanied the poll, and also Kaunda's drive away through
the dusty streets. He himself escorted the new President Chiluba on a

* The author thanks the University of Kent for a research grant that enabled him to
travel to Zambia to observe the elections.

tour of State House. In an extraordinarily peaceful poll and transfer of power it seemed like a series of scenes concocted for a film. The background to it all paints a different image. As earlier chapters in this book argue, Kaunda was forced into announcing elections. He gave himself and his party a year to reorganise and represent themselves anew; the franchise was restricted to those who already held it at the last election four years ago, thus depriving Zambians who had just come of age the right to vote, and thus seeming to deprive the MMD of its youthful support at the juncture where it would be most required; and the habits of free campaigning seemed hardly natural at first, with the opposition MMD party having to fight court battles for media space and to deny ownership of various media being transferred from Kaunda's Government to his UNIP party. As late as mid-October, Kaunda was promising to be 'merciless' with MMD leaders after a UNIP victory,[1] and UNIP officials often found it difficult to refrain from bullying tactics as they campaigned. Right up to the eve of the poll, picked up by western journalists who had decamped into Zambia after the Commonwealth summit in Harare (16–22 October), some UNIP officials indulged a flamboyant style: in Chipata, one red-shirted party boss, wearing a holstered pistol and introducing himself as the Saddam Hussein of Zambia, was accused of burning the houses of MMD supporters, and was certainly not noted for subtle canvassing.[2]

For Kaunda himself, the campaign was an ordeal mixed with more personal tribulations. His son, Kambarage, was tried on charges of murder and sentenced to death. Rumours abounded in Zambia that other members of his family might shortly be arraigned on murder charges. At the Commonwealth summit, Kaunda flew to Harare for the opening ceremony, then flew striaght back to Lusaka – the first time he had excused himself from the full duration of the summit. On Zimbabwean television, he looked pale and drawn, although it must be said that here, as in his concession speech, he tried to act in a statesmanlike manner, ensuring his photo was taken alongside Britain's John Major, and smiling determinedly for the 1,000 journalists present.[3]

The image of the peaceful transition of power is a true and

---

[1] *Times of Zambia* (Lusaka), 11 October 1991.
[2] *The Guardian* (London & Manchester), 29 October 1991.
[3] The author thanks the Nuffield Foundation for its research grant to attend the Commonwealth summit in Harare.

necessary one. The citizen-driven movements for democracy in eastern Europe are now being repeated in Africa. Zambia became the first African state in which a single-party government left office because of the ballot box. Zambia has become an example. Right up to the announcement of results, however – results that seemed painfully slow in coming at first – reports abounded of cheating and rigging. The newly-founded *Daily Express*, an MMD-supporting paper, had the headline 'Poll Scandal' on its November 1 front page, with accounts of fake ballot papers having been discovered.[4] *The Times of Zambia*, originally a pro-government and pro-UNIP paper, which had moved towards reasonable coverage of both major parties, had as its front page headline, 'Anomalies mar polling day', followed by stories of minor irregularities in different parts of the country.[5] With the nation on tenterhooks, there was a distinct tension in the air at the end of a year-long and, although largely peaceful, bitter campaign. By 11am on 1 November, however, sufficient results had been announced to indicate a landslide return for the MMD; and at 4pm that day, the Commonwealth Observer Group, monitoring the freeness and fairness of the elections, announced that 'the results . . . fully reflect the will of the Zambian people. The entire process has shown that there is a basis in Zambia for the development of multi-party democracy. There is no doubt that events on Election Day throughout the country will provide lessons for other countries which intend to change to a plural political system.'[6] But, by then, the tension had already disappeared. Drivers all over the cities of Zambia flashed the MMD hand signal from their windows, grinning and beating their car horns. There seemed little other celebration – simply a resigned feeling of relief: relief because they had ended it all, ended the Kaunda and UNIP era; resignation because the times ahead will be hard for them.

The final results were indeed a landslide, making the projections of Zambian political scientists, published in another new newspaper, the *Weekly Post*, seem cautious and modest.[7] But that itself has been a benefit of the new pluralism. Newspapers have sprung up; political debate is open; contrary to the report in an earlier chapter of this book, some modest new bookships have opened. These things are

---

[4] *Daily Express* (Lusaka), 1 November 1991.
[5] *Times of Zambia*, 1 November 1991.
[6] Commonwealth Observer Group press release of 1 November 1991.
[7] *Weekly Post* (Lusaka), Special edition 29–31 October 1991, pp 13 & 15.

important to the continuation of pluralism. Important to the reinvigo-ration of development will be the abolition of the UNIP commissar structure, which provided a parallel administration across the country to everything the government did. Often the UNIP expenditure on itself in any one region was greater than the funds government agencies had for development programmes. The programme of liberalism on which the MMD stood is meant to open Zambia to foreign investment and encourage private enterprise in an economic culture which has been centred on inefficient and unimaginative government control or monopoly.[8]

Whether foreign investors will come, or whether Zambian private business can properly function in a land of deteriorated infrastructure is another question.

More importantly, the MMD was only ever a consortium of disparate interests, united in an opposition to Kaunda. The new President Chiluba was a necessary but not popular choice for many MMD luminaries. The MMD is packed with disparate ambitions and may not be stable in office. Chiluba struggled to present his first Cabinet.[9] In the context of this book, however, what will be the foreign policy of the new government? What will be the image and reality of its behaviour in southern Africa?

In broad international terms there remains the problem of Zambian debt. In per capita terms, Zambia is the world's most indebted nation, and honeymoon writing-off or writing-down of bilateral debts will not fundamentally alter commercial bank debt or IMF debt. The IMF might itself extend some grace period to Zambia, but this cannot reduce the fact that the nation's future, and future development, have been mortgaged. Foreign policy will have an economic flavour.

In the region, the new government cannot play Kaunda's former role. The image of patron of liberation may linger but the era of liberation groups needing Zambian support ended two years before Kaunda's hold on power also ended, with agreement over Namibia. The residual conflicts in southern Africa, in Angola and Mozambique, are being mediated by non-African powers – the United States, Portugal, Italy and the Catholic church – with some Kenyan and Zimbabwean negotiating advice having been directed towards the Mozambican antagonists, but with neither country having been able

---

[8] For a summary of MMD policy, see *Times of Zambia*, 21 September 1991.
[9] *Guardian* (London & Manchester), 8 November 1991.

to act as principal brokers. The MMD hierarchy has not, for the most part, enjoyed close contact with the principal ANC negotiators and advisers to Nelson Mandela. President Chiluba has, himself, little international relations experience, although he has made a favourable impact in conferences of the international labour and trades union movement. The energies of the MMD will be devoted to domestic change and revitalisation. It will seek, as a principal regional policy, closer economic contacts with South Africa. This will mean that, unlike the attempt made by SADCC (the Southern African Development Coordination Conference), to strengthen horizontal or broadly-based transnational economic linkages in the region, Zambia will seek to strengthen the vertical linkage between itself and South Africa – bypassing the emphasis on developing linkages across what has been the frontline. The image of the frontline will itself fade from the region, and the change of government in Zambia – with the new Zambian preoccupations – will hasten this process.

Within the MMD, however, are several constitutional lawyers, some of whom are distinguished in the field of international human rights. Dr Rodger Chongwe was six years Chairperson of the Law Association of Zambia, was also President of the African Bar Association, and is President of the Commonwealth Lawyers Association, and is frequently consulted by organisations such as the International Commission of Jurists. The concerns of such individuals will continue to find a place in international fora and, because they are now government members, this suggests that the previous generalised concern of Kaunda on human rights issues will be replaced by a more detailed and sophisticated advocacy. In this field, as in its domestic programme, the MMD expects to bring to bear the weight of its technocratic wing.

Precisely because of an economically liberal and technocratic orientation, and its internal divisions, there is unlikely to be any MMD ideology or social philosophy. There will be no more Humanism, and no further appeals to a universalistic set of ideals. The new Zambia, the Third Republic, was accomplished by a citizen drive for pluralism. It is citizen-centred, not man-centred. It is concerned with constitutional rights, and not with the pastoral images of a cooperative kingdom. In Zambia, the hour has come for something beyond Kaunda. In southern Africa, and the mesh and mash of the foreign policies there, Kaunda and his images have slipped into history.

APPENDICES

Three appendices are included here. The first is a note on research which clarifies some of the author's methodology and some of the problems he faced. The second, the Lusaka Manifesto of 1969, was a milestone in both Zambian and African foreign policy formulation, and the third, Kenneth Kaunda's speech of September 1990, marked the Zambian President's move, under immense public pressure, away from the one-party state.

Appendix 1
A RESEARCH NOTE

A full research report and research diary has been lodged with the Economic and Social Science Research Council (R000 22 1089). Access to them is possible at the ESRC library, but only with the permission of the author. The following is excerpted from the report to the ESRC and comments on the difficulty of research in southern Africa.

This additional report is submitted, however, in the hope that it might be held and filed by the ESRC as a document of record. During my field research I received much interview material which is normally confidential and sensitive. Some of it is incriminating of my informants. I do not propose, therefore, to cite their names in any published work. This report, however, consists largely in a daily research diary and I wish to deposit this with the ESRC as evidence that my information was derived from identifiable and well-placed sources. It should not, as a safeguard, be consulted by the public at large without my permission.

As a final safeguard, even in this report I do not name the local military personnel who proffered detailed information on the disposition of military units drawn from SADCC countries during the April crossover of SWAPO troops into Namibia and their subsequent slaughter. I have not, however, been able to confirm this information, despite remarkably free conversations with diplomatic personnel who may be said to have an expert interest in military intelligence. If the information given me is true, then it is a major new finding, not just in the academic sense but in the context of actual international relations in southern Africa. Since I cannot confirm the information, its academic utility, even if true, is limited.

A Research Note

The problem outlined in the previous paragraph provides a distinction between political reportage and journalism on the one hand, and academic work on the other. Working on the principle derived from the natural sciences, that laboratory results should be capable of replication, I propose only to offer as research findings information that has been advanced from more than one source. My field research was successful insofar as most of my new information conformed to this condition.

The rules for interview were simple: no names would be cited in published work; discussion was to be informal, without any structured questionnaire; no notes or recordings were to be taken at the time of interview. These provided safeguards for my informants and, importantly, facilitated a relaxed atmosphere. The unspoken rule was that interviews would be prolonged and extended beyond normal professional bounds if there was an exchange of information, i.e. if the interviewee could also play interviewer and increase his own stock of information. The more I could provide to certain interviewees, the more they, in a sense of proper exchange, entrusted to me.

Many interviews were set up in the first place because of contacts and recommendations. A great number of my sources would have been inaccessible to me without either my prior association with them, as in Zambia, or the use of intermediaries, as in Zimbabwe. In the latter country, a certain High Commission was of great assistance in establishing an important initial contact. This help was offered because of consultancy work I had performed in the establishment of the High Commission. In short, I was able to call in a debt – a practice in which I engaged unabashedly on the Zambian leg of my research. From the first meeting facilitated by the High Commission I was handed on from one source to another until, by the end of my stay, when I was cross-checking information and exchanging notes with local academics, it was clear I had gained more information than those who resided and worked in Harare.

I discussed this situation with the Professor of Political Science at the University of Zimbabwe. He remarked that, in practice, local researchers operated at a disadvantage. They had no foreign pedigree to exploit and no 'new information' to exchange. This raises the question of the viability of sending research students to their own countries for field research, on the premise that they can find their way around in familiar circumstances. I had two research students under my supervision, visiting Zambia at the same time as myself. Although both were helpful to me (and themselves) in bibliographic searches, neither of them, as Zambians, enjoyed any satisfactory progress in arranging interviews with appropriately-placed persons in government. Instead, as research 'students', lowly-placed in the Zambian scheme of things, they were treated as nuisances. I developed, therefore, a significantly greater respect for the field efforts of research students, but the formula of sending people to conduct research in their own countries needs some review.

Appendix 2
LUSAKA MANIFESTO ON SOUTHERN AFRICA

Joint Statement by Thirteen Governments, Lusaka (April 1969)

The Manifesto is a joint statement agreed by representatives of Burundi, Central African Republic, Chad, Congo Republic, Congo (Kinshasa), Ethiopia, Kenya, Rwanda, Somalia, Sudan, Tanzania, Uganda, and Zambia, at the Conference of East and Central African States in April 1969.

1. When the purpose and the basis of States' International policies are misunderstood, there is introduced into the world a new and unnecessary disharmony. Disagreements, conflicts of interest, or different assessments of human priorities, already provoke an excess of tension in the world, and disastrously divide mankind at a time when united action is necessary to control modern technology and put it to the service of man. It is for this reason that, discovering widespread misapprehension of our attitudes and purposes in relation to Southern Africa, we, the leaders of East and Central African States meeting at Lusaka, April 16, 1969, have agreed to issue this Manifesto.

2. By this Manifesto we wish to make clear, beyond all shadow of doubt, our acceptance of the belief that all men are equal, and have equal rights to human dignity and respect, regardless of colour, race, religion, or sex. We believe that all men have the right and the duty to participate, as equal members of the society, in their own government. We do not accept that any individual or group has any right to govern any other group of sane adults, without their consent, and we affirm that only the people of a society, acting together as equals, can determine what is, for them, a good society and a good social, economic, or political organization.

3. On the basis of these beliefs we do not accept that any one group within a society has the right to rule any society without the continuing consent of all the citizens. We recognize that at any one time there will be, within every society, failures in the implementation of these ideals. We recognize that for the sake of order in human affairs, there may be transitional arrangements while a transformation from group inequalities to individual equality is being effected. But we affirm that without an acceptance of these ideals – without a commitment to these principles of human equality and self-determination – there can be no basis for peace and justice in the world.

4. None of us would claim that within our own States we have achieved that perfect social, economic and political organization which would ensure a reasonable standard of living for all our people and establish individual security against avoidable hardship or miscarriage of justice. On the contrary, we acknowledge that within our own States the struggle towards human brotherhood and unchallenged human dignity is only beginning. It is on the basis of our commitments to human equality and human dignity, not on the basis of achieved perfection, that we take our stand of hostility towards the colonialism and racial discrimination which is being practised in Southern Africa. It is on the basis of their commitment to these universal principles that we appeal to other members of the human race for support.

5. If the commitment to these principles existed among the States holding power in Southern Africa, any disagreement we might have about the rate of implementation, or about isolated acts of policy, would be matters affecting only our individual relationships with the States concerned. If these commitments existed, our States would not be justified in the expressed and active hostility towards the regimes of Southern Africa such as we have proclaimed and continue to propagate.

6. The truth is, however, that in Mozambique, Angola, Rhodesia, South-West Africa, and the Republic of South Africa, there is an open and continued denial of the principles of human equality and national self-determination. This is not a matter of failure in the implementation of accepted human principles. The effective administrations in all these territories are not struggling towards these difficult goals. They are fighting the principles; they are deliberately organizing their societies so as to try to destroy the hold of these principles in the minds of men. It is for this reason that we believe the rest of the world must be interested. For the principle of human equality, and all that

flows from it, is either universal or it does not exist. The dignity of all men is destroyed when the manhood of any human being is denied.

7. Our objectives in Southern Africa stem from our commitment to this principle of human equality. We are not hostile to the Administrations of these States because they are manned and controlled by white people. We are hostile to them because they are systems of minority control which exist as a result of, and in the pursuance of, doctrines of human inequality. What we are working for is the right of self-determination for the people of those territories. We are working for a rule in those countries which is based on the will of all the people, and an acceptance of the equality of every citizen.

8. Our stand towards southern Africa thus involves a rejection of racialism, not a reversal of the existing racial domination. We believe that all the peoples who have made their homes in the countries of Southern Africa are Africans, regardless of the colour of their skins; and we would oppose a racialist majority government which adopted a philosophy of deliberate and permanent discrimination between its citizens on grounds of racial origin. We are not talking racialism when we reject the colonialism and apartheid policies now operating in those areas; we are demanding an opportunity for all the people of these States, working together as equal individual citizens, to work out for themselves the institutions and the system of government under which they will, by general consent, live together and work together to build a harmonious society.

9. As an aftermath of the present policies it is likely that different groups within these societies will be self-conscious and fearful. The initial political and economic organizations may well take account of these fears, and this group self-consciousness. But how this is to be done must be a matter exclusively for the peoples of the country concerned, working together. No other nation will have a right to interfere in such affairs. All that the rest of the world has a right to demand is just what we are now asserting – that the arrangements within any State which wishes to be accepted into the community of nations must be based on an acceptance of the principles of human dignity and equality.

10. To talk of the liberation of Africa is thus to say two things. First, that the peoples in the territories still under colonial rule shall be free to determine for themselves their own institutions of self-government. Secondly, that the individuals in Southern Africa shall

be freed from an environment poisoned by the propaganda of racialism, and given an opportunity to be men – not white men, brown men, yellow men, or black men.

11. Thus the liberation of Africa for which we are struggling does not mean a reverse racialism. Nor is it an aspect of African Imperialism. As far as we are concerned the present boundaries of the States of Southern Africa are the boundaries of what will be free and independent African States. There is no question of our seeking or accepting any alterations to our own boundaries at the expense of these future free African nations.

12. On the objective of liberation as thus defined, we can neither surrender nor compromise. We have always preferred and we still prefer to achieve it without physical violence. We would prefer to negotiate rather than destroy, to talk rather than kill. We do not advocate violence, we advocate an end to the violence against human dignity which is now being perpetrated by the oppressors of Africa. If peaceful progress to emancipation were possible, or if changed circumstances were to make it possible in the future, we would urge our brothers in the resistance movements to use peaceful methods of struggle even at the cost of some compromise on the timing of change. But while peaceful progress is blocked by actions of those at present in power in the States of Southern Africa, we have no choice but to give to the peoples of those territories all the support of which we are capable in their struggle against their oppressors. This is why the signatory states participate in the movement for the liberation of Africa under the aegis of the Organization of African Unity. However, the obstacle to change is not the same in all the countries of Southern Africa, and it follows therefore, that the possibility of continuing the struggle through peaceful means varies from one country to another.

13. In *Mozambique* and *Angola*, and in so-called *Portuguese Guinea*, the basic problem is not racialism but a pretence that Portugal exists in Africa. Portugal is situated in Europe; the fact that it is a dictatorship is a matter for the Portuguese to settle. But no decree of the Portuguese dictator, nor legislation passed by any Parliament in Portugal, can make Africa part of Europe. The only thing which could convert a part of Africa into a constituent unit in a union which also includes a European State would be the freely expressed will of the people of that part of Africa. There is no such popular will in the Portuguese colonies. On the contrary, in the absence of any opportunity to negotiate a road to freedom, the peoples of all three territories

have taken up arms against the colonial power. They have done this despite the heavy odds against them, and despite the great suffering they know to be involved.

14. Portugal, as a European State, has naturally its own allies in the context of the ideological conflict between West and East. However, in our context, the effect of this is that Portugal is enabled to use her resources to pursue the most heinous war and degradation of man in Africa. The present Manifesto must, therefore, lay bare the fact that the inhuman commitment of Portugal in Africa and her ruthless subjugation of the people of Mozambique, Angola and so-called Portuguese Guinea, is not only irrelevant to the ideological conflict of power-politics, but is also diametrically opposed to the politics, the philosophies and the doctrines practised by her Allies in the conduct of their own affairs at home. The peoples of Mozambique, Angola, and Portuguese Guinea are not interested in Communism or Capitalism; they are interested in their freedom. They are demanding an acceptance of the principles of independence on the basis of majority rule, and for many years they called for discussions on this issue. Only when their demand for talks was continually ignored did they begin to fight. Even now, if Portugal should change her policy and accept the principle of self-determination, we would urge the Liberation Movements to desist from their armed struggle and co-operate in the mechanics of a peaceful transfer of power from Portugal to the peoples of the African territories.

15. The fact that many Portuguese citizens have immigrated to these African countries does not affect this issue. Future immigration policy will be a matter for the independent Governments when these are established. In the meantime we would urge the Liberation Movements to reiterate their statements that all those Portuguese people who have made their homes in Mozambique, Angola or Portuguese Guinea, and who are willing to give their future loyalty to those states, will be accepted as citizens. And an independent Mozambique, Angola, or Portuguese Guinea may choose to be as friendly with Portugal as Brazil is. That would be the free choice of a free people.

16. In Rhodesia the situation is different insofar as the metropolitan power has acknowledged the colonial status of the territory. Unfortunately, however, it has failed to take adequate measures to re-assert its authority against the minority which has seized power with the declared intention of maintaining white domination. The matter

cannot rest there. Rhodesia, like the rest of Africa, must be free, and its independence must be on the basis of majority rule. If the colonial power is unwilling or unable to effect such a transfer of power to the people, then the people themselves will have no alternative but to capture it as and when they can. And Africa has no alternative but to support them. The question which remains in Rhodesia is therefore whether Britain will re-assert her authority in Rhodesia and then negotiate the peaceful progress to majority rule before independence. Insofar as Britain is willing to make this second commitment, Africa will co-operate in her attempts to re-assert her authority. This is the method of progress which we would prefer; it could involve less suffering for all the people of Rhodesia, both black and white. But until there is some firm evidence that Britain accepts the principle of independence on the basis of majority rule and is prepared to take whatever steps are necessary to make it a reality, then Africa has no choice but to support the struggle for the people's freedom by whatever means are open.

17. Just as a settlement of the Rhodesian problem with a minimum of violence is a British responsibility, so a settlement in South West Africa with a minimum of violence is a United Nations responsibility. By every canon of international law, and by every precedent, South West Africa should by now have been a sovereign, independent State with a Government based on majority rule. South West Africa was a German colony until 1919, just as Tanganyika, Rwanda and Burundi, Togoland and Cameroon were German colonies. It was a matter of European politics that when the Mandatory System was established after Germany had been defeated, the administration of South West Africa was given to the white minority Government of South Africa, while the other ex-German colonies in Africa were put into the hands of the British, Belgian, or French Governments. After the Second World War every mandated territory except South West Africa was converted into a Trusteeship Territory and has subsequently gained independence. South Africa, on the other hand, has persistently refused to honour even the international obligation it accepted in 1919, and has increasingly applied to South West Africa the inhuman doctrines and organization of apartheid.

18. The United Nations General Assembly has ruled against this action and in 1966 terminated the Mandate under which South Africa had a legal basis for its occupation and domination of South West Africa. The General Assembly declared that the territory is now the

direct responsibility of the United Nations and set up an *ad hoc* Committee to recommend practical means by which South West Africa would be administered, and the people enabled to exercise self-determination and to achieve independence.

19. Nothing could be clearer than this decision – which no permanent member of the Security Council voted against. Yet, since that time no effective measures have been taken to enforce it. South West Africa remains in the clutches of the most ruthless minority government in Africa. Its people continue to be oppressed and those who advocate even peaceful progress to independence continue to be persecuted. The world has an obligation to use its strength to enforce the decision which all the countries co-operated in making. If they do this there is hope that the change can be effected without great violence. If they fail, then sooner or later, the people of South West Africa will take the law into their own hands. The people have been patient beyond belief, but one day their patience will be exhausted. Africa, at least, will then be unable to deny their call for help.

20. The Republic of South Africa is itself an independent sovereign State and a Member of the United Nations. It is more highly developed and richer than any other nation in Africa. On every legal basis its internal affairs are a matter exclusively for the people of South Africa. Yet the purpose of law is people and we assert that the actions of the South African Government are such that the rest of the world has a responsibility to take some action in defence of humanity.

21. There is one thing about South African oppression which distinguishes it from other oppressive régimes. The apartheid policy adopted by its Government, and supported to a greater or lesser extent by almost all its white citizens, is based on a rejection of man's humanity. A position of privileges or the experience of oppression in the South African society depends on the one thing which it is beyond the power of any man to change. It depends upon a man's colour, his parentage, and his ancestors. If you are black you cannot escape this categorisation; nor can you escape it if you are white. If you are a black millionaire and a brilliant political scientist, you are still subject to the pass laws, and still excluded from political activity. If you are white, even protests against the system and an attempt to reject segregation, will lead you only to the segregation and the comparative comfort of a white jail. Beliefs, abilities, and behaviour are all irrelevant to a man's status; everything depends upon race. Manhood is irrelevant. The whole system of government and society in South

Africa is based on the denial of human equality. And the system is maintained by a ruthless denial of the human rights of the majority of the population and thus, inevitably of all.

22. These things are known and are regularly condemned in the Councils of the United Nations and elsewhere. But it appears that to many countries international law takes precedence over humanity; therefore no action follows the words. Yet even if international law is held to exclude active assistance to the South African opponents of apartheid, it does not demand that the comfort and support of human and commercial intercourse should be given to a government which rejects the manhood of most of humanity. South Africa should be excluded from the United Nations Agencies, and even from the United Nations itself. It should be ostracized by the world community. It should be isolated from world trade patterns and left to be self-sufficient if it can. The South African Government cannot be allowed both to reject the very concept of mankind's unity, and to benefit by the strength given through friendly international relations. And certainly Africa cannot acquiesce in the maintenance of the present policies against people of African descent.

23. The signatories of this Manifesto assert that the validity of the principles of human equality and dignity extend to the Republic of South Africa just as they extend to the colonial territories of Southern Africa. Before a basis for peaceful development can be established in this continent, these principles must be acknowledged by every nation, and in every State there must be a deliberate attempt to implement them.

24. We re-affirm our commitment to these principles of human equality and human dignity, and to the doctrines of self-determination and non-racialism. We shall work for their extension within our own nations and throughout the continent of Africa.

Appendix 3
ADDRESS

by

His Excellency the President Comrade Dr Kenneth David Kaunda at the Opening of the 25th National Council of the United National Independence Party

at Mulungushi International Conference Centre
SEPTEMBER 24–29, 1990

In the name of The Almighty God, The Creator of all that is on Earth and in the Universe, and indeed, in the name of all the people of Zambia, I welcome you to this National Council Session. May He through His infinite Wisdom and Power, grant us the spirit of Love, Truth, Social Justice and Fair Play to face all our problems with rare wisdom, courage and determination!

Comrade Moderator,
Fellow Councillors,
Your Excellencies,
Comrades and Friends.

It is our time honoured custom to remember and give reverence to the fallen Members of this Council and other national leaders during the intervening period of our meeting. Since the 24th National Council met in this Hall in September, 1989, we have lost the following dear colleagues and comrades:

  (i) Comrade Axon Jasper Soko, former Member of the Central Committee;

(ii) Comrade Wilson Mofya Chakulya, former Member of the Central Committee and Cabinet Minister;

(iii) Comrade Unia Gospel Mwila, High Commissioner and former Cabinet Minister;

(iv) Comrade Sunday John Kazunga, Ambassador and former Special Assistant to the President;

(v) Comrade David Tonga, Member of Parliament;

(vi) Comrade Clifford Lubanza Ngalande, Member of Parliament;

(vii) Comrade Sandie Goma, former District Governer;

(viii) Comrade Paul L. Mukangwa, District Youth League Chairman, Mbala;

(ix) Comrade Musiya, District Youth League Chairman, Mpika;

May I now invite you all to be up-standing so that we all join together in observing a minute of silence in honour of these fallen fellow leaders!!

Comrade Moderator, 1990, like the red letter years of 1964 and 1973, will go down in the history of our Party and indeed the country as a significant turning point in the dynamic political process of our fast growing young nation. As a Party, we found it necessary in March this year to call a National Convention to examine for ourselves the political upsurge around the world, beginning in the Soviet Union and Eastern Europe, and how these might affect our beloved country.

That Convention was followed by a brief sitting of the National Council. And thereafter, at the end of May, we once again met in an Extraordinary Session of the National Council to conclude our discussion of the meaning of the political upsurge of the Gorbachev Revolution to us in Zambia where we have been building our political life on the basis of socialism leading to Humanism through the instrument of One Party participatory Democracy.

We concluded our discussion at the Fifth Extraordinary Session of the National Council by making two historic decisions of far-reaching consequences on the political process of our country. First, the National Council of the Party decided that there will be held a referendum in the nation for each person individually and for the people collectively to express themselves whether they want for Zambia the continuation of the One Party Participatory Democracy or the opening up of the nation's political process to a multi-party democracy.

Secondly and equally important, the National Council of the Party decided that in the national referendum, the Party, i.e. all its members, was to support the continuation of One Party Participatory Democracy as the nation's proven and stable political road that has made possible the rare political peace and national unity that have been the bulwark of our nation's resistance and resilience against and in the face of seemingly insurmountable forces of economic and political adversity inside the country and everywhere in our region and continent.

In making this second decision for the whole Party and for each and everyone of its members, the Party examined critically the track record of our nation's political life observing that this nation was not born as a One Party Participatory Democracy but that indeed it was born a multiparty democracy. This nation became a One Party Participatory Democracy to bring to an effective end endemic multiparty violence, destruction and death that threatened to undermine and to kill in the bud the very freedom and political independence that the people fought so hard to obtain. And since One Party Participatory Democracy replaced multiparty democracy, there has been peace despite great economic and liberation struggle difficulties the people of Zambia individually and collectively as a nation have faced inside the country and in the region of Southern Africa.

For the past seventeen years of One Party Participatory Democracy, Zambia has been an oasis of peace in the deserts of apartheid and oppression in Southern Africa.

What is more from this oasis of peace and stability Zambia has worked in a spectacular manner to help bring freedom to the rest of Southern Africa and to build a political stature in the African and world public affairs which is far in excess of its territorial, demographic, political and economic size. Today, politically Zambia counts as a giant country among nations.

While, therefore, the people of Zambia are to be free to choose multiparty democracy or One Party Participatory Democracy, the Party had to be true and sincere to the people on the basis of the Party and the people of Zambia's practical experience in the development and defence of the people's political process over the past 26 years of freedom and independence. For the Party not to have used this practical experience as the yardstick for its role in the referendum would have been an attempt to put up a performance of deception and infidelity calculated to cheat itself and the people on the Party's and the people of Zambia's own track record.

Before I come to make my contribution on some of the matters that this session of the National Council might consider, I want, Comrade

Moderator, to make some observations on the events that have taken place since the two basic decisions which we made at the National Council of last May. As leader for the time being of this Party and the elected President of this country, I have an unavoidable obligation to make these observations. I have to guide at every critical turn the political process of our nation. I have to show the way forward.

First, the referendum, for the Party, for the Party members, for non-Party members and for all those who want to agitate this question on either side, the referendum is a landmark in testing the national political maturity of our young country. This is a political maturity which makes it possible for a Zambian to stand by a Zambian and if need be to die for a Zambian because he and she is a fellow citizen without reference to political views held or not held. This nation will not hold together and survive the future without this spirit. It is a spirit of national love and identity. We need this foundation of an unquestioning loyalty and commitment first and foremost to ourselves as fellow countrymen and women in our own country and wherever we may be. Whatever political instruments which we create and use to organise ourselves should be to build and support this common active identity and commitment to ourselves.

This requirement for ourselves is an imperative political necessity regardless of the direction our national political process may take during any phase of our nation building. This automatic commitment will and must be there whether we continue to march as a nation, in action for itself, in the direction of One Party Participatory Democracy of whatever characteristics; or we march into the direction of multi-party democracy of whatever characteristics. In either case we must be proud of the Zambian man and woman. This is a basic commitment. After everything is said and done, we must always remain what we are. That is, we are all Zambians – loving one another, true to one another, fair to one another, great to one another!

Early this year I made a statement to the nation that 1990 was going to be a year of action. This is now September and in these nine months many things have happened. Naturally some have been very good and others have been very bad. Indeed, it can be said and rightly so, that some of the bad things have been the worst this nation has ever experienced. We have a responsibility to this nation to analyse these issues in an honest and sincere manner so that we can work out meaningful solutions. The Central Committee has empowered me, as usual, to start the ball rolling.

We all know that the last week of June 1990 will go down in history as a week of serious rioting in Lusaka, Kabwe and Kafue. The climax of these riots in which we lost twenty-seven lives and unquantified loss of property was an attempted coup. After the 30th of June, 1990, the leadership of this nation guided by the Central Committee has undertaken a number of programmes to meet the challenges of a NEW BEGINNING! I declared a general amnesty on behalf of the nation as a whole. In this amnesty the following groups of people were released:

1. Mr Shamwana and his fellow-coup plotters who were arrested, charged with treason, tried and sentenced to death by the High Court of Zambia, and on appeal the Supreme Court of Zambia confirmed the death sentence. I, on behalf of the people of Zambia reduced the death sentence to one of life imprisonment.

2. Mr Tembo and his fellow-coup plotters were arrested and charged with treason. The trial was going on when I declared on behalf of the people of Zambia this general amnesty. They have benefited from it and the State entered a nolle prosecui.

3. Mr Luchembe who announced the attempted coup on the morning of 30th June, 1990. He too was released unconditionally.

4. The looters in Lusaka and who were being tried were also released unconditionally.

5. University students who were accused of participating in the organisation of the riots were also released unconditionally.

We extended an olive branch to all these people. But the whole country knows from their activities that there has been no reciprocity.

If there are any people in this country or abroad who had any doubt about the threat to State security by the people we pardoned, they must have heard for themselves the pronouncements that have been made at multi-party rallies in this connection.

The Central Committee did all this not out of weakness, but out of a genuine desire to start afresh. Hence my use earlier on of the phrase 'New Beginning'. We are determined to give everybody a chance in this new atmosphere. On the economic front, our national programme of economic reform is, as I will indicate later, on course. It gives us new hopes especially for the poorest of the poor.

I should, however, here point out that there is now an extremely serious threat to our Economic Recovery Programme. The Gulf situation has of course sent oil prices rocketing. They have already very adversely affected our economy. This is a very serious and rather terrifying development. Obviously we must place this top on the agenda of this National Council Session.

In my introductory remarks I have referred to the fact that in the earlier part of this year we held the Fourth National Convention and the Fifth Extra-ordinary National Council Session and that it was at these meetings that we decided to accept the call for a referendum on whether or not we should continue as a One Party Participatory Democracy. The campaign has been going on for a few months and I now want to discuss this whole issue in detail.

I have been thinking about the situation that has been created by multiparty Party Campaigners. I use the definition Party deliberately even though these campaigners are saying that they are not a political party. But what else are they? Certainly they behave as such!

They are trying to present themselves as the saviours of this country from the so-called oppression and slavery of UNIP. They say they want to reintroduce democracy in Zambia! But if there was no democracy in Zambia, how is it that they are able to organize, raise funds (most of which are from dubious sources) and hold political rallies to which they transport by bus people from all over the country in order to show a larger following than they command?

I want to tell these people that I am not Sir Arthur Benson and UNIP is not the Colonial Government. Maybe I should explain who Sir Arthur Benson was. Some of you comrades were not even born at the time he was here as Governor of Northern Rhodesia. He was the Governor who banned the Zambia African National Congress (ZANC) and arrested us on the grounds that we were running, as he called it, 'murder incorporated'. In other words, we were planning to assassinate him and all the whites in the country.

He banned ZANC, but we created UNIP and we fought for Independence which we achieved in 1964 and have been in government ever since.

We did our best to develop this country and to improve the living standards of our people. We have had many achievements and inevitably we have had many failures too. But looking back, I am satisfied with most of what we did and I am sure that nobody could have done any better.

Let me delve into the past a little. Our country is very young and the majority of the people were born after Independence.

In fact when I think of it there are probably less than one million out of the eight million people of this country who are old enough to remember what the country was like before we liberated ourselves from the colonial yoke.

We had no university and had only about 100 university graduates at Independence and only a handful of secondary schools and 1,200 people with senior secondary school certificates. Out of those there were less than a dozen lawyers; less than a dozen doctors; only one Zambian engineer; no Zambian manager; no Zambian banker; no Zambian accountant; a handful of Zambian shopkeepers and very few trained artisans. We had 12,000 expatriates running the mines and the highest positions of Zambians on the mines were personnel officers known as 'bamakobo' and in the actual mining divisions only 'Capitaos'. In fact these personnel officers dealt only with black workers. The whites who stayed on in Zambia after Independence used to mock us and say 'lo government enakawena lo mali anakatina'. This means 'Government is yours but wealth is ours.'

I am happy to look around me now and find that Zambia has truly achieved Independence. In all walks of life Zambians are now at the top. In the professions; in business; on the mines; in the banks; in property; in trading; in education; in farming; everywhere! We now have less than 800 expatriates on the mines; we have Zambian owned banks; we have Zambian conglomerates and more importantly we produce all the staple food we need to eat, as long as the Almighty allows us good rains; not through commercial farmers only – who are all shades of colour – but in fact mainly through Zambian peasants in the countryside.

We have often been told that before Independence 200 white farmers used to feed the whole of Northern Rhodesia, and that since Independence we have not been able to feed ourselves. Let me put the record straight. Before Independence about 200 white farmers, highly subsidized by the Federal Government, may have fed the people of Northern Rhodesia in the 1950's but the population was less than two million. There was no peasant production to speak of because there was a different Ministry of Agriculture for the blacks (The Ministry of African Agriculture) which had virtually no money to spend and did very little for the development of peasant farming.

We are now eight million people and, not only do we feed ourselves and have surpluses for export; we do so mainly through the peasant farmers and even the Northern Province which had no agricultural tradition except the Chitemene System produced 2½ million bags of maize last year.

So, we have achieved a great deal comrades, even though our critics do not want to acknowledge it.

To get where we are we embarked upon very bold policies. We established primary and secondary schools in each district, we established two universities and many other institutions of higher education and training. We instituted the Mulungushi Economic Reforms in 1968. These, together with our very aggressive educational policies immediately after Independence have made the biggest contribution to the development of indigenous business in this country.

I know that the Parastatal Sector is resented by some people both locally and abroad but I wish to submit to you comrades that if we did not do what we did in 1968 and 1969 our economy would still be dominated by the multinational companies and by the white settlers. Nobody was interested in training Zambians; nobody was interested in promoting Zambians to more responsible jobs. The mining companies of the day used to talk of Zambianisation sometime in the 21st Century. Some, if not most, of our critics amongst the Multiparty Party campaigners would not have been where they are if we had not given them the opportunity by training them as businessmen in the Parastatal Sector and by assisting them with finance afterwards.

Comrades, we have achieved a lot and more importantly we have achieved it without social disruption and without resorting to oppressive measures.

Our critics can say what they like but the record is there to see. We have had no major upheavals in our history of 26 years. We have no Zambian refugees in other countries who have run away from our policies. Our prisons do not have political prisoners even though some of our people have misbehaved from time to time.

We have achieved all this through our Philosophy of Humanism and the leadership of UNIP. We have achieved all this because our political philosophy has its roots in our history, in our tradition and in our culture because it cares about the welfare of our people and because it believes in the paramountcy of MAN. We have always taken care to do what is in the best interest of human beings and not what hurts them. Our Party organisation was able to spread our message to all levels of society and right through the country. In wards, villages, towns and districts there are leaders who take care of our people and their everyday problems at all times.

I have said all this knowing full well that we have problems, many problems. Some of them are certainly of our own making but a lot of them are the result of economic circumstances beyond our control. Difficulties started in the mid 1970's with the oil crisis and the inflationary pressures that it produced on the world economy which led to the recession of the early 1980's and the decline in the net value of primary commodities.

Comrades, you may hear that the price of copper is at the moment £1,500 per tonne. This amounts to three times as much as the £500 per tonne that it was in the 1960's. But with £500 in the 1960's you could buy a tractor whereas now you need £12,000 to buy the same tractor. In other words, whereas our one tonne of copper could buy us a tractor in the 1960's we now need eight tonnes of copper to buy a tractor. And our mines are getting exhausted as ore grades decline and equipment gets older.

Furthermore, in the 1960's we used to produce over 600,000 tonnes of copper as against the current 450,000 tonnes of copper per annum. At the same time the population has quadrupled. All these factors have made our economic situation rather difficult.

I have delved into the history in order to explain the position we are in today. However, wise men do not live in the past. They live in the present and prepare themselves for the future. We have to be pragmatic, face the situation we are in squarely and determine our future policies. Thank God the intervening years have moulded us together as one nation and we are better able to cope with adversity.

Our society seems to me to be restless and seems to want change. In order to determine what is best for us, we established a Special Parliamentary Select Committee and asked it to advise us on what we should do in order to improve our political Party so as to face these difficult economic times and a changing world as a united people. The Special Parliamentary Select Committee has come forward with some sensible and inspired recommendations. I wish now to thank Comrade Mr Speaker, the Committee and, indeed, all Comrade Honourable Members of Parliament for a job well done! The main recommendation of the Committee is that we must democratise the Party. And this is what we must do. We shall embark upon this and other recommendations aimed at democratising further the Party and keeping it as the foremost political force in the country that it has always been.

I believe that a reorganized, and more democratised UNIP is the only Party that the country needs. I believe too that as a developing nation we cannot afford the luxury of political debate for its own sake which will only delay development.

It is clear that if we allow the present campaign which is not addressing itself to the core issue of the referendum to continue, there will be divisions in the nation that can end up in bloodshed.

Being not a government, the Multiparty Party campaigners have been making irresponsible statements and making promises which they cannot fulfil in the unlikely event they came to power. For example, the economic restructuring programme which they are using to woo support from the poor among us has the full endorsement of the leading world financial institutions and the international community which has pledged a lot of support for which we are grateful. This support includes the Social Action Programme aimed at alleviating the suffering among the poorest of the poor in our society who have become target group of the Multiparty Party advocates. The Zambian society has not idolised lawlessness. I do not want to split the country into two camps. I do not want to encourage the campaign for or against multi-party because I see bloodshed at the end of the road and I see disaster for the country.

So, I say, why hold the referendum! Why allow them to divide our people. We are not afraid of them! UNIP is a great Party and it will win any General Election against **any** other party. Let us make these people who are now hiding behind empty multi-party slogans, who are shielding behind false accusations of oppression by UNIP sit down and think what it is like to run a real political party. Let them produce people who are more capable of running the country than those UNIP is capable of producing. Let us see what kind of economic and social policies they are capable of producing. Let us take them on comrades. Personally, I am more than ready to lead UNIP in an election against any party or parties in this country.

I am proud of our record. I have faith in the wisdom of the common man. When the chips are down he will choose the people he can trust; the people he knows best; the people who care for him; who listen to him; who live with him; who think like him; who are part of him. Not the people who live in ivory towers who think they are cleverer and look down on the common man, who are out of touch and who achieved very little in life despite a very expensive education and a privileged start.

So comrades with these thoughts the Central Committee decided to recommend to you that we do not carry on with the referendum which was an excellent idea if everybody was prepared to behave in a civilised fashion but which has now been turned into an instrument for creating anarchy in the nation by some individuals and organisations not known for their democratic values, principles and practices. Instead the Central Committee is recommending to this National Council that this Council decides that the Government of the Republic of Zambia appoints a Commission to determine the necessary amendments to the Constitution of the Republic.

Democratisation of the Party and the call for political pluralism, entails political and social liberalisation. We have therefore decided to recommend to this National Council that the right to choose a Party and the Government must extend to the right to form and to belong to a trade union and the right of a union to be or not to be affiliated to the Zambia Congress of Trade Unions. In this political process therefore, affiliation by a trade union to ZCTU cannot be mandatory and supported by statute. In this regard, that part of the law in the Industrial Relations Act making it obligatory for a trade union to be affiliated to ZCTU will be repealed.

I now want to explain the broad features of what we have in mind. It is pertinent to observe the fact that for peace to endure in any country there should always be a smooth and peaceful way of changing constitutions.

We all must believe there is a need for continuity in the political life of the country instead of a complete change after every five years. The new constitution therefore should be so arranged that the terms of the President and the Parliament are not coterminous. Moreover, there should be a complete separation of the powers of the Legislature, the Executive and the Judiciary. In addition it is proposed that a Constitutional Court should be established whose function is to ensure that the provisions of the constitution are strictly adhered to and that neither the President nor parliament can abuse their powers and where any man will seek redress if he feels that his rights have been abused.

The Legislature

The new constitution would provide for a Parliament of 150 members, all of them elected. The President would have no right to appoint

Members of Parliament. The parliamentary term would be five years as at present. The President would have no right to dissolve Parliament. The Parliament would have the right to dissolve itself by a two thirds majority vote but re-election will only last to the end of the term of the dissolved Parliament.

Parliament's main function will be as it is now, the enactment of legislation submitted to it by the Executive but it will also have the right to initiate its own legislation except on subjects relating to Defence, Security and Foreign Affairs where the President has the power of veto.

With regard to Budget and other Bills involving expenditure Parliament will have the right to make adjustments as regards the distribution of the total expenditure amongst various expenditure votes but shall have no right to change the total figure.

Parliament will establish committees corresponding to the various ministries and each committee will first review legislation of its competence before such legislation is submitted to the full Parliament with a recommendation for approval or rejection.

The Ministers will not be Members of Parliament. If the President appoints a Member of Parliament to a Cabinet post that member will have to resign his or her parliamentary post before he or she accepts the position of Minister.

Parliament will elect its own Speaker and Deputy Speaker. The President will have no right to appoint them.

The Executive

There shall be a President elected directly by a majority vote. If nobody attains majority during the election there will be a re-run two weeks after between the two candidates who have attained the highest number of votes. The President's term of office under this constitution is, like Parliament's, five years. However, in order to arrange that the term of Parliament and the term of the President are not coterminous, the First President elected under this constitution will have a first term of 7½ years. So the first President under this Constitution will be elected on the same day as the new Parliament and his term will begin not later than October, 1991 to the end of 1998.

The President will appoint a Vice President but Parliament will have the right to ratify this appointment. The President will have the right to appoint up to 15 Cabinet Ministers who will not be Members of Parliament.

The President shall have the power of veto over Defence, Security and Foreign Affairs.

The President shall have an advisory council consisting of two representatives from each Province chosen by the President at his own discretion from amongst prominent citizens of such Province. Such members could include traditional rulers. The function of the President's council is purely advisory.

The Judiciary

The Judiciary shall be completely independent of the Executive as at present but in addition there will be a Constitutional Court whose functions I have already explained. This Court will have a Chairman appointed by the President for a specific term and two Judges also appointed by the President but whose appointments must be ratified by Parliament.

Comrades, these are the main features of the new Constitution I am putting before this extremely important National Council Session which, if approved, will be submitted to the Commission. These proposals are a clear demonstration of our total commitment to the importance of man as God made him. This is a translation of our Philosophy of Humanism into constitutional arrangements. Human rights are at the centre of these proposals.

The next question of great importance to all of us as UNIP members and leaders is where is the United National Independence Party in this scheme of arrangement?

UNIP's Revival

The place of UNIP in the new set up is certainly assured. But it is assured only on the basis of a strong revival programme. Therefore, the biggest job ahead of us now is the reorganisation and renewal of UNIP into the Party of the future. UNIP must now begin to prepare itself for the next elections by, among other things, putting its house in order. What is now required is a well thought out programme to overhaul totally the internal and external working of the Party; to shake off the outdated images of the past, and to emerge into the new political arena as the **PARTY OF THE FUTURE.**

I believe, beyond any shadow of doubt, that UNIP will win the next election against all comers. But let us not get complacent. The key to our winning is going to lie both in our bringing the Party totally up-to-date, and in the working out of a many-sided programme designed to provide what the public wants and needs.

Today I wish to outline the areas which the Party will have to address in establishing its NEW IMAGE as details will have to be worked out later.

Cultivating the New Look

The Party will have to begin to reform itself from the ground up: cultivating an entirely new modernized image; totally eradicating the paternalism of the past; replacing the 'founding fathers' image – which will always be revered as the important hall-mark of the Party's founding role in Zambia – with the image of the 'PARTY OF THE FUTURE'. The Party must clearly identify itself as the exclusive initiator and custodian of the economic reform programme and thus with the position that, for Zambians, 'prosperity need not be only a dream.' We must actively recruit into the Party high-profile people with respected reputations in business and the professions, opening up new channels for their input into Party policy-making and administration.

Leaders of the Party must become more high-profile, more visibly involved in a hands-on way with the things they are responsible for. Speeches telling the people what to do are no longer enough. The people want to see what the leaders are doing, and take their example. We must indeed develop a brand new approach to the electorate. The Party must be vital, and talk instead about the boundless opportunity that Zambia offers to people who have the vision to see it, and the courage to undertake new things on the land or in the towns.

What I visualize, in short, is a **wholly new UNIP PARTY** entering the next election – possibly unrecognizable from its former self; every leader hard-working, short on speeches and long on action; the Party which both pioneered the Reform Programme and is seeing it through; the Party to which thinking businessmen and workers alike will be proud to ally themselves because of its sensible and sympathetic grasp of their problems; the Party which stands for the values of Church and family; the Party which respects and encourages initiative and competition in enterprise; the Party which is seen as the facilitator to make it easier for legitimate business to operate, and the intervener only when necessary to ensure that the laws of competition, of standards, of fair wages, of social programmes for employees, and other essential laws, are obeyed; the Party which taxes fairly to ensure provision of infrastructure and programmes of medical and social services for the people. The Party which cares for the poor and the less privileged in our society. In short, the **NEW UNIP; THE PARTY OF JUSTICE AND PROSPERITY!**

A tall order? Yes. But not too big for people who believe in what is needed to get Zambia going again.

The Party needs only men and women of integrity, patriotism and commitment to the cause of the country.

We are analysing the prevailing situation in the country. This analysis will not be complete without pointing out that we see thousands of our people trooping to attend rallies of the multi-party people. Those are protest rallies. Our people are calling for cheaper mealie meal; more and cheaper housing; they are calling for more and better schools; they are calling for more jobs. You and I know that the multi-party people cannot produce these at all. After all, the track record of their leaders is well known! They are merely cashing in on the difficult economic situation that we face. UNIP must go full scale ahead to remove this scourge of Poverty and all its off-shoots! The beginning point is the reduction on prices of mealie meal. In this respect I am glad to say that we all know we have begun to do this. Only ten days ago parastatal companies announced some very meaningful or substantial reductions in the prices of roller meal and breakfast meal. This was done after the liberalization of the maize and fertilizer business in accordance with the policies we have been following since May 1987. All this shows our commitment to the people of Zambia.

Let Us Remember This When We Look Back Upon Our Past:

The worst is over now! Our past is behind us! We must move with confidence into the future, for the future is Zambia's!

And above all, let us remember the boundless promise of this land.

NOTHING – NO, NOTHING – CAN STOP ZAMBIA'S ADVANCE TO PROSPERITY ... NOTHING EXCEPT ZAMBIA ITSELF!!

Long live the humanist Revolution!
Long live the Republic!

As I say: May God bless the Republic
I also say: Members of UNIP I give you the future!

Thank you.

SELECT BIBLIOGRAPHY

Books by Kenneth Kaunda

Kenneth D. Kaunda, *Zambia Shall be Free*, London: Heinemann, 1962
Kenneth D. Kaunda and Colin Morris, *Black Government? A Discussion*, London: United Society for Christian Literature, 1960
Kenneth D. Kaunda, *A Humanist in Africa – Letters to Colin Morris*, London: Longman, 1966

By Kenneth Kaunda on Foreign Policy

Kenneth D. Kaunda, *Kaunda on Violence*, (ed, Colin Morris), London: Collins, 1980

Works on Kenneth Kaunda

Favourable

Philip Brownrigg, *Kenneth Kaunda*, Lusaka: Kenneth Kaunda Foundation, 1989
Richard Hall, *The High Price of Principles: Kaunda and the White South*, London: Hodder and Stoughton, 1969
John Hatch, *Two African Statesmen*, London: Secker & Warburg, 1976

Even-handed

William Tordoff, 'Zambia: The Politics of Disengagement', *African Affairs*, Vol. 76, No. 302, 1977

Critical

Douglas Anglin and Timothy M. Shaw (see Shaw's contribution), *Zambia's Foreign Policy: Studies in Diplomacy and Dependency*, Boulder, Colorado: Westview, 1979
Kenneth Good, 'Debt and the One Party State in Zambia', *Journal of Modern African Studies*, Vol. 27, No. 2, 1989
Kenneth Good, 'Zambia and the Liberation of South Africa', *Journal of Modern African Studies*, Vol. 25, No. 3, 1987

The Structuralist View of the International Political Economy

Samir Amin, *Unequal Development: An Essay on the Social Formations of Peripheral Capitalism*, Hassocks: Harvester, 1976
André Gunder Frank, *Capitalism and Underdevelopment in Latin America – Historical Studies of Chile and Brazil*, New York: Monthly Review Press, 1969
Timothy M. Shaw, *Towards a Political Economy for Africa*, London: Macmillan, 1985
Immanuel Wallerstein, 'The Rise and Future Demise of the World Capitalist System: Concepts for Comparative Analysis', *Comparative Studies in Society and History*, Vol. 16, No. 4, 1974

Works on Zambia

Marcia M. Burdette, *Zambia: Between Two Worlds*, Boulder, Colorado: Westview, 1988
Kwaku Osei-Hwedie and Muna Ndulo (eds.), *Issues in Zambian Development*, Boston: Omenana, 1985
William Tordoff, *Politics in Zambia*, Manchester, Manchester University Press, 1974
William Tordoff, *Administration in Zambia*, Manchester: Manchester University Press, 1980

Works on Humanism

Stephen Chan, 'Humanism, Intellectuals and the Left in Zambia', in Kwaku Osei-Hwedie and Muna Ndulo, (eds.), *Issues in Zambian Development*, Boston: Omenana, 1985

Bastiaan de Gaay Fortman, *After Mulungushi: The Economics of Zambian Humanism*, Nairobi: East African Publishing House, 1969
Timothy Kandeke, *Fundamentals of Zambian Humanism*, Lusaka: NECZAM, 1976
Henry S. Mebeelo, *Main Currents of Zambian Humanist Thought*, Lusaka: Oxford University Press, 1973
Patrick Ollawa, *Participatory Democracy in Zambia: The Political Economy of National Development*, Ilfracombe: Arthur Stockwell, 1979

Foreign Policies in Southern Africa

Stephen Chan, *Exporting Apartheid: Foreign Policies in Southern Africa, 1978–1988*, London: Macmillan, 1990
Kenneth W. Grundy, *The Militarization of South African Politics*, Oxford: Oxford University Press, 1987
Joseph Hanlon, *Beggar Your Neighbours – Apartheid Power in Southern Africa*, London: James Currey, 1986

Zambia in the Commonwealth

Stephen Chan, *The Commonwealth in World Politics: A Study of International Action 1965 to 1985*, London: Lester Crook, 1988

INDEX